Performance-
Driven
Organizational
Change

To David J. Hickson
teacher and mentor

Lex Donaldson

Performance-Driven

Driven

Organizational

Change

The Organizational Portfolio

SAGE Publications
International Educational and Professional Publisher
Thousand Oaks   London   New Delhi

For information:

SAGE Publications, Inc.
2455 Teller Road
Thousand Oaks, California 91320
E-mail: order@sagepub.com

SAGE Publications Ltd.
6 Bonhill Street
London EC2A 4PU
United Kingdom

SAGE Publications India Pvt. Ltd.
M-32 Market
Greater Kailash I
New Delhi 110 048 India

Printed in the United States of America

Library of Congress Cataloging-in-Publication Data

Donaldson, Lex.
    Performance-driven organizational change: The organizational portfolio / by Lex Donaldson.
        p. cm.
    Includes bibliographical references and index.
    ISBN 0-7619-0354-2 (cloth: acid-free paper) ISBN 0-7619-0355-0 (pbk.: acid-free paper)
    1. Organizational change. 2. Organizational effectiveness. I. Title.
HD58.8 .D66 1998
658.4′063—ddc21   98-25383

99 00 01 02 03 10 9 8 7 6 5 4 3 2 1

Acquiring Editor:	Marquita Flemming
Editorial Assistant:	MaryAnn Vail
Production Editor:	Diana E. Axelsen
Editorial Assistant:	Nevair Kabakian
Copy Editor:	Joyce Kuhn
Typesetter:	Marion Warren

Brief Contents

132691

Detailed Contents

Preface

This book is the fourth I have written about organization theory. The previous three books defended structural contingency theory and debated against its critics. The present book is different; there is no debate or criticism of other theories. Instead, the book offers a new theory and thus is wholly constructive in tone. It builds upon contingency theory and takes it off in a new direction. In the process, the focus widens considerably from organizational structure to include all aspects of the organization.

Structural contingency theory research has sought in the past to identify which structures fit each of the contingency factors, such as size, strategy, technology, and so on. Thus incremental research contributions within this approach seek to add a new structural variable, identify a new contingency factor, or demonstrate the effect of fit on performance and so on. These are important refinements for the structural contingency approach, but they are not, however, the approach taken here. Structural contingency theory has postulated a particular model of how organizational structure changes in response to changes in the contingency factors. This adaptation process is the focus of the present inquiry.

Structural contingency theory research argues that an organization with a structure that misfits its contingency factors has, as a consequence, lower organizational performance. However, this lower performance from misfit is not enough to cause the organization to change its structure and thereby regain fit and performance. Other causes of organizational performance have to be depressing it, so that, in combination with misfit, overall performance becomes low enough to cause structural change. Performance has to drop considerably because organizational managers seek to attain not maximum organizational performance but, rather, a satisfactory, or satisficing, level that is substantially below the maximum performance level. Thus an organization in misfit can remain there for a lengthy period until other causes force its performance below the satisficing level. In the 1980s I conducted an empirical test that confirmed this model. This caused me to start thinking about the way that performance drove organizational change.

The more I thought about performance driving organizational change, the more numerous the insights that occurred to me about various implications of this basic idea. This took me off into areas that were not the customary province of organization theory. My thinking was informed by some ideas from finance and economics about risk, portfolios, business cycles, and competition. This seemed to mark a fruitful infusion from other disciplines with which tradition-ally organization theory has had little contact. The result is a formal theory consisting of a large number of propositions. The subject matter has broadened considerably from organizational structure to adaptive organizational change of any kind, such as change in strategy, human resource management, and information technology. Thus the topic is organizational change in general and in both of its two dimensions of organizational adaptation and growth.

There is theoretical reason to believe, and empirical evidence to support, the idea that a crisis of poor organizational performance is required to trigger adaptive organizational change in many aspects of the organization. There has been much study of the politics and conflict that accompany organizational change and much research into the psychological processes of organizational change. These political and psychological theories have produced prescriptions about how to manage organizational change processes. Similarly, there has been much research to define which organizational designs and human resource management practices are optimal for each organizational situation, and this also leads to prescriptions. Thus there is much prescriptive advice on offer. Yet without a performance crisis, there is a good chance that needed organizational changes will not be forthcoming. Moreover, the adaptive change induced by the crisis creates the capacity for fresh organizational growth. Through a series of adaptations and resulting growth spurts, the organization grows larger and more effective. Hence the organization requires recurrent crises of poor per-formance. This argues for more study to better understand the dynamics whereby performance-driven organizational change comes about. Hopefully, the present book is a modest step toward providing a theoretical framework to guide future empirical research in this area.

Acknowledgments

I should like to thank those who have supported me in this book project. Fred Hilmer, as Dean of the Australian Graduate School of Management from 1989 to 1996, generously provided me with the sabbatical leave to work on the book, and my colleagues in the Organizational Behavior group of the AGSM, such as Dexter Dunphy, Boris Kabanoff, and Bob Wood, encouraged me in my endeavors.

Those in the Organizational Behavior Department of the Graduate School of Business at Northwestern University were good enough to have me spend my 6-month sabbatical with them where the first draft was completed. I enjoyed their good fellowship and made many friends there, including Paul Hirsch, Andy Hoffman, Willie Ocasio, and Marc Ventresca.

The staff of the library at the AGSM, under Pam Taylor and then Sue Hornby, provided help in gathering sources and information. June Ohlson, as head of the Research Library of the Reserve Bank of Australia, helped find material on business cycles. We discussed the role of business cycles in organizational life extensively. As a freelance editor, June provided incisive, critical feedback on the book that made it more accessible and also improved its intellectual coherence.

A number of scholars were kind enough to give me comments on draft chapters: Philip Bromiley, Richard Cyert, Jerald Hage, William McKelvey, Andrew Van de Ven, David Whetten, and Edward Zajac. Peter Heslin gave me comments on the entire book. I am grateful to them for their help, but, of course, I remain responsible for the errors and omissions in the final book.

Organizational Portfolio Theory

In this book we seek to offer a theory of the organization as a portfolio. There are various internal and external causes that affect organizational performance. In turn, organizational performance drives organizational change and adaptation. For an organization that is maladapted, the adaptive change that it needs tends to occur when poor organizational performance leads to a crisis. Such poor performance comes about through the maladaptation together with other causes depressing organizational performance. The theory states how each of these causes interacts with organizational maladaptation to determine the level of organizational performance. Variations of these causes over time define the performance fluctuations that are the motors of organizational change. Sometimes, these causes reinforce maladaptation so that organizational performance is driven to the low value that triggers adaptive change. However, at other times, the causes nullify the effect on performance of maladaptation so that no change happens. The concept of a portfolio explains how this can occur. The theory of the organization as a portfolio applies this idea to offer a new perspective on organizational life.

Theories of organization have written of the organization adapting to its environment (Thompson 1967). They have specified which structures are required to fit with each environment (e.g., Burns and Stalker 1961). However, organizations tend not to adopt these required structures until their performance drops so low as to create a crisis (Chandler 1962; Williamson 1964; Child 1972). Thus organizational performance is the trigger of organizational adaptation. Although widely believed to be key, this idea that performance drives organizational change has received relatively little theoretical analysis. Yet a consideration of this seemingly simple idea reveals many theoretical implications. The task of this book is to systematically develop a theory of performance-driven organizational change. The theory seeks to explain why organizations change and also why they fail to change. It potentially applies to adaptations of any kind (e.g., organizational structure, strategy, human resource management, or information technology). Because organizational performance is the key, we have to attend closely to its causes, both external and internal to the organization.

There is a paradox that high organizational performance, while clearly being positive for the organization, has longer-term adverse effects. The high performance boosts organizational growth that leads the organization to become ill-fitted to its existing structure and other characteristics. This maladaptation reduces performance so that it becomes suboptimal, but performance may nevertheless remain satisfactory so that the organization continues maladapted. The persistent maladaptation robs the organization of the further growth and performance that it would have gained. Thus stable medium to high performance is beneficial in the short term but costly over the long term. Stable satisfactory performance carries the seeds of its own undoing, in that high performance leads to lower performance. This is the stuff of classical tragedy. In that sense, there is a price to success. This price has largely gone unnoticed to date, although it is implicit in the idea that low performance is required to trigger adaptive organizational change. This book is an effort to think through this paradox. Clearly, the idea that high performance is undesirable runs counter to common sense and so strikes most people as an alien notion. However, as will be seen, it is well based in research, so I invite you, the reader, to suspend your preconceptions and embark on a conceptual journey into a new land.

To better analyze organizational performance, we may apply the portfolio theory from finance (Sharpe 1970; Brealey and Myers 1996). We typically assume that change in one aspect of an organization leads to change in other aspects. However, portfolio theory reveals how change can lead to lack of change, in that change in one aspect is offset by change in another. Further, we can learn to examine the workings of the organization in terms of risk. The focus thus moves from the conventional one of just considering the level of organizational performance to examining how much that level fluctuates over time, which is captured by the concept of risk. This leads us to become interested in factors that affect risk both external and internal to the organization. The external factors include the business cycle and competitors. The internal organizational factors include strategy and structure. Risk is a key ingredient of the way performance drives adaptation. Thus organizational theory may benefit from using the concepts of portfolio and risk.

Organizational performance is strongly affected by the external economic environment. Conceiving of the economic environment broadly, the recurrent cycles of economic activity, such as the business cycle, come into view (Van Duijn 1983; Kuczynski 1986). What are the implications for organizational adaptation of the business cycle? How do the upswings and downswings of the business cycle influence the organization in terms of its adaptation and growth? Turning to more localized aspects of the economic environment suggests a consideration of the effect of competitor firms on the firm. How is the adaptation of a firm affected by its competitors? These are new questions for organizational theory and constitute interesting issues for theorizing.

The firm itself affects its performance level by internal factors. Structural contingency theory examines whether the organization is in fit or misfit between the structure and its contingencies, and this, in turn, affects organizational performance (e.g., Drazin and Van de Ven 1985). However, the firm itself is a portfolio. Its different components vary so that they may reinforce each other or they can be offsetting (Salter and Weinhold 1979). If one source of performance is rising while another is declining, then these two sources of performance tend to cancel out each other. For example, if the performance of one division is increasing while the performance of another is decreasing, then the overall corporate performance tends to remain stable. The causes of organizational performance thus may not amplify each other but, rather, dampen each other. The result is that tendencies for performance to swing greatly from high to low are reduced. This has strong consequences for organizational adaptation, which would be driven by performance swings. As we shall see, the seemingly benign tendency of one variable in the organization's portfolio to counter and smooth out fluctuations due to a second variable can have effects that are anything but benign.

Many firms have been undergoing reorganization, although not necessarily with the results expected. A consideration of the dynamic interplay between the internal and external causes of organizational performance that operate as the firm undergoes adaptive reorganization offers a solution to this puzzle.

The topic of corporate governance can also be approached from the organizational portfolio theoretical perspective. The traditional view is that large corporations, to a puzzling or worrying degree, use weak forms of corporate governance. This refers to widespread practices such as CEOs (chief executive officers) chairing the board and directors who are also managers (Kesner and Dalton 1986). These structures are held to compromise the independence of the board of directors so that it cannot perform its role of policing management (Jensen and Meckling 1976). Such practices are widely lamented and lead to the view that boards are too weak and consequently that the personal interests of managers are too well served. Yet the desirability of boards as an impartial check on managers, to rein in managerial abuses, has been well understood by many members of the community for many decades, so how can this phenomenon exist? The organizational portfolio theory offers fresh insights into the puzzles of corporate governance. The portfolio features of large corporations lead to the adoption of forms of corporate governance other than those normatively and theoretically prescribed.

Prospects of Cross-Fertilization
From Economics and Finance

An organization is a set of people arranged to produce outputs through their collective actions, which lead in turn to organizational performance. Thus performance is a consequence of organization. Performance is also the cause of organization, in that the striving for performance is the reason that organizations are brought into being (March and Simon 1958). Performance is thus both the consequence and cause of organization.

Most organizations are economic organizations, in that small firms are the most numerous type of organization (Aldrich 1979). It necessarily follows, therefore, that economic factors affecting the organization are intimately involved in the organization and its functioning. However, this has not been the prevailing way in which organizations have been approached by organizational theory to date. The aim of this book is to help fill this gap. It offers a treatment of the organization interacting with diverse economic phenomena. The concepts have application outside the economic realm, for example, to performance-driven change in governmental and not-for-profit organizations, but our focus here is on the economic realm in order to make the analysis more concrete.

Accordingly, in some places we use the word *organization* to refer to the subject of our theory, to signal the generality of the theory, potentially to organizations of all types (i.e., business firms, not-for-profit, and governmental organizations). However, in other places we signify that the argument is being developed primarily for business, profit-seeking organizations and thus use the terms *firm* or *company*, depending on the context. In other places where the focus is on the large business firm, we use the term *corporation*.

Much of modern organizational theory has its roots in sociology (Scott 1992). The organization is seen as a social structure composed of recurrent social relationships. Prominent among these social relationships are authority, bureaucracy, and compliance (Weber 1968; Etzioni 1975). Power is also important both for functionalist scholars (Parsons 1963) and for radical, critical theorists for whom power is the centerpiece (Clegg and Dunkerley 1980). The sociological tradition also leads to norms as central concepts, with a modern emphasis on institutionalization and taken-for-granted cognitive structuring of organization (Powell and DiMaggio 1991). Similarly, ideas held by organizational members are seen as important causes of organizational strategy and structure by strategic choice theorists (Child 1972). In contrast, the population-ecology tradition of organizational sociology emphasizes the environment selecting organizational forms that fit their ecological niche (Hannan and Freeman 1989). This marks a synthesis of sociological with biological thinking. A psychological tradition of theorizing about organizations makes the attitudes, values, and needs of organizational members central to its analysis and to the explanation of organizational form (Argyris 1964).

Modern organizational theory is selective in the phenomena it considers. Theories of organizational structure make links to technology, strategy, and the information requirements posed by uncertainty (Woodward 1965; Galbraith 1973; Khandwalla 1974; Galbraith and Kazanjian 1988). They say almost nothing about business cycles (as distinct from long waves; Abrahamson 1997). Equally, although there has been considerable use of the social psychological model of the organization as a social group (Brown 1954; Yukl 1994; Bettenhausen 1995), there has been little formal consideration of profit or risk. Organizational theory has drawn deeply from the disciplines of sociology and psychology and certain narrow strands of economics but not from financial economics and macroeconomics. Yet these also are intellectually strong disciplines. Moreover, they are cognate with organizational theory as neighboring disciplines in the multidisciplinary business schools. This suggests that some drawing from these disciplines might help give organizational theory some new insights and greater relevance.

There has, however, been economic theorizing about organizations. Some of this has dwelt on the problems of individuals maximizing their self-interest to the detriment of the interests of others. Agency theory deals with the agent, the organizational manager, potentially acting against the interest of their principal—that is, the owner of the corporation (Jensen and Meckling 1976). Transactions costs economics deals with the potential problem of one company taking unfair advantage of another, leading to vertical integration (Williamson 1985). Such theorizing closes the gap somewhat between organizational theory and economics. However, it elects to do so in a way that is only one of the possible derivations from economic thought. In particular, it emphasizes conflicts of interest by taking a negative view of the manager (Barney 1990; Donaldson 1990a, 1990b, 1995, 1996a; see also Fligstein and Brantley 1992).

We will try to show how economic concepts can be fruitfully used to explain organizations without adopting a negative model of the manager as found in agency theory and transactions costs economics (Jensen and Meckling 1976; Williamson 1985). Instead, we draw on the theory that managers are boundedly rational, lacking the knowledge to choose the optimal course of action and so having to take a course of action that is merely satisfactory, that is, satisficing (Cyert, Simon, and Trow 1956; March and Simon 1958; Simon 1976, 1979, 1983).

Economics focuses attention on profits, costs, sales, risk, business cycles, and so on. These seem to us to be foundational for any theory of organizations, especially of business firms (L. Donaldson 1994). Not only are such concepts central in economics, but they are central also in the accounts of organizations given by the people in and around business firms (and increasingly also government organizations). These economic concepts of profit, cost, risk, and so on are the everyday language of business owners, organizational managers, investors, government officials, consumers, union officials, and increasingly of employees. In contrast, much of traditional organizational theory has been free of such concerns. Under the influence of organizational sociology, the central concepts are power, conflict, environmental uncertainty, and others. Under the influence of organizational psychology, central concepts are job satisfaction, perception, empowerment, participation, and so on. These all give organizational theory a quality of innocence that sits uncomfortably with its claim to deal with a tough world. Perhaps this is part of the reason why organizational theory and organization behavior seem, in some quarters, to be losing ground to economics that appears to offer a tougher and more realistic approach. If organizational theory adopts some economic concepts, its analyses may become more valid and widely accepted.

The economic self-interest of most firms and corporations is to make more profit for themselves. This suggests that profit performance is the driver of change within the corporation. The primary cause of corporate conduct will be the internal cash flow of the corporation. This is the lifeblood of the body corporate. Understanding how it circulates around the corporation is key. Gordon Donaldson (1994) recognizes the pivotal role of corporate cash flow as a trigger for change in his empirical study of the Armco Steel Corporation: "For Armco it was the event of sudden, large, and unexpected losses and life-threatening, persistent cash flow deficits that had such an effect [initiating substantial organizational change]" (p. 39). Cash flow is as important to organization theorists trying to understand organizations as it is to economists trying to understand the circulation of money in the economy.

Organizational behavior and organizational theory offer normative (that is to say, prescriptive) theories about which behaviors or structures managers should use to attain high organizational performance. For example, effective leadership styles (Likert 1961; Yukl 1994) or effective organizational structures (Galbraith and Kazanjian 1988) are prescribed. In contrast, economics aims more for positive theories, that is, theories that explain how things happen rather than prescribing what should be done. The focus in economics is on how adaptation emerges without being the result of people following prescriptions. For example, the market allocates resources so that the total of human welfare is maximized without the people in the market intending to bring that about. This emphasis on adaptation in economics is potentially instructive for organization theorists and suggests that it may be fruitful to analyze organizational adaptation through developing positive theory of how it actually occurs.

Both qualitative case histories (Chandler 1962) and quantitative studies (Donaldson 1987; Hamilton and Shergill 1992, 1993) of organizational adaptation have confirmed each other. The associated theorizing has developed models of how the organization adapts to its situation, revealing its stages and processes (Donaldson 1987; Hamilton and Shergill 1992, 1993). In such a way, a theory of organizational adaptation has begun to be created. This suggests building on such work to construct a more refined and articulated theory of organizational adaptation. Such a theory of organizational adaptation is positive (i.e., explanatory) rather than normative or prescriptive.

The key is that organizations whose structure and contingency factors are in misfit need to experience a crisis of poor performance before they make the required structural changes (Chandler 1962; Donaldson 1987; Hamilton and Shergill 1992, 1993). Thus we have uncovered a principal element of the dynamic process whereby organizational adaptation takes place. More detailed prescriptive theories, and managers better educated in them, may not lead to more effective structures if the impetus for organizational adaptation—poor organizational performance—is missing. To more fully understand organizational change, we need to analyze the fluctuations in performance that make it happen.

Moreover, a crisis of poor performance may be needed before organizational changes of many different kinds occur (e.g., strategy, human resource management, or technology) because each of these needed organizational changes would only be implemented when organizational performance drops below the satisficing level. Poor performance is the master cause of organizational adaptation of any kind. Hence clarifying the exact nature of this performance-driven change process becomes important. Organization studies may benefit from the study of performance as the cause of organizational adaptations of diverse types (e.g., structure or strategy or technology). At the least, given the relative neglect of performance-driven adaptation to date, it seems sensible to give these processes more attention than they have received in the past.

In elaborating a positive theory of organizational adaptation, it may be fruitful for organizational theory to draw more specifically upon economics and finance for certain concepts and theories. The portfolio theory in finance and the business cycle concept in macroeconomics may hold promise for organizational theory, as argued below.

Financial economics focuses on investments by property holders. Investors owning several assets may consider them as a portfolio. Each asset has a rate of return (i.e., profit) and bears a risk. The risk is the variation in the rate of return—that is, the volatility of the return as it fluctuates from period to period about its average (Sharpe 1970; Brealey and Myers 1996). Each asset is correlated with each other asset, either positively or negatively, to a greater or lesser degree. Hence the correlation between assets is an important characteristic of the portfolio. Risk may be reduced not only by holding assets of low risk but also by holding assets that correlate negatively with each other, in other words, the portfolio effect. We will argue that this portfolio model can be applied to an individual organization.

From the macroeconomics perspective, the organization, as a firm, exists in an economic environment composed of fluctuating variables such as consumer demand, prices, interest rates, and exchange rates. Several of the key economic variables fluctuate together over time constituting the business cycle in the macroeconomy (Van Duijn 1983). There are cycles of different frequencies, and they occur in different sectors of the economy at somewhat different times (Kuczynski 1986). Business cycles are a major cause of performance variation for the organization. Moreover, their correlation with other causes of organizational performance varies over time in ways that affect organizational change.

Point of Theoretical Departure

There are numerous theories of organization (Davis and Powell 1992; Scott 1992), many of which I reviewed elsewhere (Donaldson 1985a, 1995, 1996a). This has led me to conclude that the most valid theory of organizational structure is contingency theory (Lawrence 1993; Donaldson 1996b). The contingency approach has been applied in many topic areas, such as leadership (e.g., Vroom and Yetton 1973) and strategic management (Hofer 1975). When applied to organizational structure, it is termed *structural contingency theory* (Pfeffer 1982).

Structural contingency theory holds that there is an organizational structure that fits the level of the contingency factor, such as the size, strategy, or environmental uncertainty of the organization, so that an organization in fit has a superior performance to an organization in misfit. This idea that fit between organizational structure and contingency factor leads to superior performance has been empirically supported in both qualitative (Burns and Stalker 1961; Chandler 1962) and quantitative studies (Lawrence and Lorsch 1967; Khandwalla 1973; Child 1975; Drazin and Van de Ven 1985; Donaldson 1987; Powell 1992; Hill, Hitt, and Hoskisson 1992; Hamilton and Shergill 1992, 1993; Jennings and Seaman 1994). Regarding organizational change, structural contingency theory holds that because of the imperative to maintain performance, organizations adapt their structure to fit with their contingencies of size, strategy, and so forth.

In contrast, *population-ecology theory* argues that organizations are inertial and tend not to make adaptive change, and so adaptation occurs at the population level through disbanding unfit organizations and founding fit ones (Hannan and Freeman 1984, 1989). However, evidence exists supporting the structural contingency view that individual organizations make changes in order to adapt to their environments, but there is a relative paucity of evidence supporting the idea of population-level adaptation (Donaldson 1995). Although there is some evidence of population-level adaptation for smaller organizations (Usher and Evans 1996), evidence exists that for large corporations, a focus of this book, organizational-level adaptation is stronger than population-level adaptation (Donaldson 1995). Therefore, adaptation at the organizational level is the object of the present inquiry.

Structural contingency theory describes a dynamic process of organizational structural adaptation: Change in contingency causes adaptive change in structure (Woodward 1965; Burns and Stalker 1961; Chandler 1962). The causal process occurs through several intervening steps (see Figure 1.1). Retaining the old structure after changing the contingency brings the organization into misfit, which lowers performance. When performance becomes sufficiently low so that it is less than the satisfactory (i.e., satisficing) level through misfit and other causes, a new structure is adopted. This brings the organization into a new fit and restores performance. Thus misfit and resulting low performance are crucial intervening stages connecting contingency change to structural change (Donaldson 1987, 1995). For example, if a corporation is undiversified and has a functional structure that fits that strategy, this fit raises organizational performance (see Figure 1.2). The corporation then diversifies while retaining the functional structure that is a misfit to the new strategy and so produces lower performance (Donaldson 1987). When the performance eventually drops low enough, the corporation adopts a new structure, the multidivisional form, and thereby regains fit and performance. The change is adaptive in that the new structure is a fit and replaces the old one that did not fit the new diversified strategy. Overall, change in the contingency, that is, diversifying, has led to change in structure but through the intervening state of misfit and consequent low performance. Only when performance drops to a low point is crisis experienced, triggering structural change. Concretely, low levels of sales, profit, and earnings per share produce structural change among corporations that are in misfit (i.e., have diversified but retained a functional structure; Donaldson 1987).

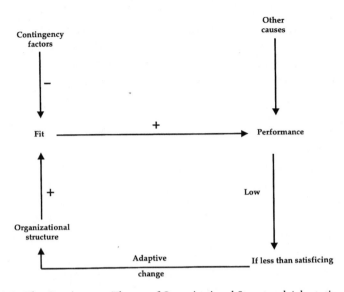

Figure 1.1　The Contingency Theory of Organizational Structural Adaptation

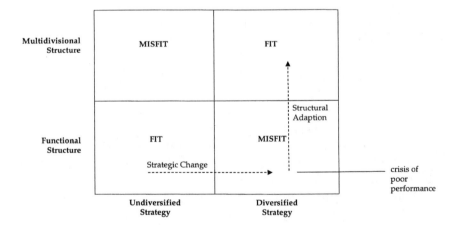

Figure 1.2 Change in Strategy Causes Change in Structure—The Dynamics of Structural Adaptation

This theoretical model is of structural adaptation to regain fit (Donaldson 1987, 1995). It is a crystallization of the causal change model that underlies many of the pioneering contributions to structural contingency theory. These contributions talked about how one particular contingency variable, such as technology, causes structure (Woodward 1965). The theoretical model abstracts the commonalities in the underlying change process that run across these contributions to theorize the effect of contingencies-in-general on structures-in-general.

The theoretical model of structural adaptation to regain fit has been supported by empirical research (Donaldson 1987; Hamilton and Shergill 1992, 1993) and so constitutes a valid basis for contemporary theorizing. It is a point of departure in that there is more to be said about organizational change to create a more dynamic model. Organizational performance plays the role in structural contingency theory of being the result of structural fit, and it is also the trigger that feeds back to cause structural adaptation. The new theory examines how organizational performance is caused by factors other than just structural fit. And organizational performance feeds back to affect more than just the structure. Whereas in structural contingency theory the focus is on structural adaptation, in the new theory the adaptation of many aspects of the organization other than just structure are included. The new theory deals with repeated cycles of change that produce cumulative growth and development over time.

Greiner (1972) argues that the development of an organization rather than being a smooth series of transitions is marked by a series of crises, each of which leads to a revolutionary transformation. A crisis is required to open the door for the required change. In the model discussed here, the crises are each of poor performance, and there can be many of them in the life of an old organization that has grown large and complex through making successive adaptations to resolve each crisis. In the spirit of Greiner, and by analogy with certain theories of individual development, meaningful organizational change comes as the result of therapeutic crisis. The crisis is uncomfortable but also therapeutic in that it shocks the system into addressing the need for change and gives it the impetus for taking the developmental step forward.

Much of the preexisting theory about organizational change focuses on sociological or psychological variables. Thus change is analyzed sociologically in terms of political interests and resistance to change and mobilization of power resources to force change (Pettigrew 1973, 1985; Dougherty and Hardy 1996). Or again, change is analyzed psychologically in terms of the perceptions about requirements for change or about the motivations of managers to engage in change (e.g., Argyris 1964; Dunphy 1981). These are intergroup, interpersonal, and intrapersonal levels of analysis. As such they are intervening variables and processes between the situation and the occurrence of change. However, from the perspective of organizational portfolio theory, the prime mover of organizational change is organizational performance. This leads to change via the sociological and psychological process, that is, through the perceptions and actions of managers and other people who can influence the decision making of the organization. These managerial perceptions and actions are the immediate causes of organizational change; however, they are in turn triggered by crises of poor performance. Whereas these sociological and psychological causes of organizational change have been much studied and discussed (e.g., Jaques 1951; Likert 1961; Bennis 1971; Argyris 1970; Cohen, Fink, Gadon, and Willits 1976; Hage 1974, 1980, 1988; Perrow 1986; Cummings and Huse 1989; McLennan 1989; Dunphy and Stace 1990; Stace and Dunphy 1994; Finkelstein and Hambrick 1996), organizational performance has been less so. Thus an extended analysis, the intent of this volume, is warranted.

Overview of Organizational Portfolio Theory

Performance as a Cause of Organizational Change

Organization theorists have argued that organizational performance has to become low before it triggers organizational adaptation (Chandler 1962; Williamson 1964; Child 1972). Merely a decline of organizational performance from the maximum level will not cause adaptive organizational change. Organizations satisfice rather than maximize (Simon 1976). There exists a satisficing level of performance that the organization strives to maintain, which is substantially below the maximum level. The satisficing level is that level of performance that organizational managers consider satisfactory or acceptable. The main reason why organizations satisfice rather than maximize is due to bounded rationality, that is, to limits on the decision-making capacity of managers, given inadequacies such as in their knowledge (March and Simon 1958). Managers solve problems to restore performance to regain the satisficing level.

Organizational portfolio theory attends to the causes of organizational performance both from within the organization and from the external economy. These factors have been relatively neglected in that there has been no systematic *theoretical* treatment of organizational performance as a cause of adaptive change. There is widespread acceptance that low performance is a trigger of adaptive change (Chandler 1962; Williamson 1964; Child 1972), but little formal theory beyond that basic point. Given that organizational performance is accepted as a cause of adaptive organizational change, it behooves us to consider fully the implications of this insight. Its ramifications need to be developed in order to maximize the explanatory power that may be obtained. This book seeks to advance a systematic theory of organizational performance as a cause of organizational change. This leads to an extended consideration of how the variables in the organizational portfolio interact with organizational maladaptation to produce change and stasis. It further leads to an analysis of the different kinds of organizational change that flow from different values of organizational performance, such as low and high performance.

In this way, the present book develops the implications of the idea that organizational change is performance driven. The argumentation is distilled into a series of theoretical propositions. These are intended to provide guidance for future empirical research. The theoretical propositions may be readily turned into testable hypotheses by expressing them in terms of measured variables. Such future empirical research will establish the validity or otherwise of the theory. Bold conjectures that go beyond the existing view provide the opportunity for scientific progress and also the possibility of falsification (Popper 1963).

The theory that managerial decision making is satisficing and the derived implication that organizational change is performance driven have existed in the literature for many years and enjoyed wide acceptance. Thus it is not premature to more fully probe the adequacy of these ideas, and one way to hasten this process is to tease out a large number of their testable implications. Such testing may confirm the theory or lead to it being modified to accommodate real-world complexities or lead to its refutation, which would open the door to a radical revision of the theory of organizational change. Enough evidence has been accumulated to date to believe that the basic idea that low performance drives organizational change has some validity, so the wholesale refutation of the theory seems an unlikely outcome of empirical testing, but the extent of confirmation and disconfirmation of the theory is a matter for future empirical work.

Theory construction is, by its nature, a process of abstraction, in which many complexities and other causal mechanisms are waved away by caveats such as "other things being equal." This gives an extended theory that occupies a whole book, such as the present one, a sometimes narrow or tendentious quality. There are numerous other aspects to organizational change other than the way it is affected by organizational performance. However, focusing a book on just the performance-driven aspect of organizational change may help us understand this aspect more fully so that eventually it may be combined with others to attain a more complete understanding of organizational change. By stating the theory clearly and starkly, we hope to provide a stimulus to fresh thinking about organizational change that will prompt future research.

Organizational adaptation involves a move from maladaptation to adaptation (i.e., from misfit into fit). As noted above, the theory is concerned with organizational adaptation of any kind (e.g., organizational structure, strategy, human resource management, information technology, and environmental scanning). Throughout the book, it will often be convenient when talking about adaptations to make reference to structure to provide concrete examples, but this is just for illustration and the arguments apply generally (unless stated otherwise). Adaptation or fit can involve an organizational characteristic that is internal to the organization (e.g., its structure) or external (e.g., an alliance with another organization). These organizational characteristics are adapted or fitted to states of the environment (e.g., technological change in the market) or to states inside the organization (e.g., organizational size, that is, the number of employees). These environmental or organizational states are considered situational or contingency factors. They are contingency factors in that the level of organizational performance is affected by the degree of fit (i.e., adaptation) of the organizational characteristics to these contingency factors. Therefore, performance resulting from the organizational characteristic is contingent upon the level of the contingency factor (Lawrence and Lorsch 1967).

Maladaptation or misfit between organizational characteristic and situation lowers organizational performance. Adaptation into fit will occur when organizational performance becomes low, that is, when it drops below the satisficing level. Thus while change in the situation inclines the organization to make adaptive change, whether it does so or not is affected by its overall level of performance. Performance mediates the impact of situational changes on organizational adaptation. Hence understanding when organizational adaptation will occur requires understanding the level of performance. Because organizational performance is the result of a number of factors, the causes of performance need to be analyzed.

Misfit depresses organizational performance but usually not enough for performance to become unsatisfactory. To become unsatisfactory, performance usually requires causes additional to misfit to make it drop below the satisficing level. Therefore, adaptive change from misfit into fit is often caused by other causes combining with misfit to cause unsatisfactory performance. The conjunction between misfit and other causes of performance is key for organizational adaptation. The various causes combine to produce the level of performance. As these causes and their interactions vary over time, the level of performance fluctuates. The issue is whether the fluctuation of performance goes low enough to trigger organizational adaptation. Conversely, there is also the issue of whether performance rises high enough to cause organizational growth.

An organization whose internal organizational characteristics and its situation are in fit, has, as a result, higher organizational performance. This higher performance tends to lead the organization to expand, such as by growing in size, increasing its geographical scope, or adding new products or services. Such growth is more likely and likely to be faster and more sustained when performance is boosted by the causes of performance additional to fit. Therefore, the conjunction of fit and these other causes raising performance will tend to lead to high growth. Conversely, the conjunction of fit with the other causes lowering performance will reduce growth or even prevent it. Hence the key to growth is the conjunction between fit and the other causes of performance.

Both adaptation and growth are affected by performance: Low performance is necessary for adaptation, and medium to high performance increases the probability and extent of growth. The level of performance is a crucial ingredient for both adaptation and growth.

Explaining Cumulative Organizational Change

If the organization experiences low and then high performance, it will tend to make an adaptation and then tend to have a growth increment. If the organization experiences repeated episodes of low performance and then high performance, it will have repeated increments of adaptation and growth, thereby becoming internally complex, large, and successful. To experience such cumulative growth in size and structure, the organization must go through the

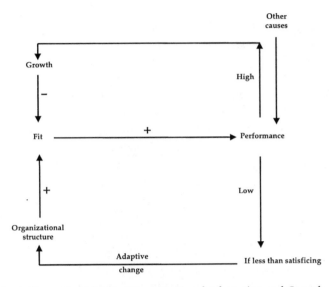

Figure 1.3   A Theoretical Model of Organizational Adaptation and Growth

cycle of incremental growth and adaptation again and again. But when the organization has made a structural adaptation and regained fit, why does it not remain there? Why does the organization make a new growth increment and then another structural adaptation? How can it do this if fit is an equilibrium state so that once the organization has regained fit it remains there?

Increments of growth and adaptation often follow each other because fit is not an equilibrium. It is not the case that once an organization has gained fit it remains there indefinitely. Fit produces higher organizational performance that tends to lead to organizational growth that, in turn, leads to misfit (as signified by the negative effect of growth on fit in Figure 1.3). Growth in size causes the organizational size to become too great for its existing organizational structure. Thus fit tends to lead to misfit (shown as the upper pathway in Figure 1.3). This misfit causes lower performance and eventually tends to lead into fit (shown as the lower pathway in Figure 1.3). Fit leads to misfit again, thus restarting the cycle once more so that it repeats again and again. (Each cycle alternates between the upper and lower pathways in Figure 1.3.) Thus the organization is seldom static and tends to be restlessly moving into fit and then into misfit. This leads to recurrent increments of adaptation and growth that cause cumulative organizational elaboration (e.g., structural complexity) and growth.

For example, as shown in Figure 1.4, a growth increment in organizational size leads the organization from fit (at point A) to misfit (at point B), which triggers a structural adaptation so that the organization regains fit by increasing its organizational structural formalization so that it moves to point C. This new fit causes a further growth increment (to D) so that the organization subsequently moves to another fit at point E. The repetition of this cycle of adaptive change and incremental growth causes the organization to grow from low to high size and from low to high organizational structural formalization. Thus the occurrence of cumulative change can be explained by the present model because fit is not an equilibrium state. The frequency of these movements between fit and misfit is affected by the other causes of performance besides fit and misfit so that the fluctuations in the overall level of performance are key.

Of course, growth is not an inevitable consequence of fit, for if the other causes are depressing enough, decline may ensue. Similarly, misfit may not lead to fit if the other causes boost performance sufficiently. This again places the focus on the interaction between fit and the other causes of performance. Cumulative growth and elaboration will thus not occur for all organizations; some will remain static or in decline.

Risk and the Organizational Portfolio

Let us now return to the idea that organizational change is performance driven. For an organization to experience low performance and then high performance, its performance must fluctuate considerably over time. The greater the performance fluctuation, the higher the probability that the organization will experience low performance that triggers adaptation and also high performance that leads to growth. For recurrent episodes of low and then high performance to occur, the organization needs to have quite rapid performance fluctuations. Risk is a measure of variations in performance over time (i.e., the amount of fluctuations). Higher risk leads the organization to have the low performance that leads to its adaptation and then the high performance that leads to its growth. To understand whether an organization is likely to make adaptive changes or not, and whether it is likely to grow or not, we need to understand its degree of risk.

Understanding the risk of an organization entails applying *portfolio theory*. In finance, a portfolio consists of several assets, each with an average return (e.g., profit) and a risk, that is, a variance over time in that return (Sharpe 1970; Brealey and Myers 1996). The higher the risk of each asset, the higher the risk

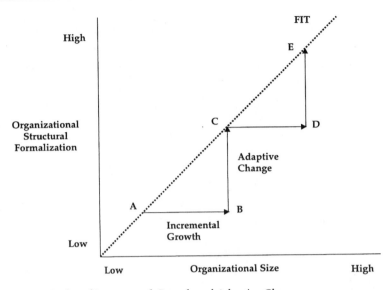

Figure 1.4 Cycles of Incremental Growth and Adaptive Change

of the portfolio. However, the risk of the portfolio is also affected by the correlations between the assets. Negative, or even low positive, correlations between assets reduce the risk of the portfolio. The overall risk of the portfolio is the result of the risks of the assets and the correlations between the assets. The reduction in the risk of a portfolio from having low positively or negatively correlated assets may be termed the *portfolio effect*.

The organization can likewise be seen as a portfolio in that it contains several assets with certain returns, risks, and correlations that interact to produce overall organizational return and risk (Ball and Brown 1980; Amihud and Lev 1981; Helfat and Teece 1987; Hoskisson 1987; Miller and Leiblein 1996). Organizational theory may be enriched by considering the organization in terms of such a perspective. The key is to understand the risk of each element of the organization and the correlations between them as positive or negative, thereby constituting a portfolio.

More specifically, the causes of organizational performance can be considered to form a portfolio, and each cause can be termed a factor in the organizational portfolio. These organizational portfolio factors include causes of organizational performance inside the organization (e.g., diversification) and outside it (e.g., competition). Each factor has a risk, and each is correlated to a varying extent, positively or negatively, with every other factor. The higher the risk of the factors and the more they are positively correlated with each other, the higher the risk of the organization and so the more it will adapt, grow, and succeed. The lower the risk of the factors or the more they are negatively correlated with each other, the lower the risk of the organization and so the less it will adapt and thus stagnate. Therefore, in analyzing each factor of performance, we need to understand how much it varies over time (its risk) and whether it is positively or negatively correlated with misfit and the other factors of performance.

The organizational portfolio is composed of organizational adaptation, that is, whether the organization is in fit or misfit on any aspect (e.g., structure or strategy), together with eight other organizational portfolio factors, which are causes of organizational performance other than organizational adaptation. The theory of performance-driven organizational change seeks to explain when a maladapted organization will make the needed adaptive change and subsequently grow. The explanation is in terms of the level of organizational performance that results from the organizational maladaptation together with other causes. The focus is on whether the performance effect of organizational maladaptation is reinforced or countered by each of the other organizational portfolio factors. Hence the interest is on the correlation between organizational maladaptation and each other portfolio factor. Therefore, the discussion is cast in terms of the adaptation and growth by the organization as conditioned by the eight other organizational portfolio factors, which are the business cycle, competition, debt, divisional risk, diversification, divisionalization, divestment, and directors. The role of each organizational portfolio factor is explained below.

In analyzing organizational change, we distinguish between change at the organizational, or corporate, level and change at the divisional level. We first discuss corporate-level adaptive change and then divisional-level adaptive change.

Portfolio Analysis of Corporate-Level Change

There are four organizational portfolio factors that affect organizational performance and lead to adaptive organizational change at the corporate level: the business cycle, competition, debt, and divisional risk. There are also four organizational portfolio factors that lead to a lack of adaptive organizational change at the corporate level: diversification, divisionalization, divestment, and directors. Each is briefly discussed here in turn. Refinements and qualifications are offered in the fuller analysis and argument in the ensuing chapters.

Portfolio Factors Leading to Corporate-Level Change

The Business Cycle

The organizational performance level is greatly affected by the business cycle, which contributes much to performance variation over time. The rising business cycle leads to growth and so misfit, as organizational size outstrips internal characteristics such as organizational structure. Although misfit depresses performance, this is more than offset by the buoyant business conditions around the peak of the business cycle, preventing performance from becoming low and preventing adaptive change so that the organization remains in misfit. Buoyant business conditions raise organizational performance, whereas misfit depresses it. Thus the effect on organizational performance of the business conditions is negatively correlated with the effect of misfit. This is a portfolio effect whereby the buoyant business conditions offset misfit, and so needed organizational adaptation fails to occur.

When the business cycle subsequently falls, it drags down organizational performance. Now the business cycle is positively correlated with misfit, and both are depressing performance. This causes performance to become low and unsatisfactory, so causing adaptive change. The organization moves from misfit into fit by adopting better-fitting internal characteristics, such as its organizational structure.

Thus the business cycle contributes strongly to fluctuations in organizational performance and constitutes a high-risk factor in the organizational portfolio. The business cycle correlation with misfit alters from negative to positive with the rise and fall of the cycle, thereby alternating between retarding and prompting organizational adaptation. These alternations in the sign of the correlation happen every cycle so that the business cycle can drive recurrent organizational adaptation and growth, thus producing a large, successful organization with elaborate internal characteristics, such as organizational structure.

Competition

Another environmental factor affecting organizational performance is competition. Stronger competition increases organizational adaptation and decreases organizational growth. Stronger competition comes from several sources, including from having more competitors who are each well organized—that is, they are in fit. When an organization is in misfit, its performance will be depressed if its competitors are in fit because they can take business away from the firm. However, if the competitors are in misfit, then they are as disorganized as the firm and so it will not suffer loss of business to its competitors and its performance will not be depressed, ceteris paribus. Thus low performance and the resulting organizational adaptation of a firm in misfit are more likely when its competitors are in fit.

Organizational adaptation is less likely when the misfit of a firm is offset by the misfit of its competitors. Then the normally depressing effect of misfit on performance is countered by the effect of competitor misfit in raising firm performance. The boosting effect of competitor misfit on the performance of the firm is negatively correlated with the depressing effect of the misfit of the firm on its performance. Thus the portfolio effect again comes into play, keeping organizational performance satisfactory and thus preventing needed organizational adaptation. Again, what is required for change to occur is for the portfolio effect to be switched off; that is, the negative correlation has to become positive. This occurs when the competitors move into fit, thereby depressing firm performance and reinforcing the effect of firm misfit, so causing the firm to adapt.

Debt

Debt leads to the organization making needed adaptations. It tends to raise the level of organizational performance that the organization's managers regard as satisfactory because interest payments have to be made regularly. A certain minimum operating profit has to be made to cover the interest payments. This amount has to be made before there is any profit to declare to shareholders and reinvest. Thus the satisficing level is raised by debt. This implies that organizational adaptive change is triggered at higher levels of performance with debt than without it. For example, a firm that might be making a satisfactory annual operating profit at $5 million, with debt may need to make $10 million to be satisfactory. Thus an operating profit of $8 million that would not have triggered change previously now causes the firm with debt to take adaptive action. Debt depresses performance and therefore reinforces any depressing effect on performance due to misfit. Thus debt and misfit can be positively correlated within the organizational portfolio. In this situation, debt inclines the organization to make needed adaptive changes.

Divisional Risk

The preceding three factors operate at the level of the whole organization (i.e., the corporation). However, the fourth factor operates at the level of a part of the organization, the division, which feeds up to effect change in the overall organization. High-risk divisions have large fluctuations in their performance, which directly contribute to fluctuations in overall organizational performance, thereby raising the risk of the overall organization (i.e., corporate risk). The large performance fluctuations of the corporation lead it to make needed adaptive changes and thereby lead the corporation to tend to grow and succeed long term. In contrast, low-risk divisions have small fluctuations and so produce only limited corporate risk and organizational change. Divisional risk affects corporate risk when they are positively correlated. This aspect of divisional risk is termed here *systematic divisional risk,* and its magnitude is measured by the divisional beta coefficient, which is analogous to the beta coefficient in finance.

The high risk of a division can arise from it being in a high-growth industry that causes the division to grow rapidly so that it cycles in and out of fit with resulting fluctuations in divisional performance. Conversely, the low risk of a division can arise from its dominant position in its industry, such as being an oligopolist that has high market share and can control prices. Because of differences in position in their industry, divisions within the same corporation can vary considerably in their risk. Notwithstanding such differences among divisions in their risks, the higher their average risk, the higher the risk of the corporation.

Portfolio Factors Leading to Lack of Corporate-Level Change

Diversification and Divisionalization

As a firm expands during growth, it may diversify. Diversification combines multiple business cycles from each product market, so lowering risk (i.e., smoothing out performance fluctuations). Diversification also leads to adoption of the multidivisional structure in place of the functional structure. The multidivisional structure also lowers risk. The manager in charge of each division seeks to smooth out fluctuations in the performance of the division, thereby reducing its risk and that of the corporation. Moreover, the autonomous decision making of each division reduces the positive correlation between their performances and increases the negative correlations between them, so intensifying the portfolio effect of diversification. Thus corporate risk is reduced by the divisional structure, which reinforces the tendency of diversification to reduce risk. This leads to less adaptation and growth long term for diversified, divisionalized corporations.

Divestment

Corporations can respond to low performance by divestment, particularly if the corporation has diversified so that it can divest one division without affecting the remaining divisions. Divestment increases organizational slack so that its performance becomes satisfactory again without having to make an adaptation. Thus divestment by a corporation can allow it to avoid adaptation. Divestment has a boosting effect on organizational performance, and, because it frequently occurs when performance is low, divestment offsets the causes of that low performance, such as organizational maladaptation. Thus the effect of divestment can be negatively correlated with the effect of organizational misfit. Hence divestment is another way that the portfolio effect can be introduced, thus preventing needed organizational change. The result of divestment leads to less adaptation and growth long term.

Directors

The shorthand term *directors* in our list of factors should be understood as referring to non-executive directors. (Besides having the virtue of brevity, this use also accords with the everyday use of the word *director* to refer to a non-executive director when that is the only role they hold in the company, the executive directors being also managers of the company.)

Non-executive directors reduce corporate risk. A board dominated by non-executive directors constrains management and reduces corporate risk, which impedes adaptive organizational change. Thus non-executive directors reduce corporate risk and thereby corporate change. In contrast, executive directors on the board lead to the adoption of riskier corporate strategies that produce more fluctuation in corporate performance. These greater fluctuations foster organizational adaptation and growth. However, the greater performance fluctuations increase the probability of a crisis of poor performance so that, in that situation, executive directors are replaced by non-executive directors.

Corporate governance is also affected by the other organizational portfolio factors. Diversification, divisionalization, and divestment help keep corporate performance satisfactory. In these circumstances, boards of directors allow managers to gain power by becoming directors and board chairs, thus undercutting the ability of the board to exercise independent control of managers on behalf of shareholders. However, adverse economic circumstances, through declines in the business cycle, increased competition, and vulnerability brought on by greater corporate debt, lead to low performance and criticisms of managers and directors as failing in their duties. Boards are reformed to decrease the role of managers and increase the representation of shareholders so that they are more independent (i.e., a higher proportion of non-executive directors and a non-executive chair). However, when the business cycle turns back up and corporate performance is restored, managerial credibility is renewed, and boards change their composition to become less independent of managers again. Thus the interaction of the organizational portfolio factors that determine corporate performance shapes board structure.

In summary, there are forces that push firms to adapt and grow and forces that push them not to adapt and so not grow. The forces that push them to adapt and grow are those that amplify the swings downward and upward in organizational performance, that is, those that raise the risk of the organizational portfolio. These are the business cycle, competition, debt, and divisional risk. The forces that retard adaptation and growth are those that mainly dampen swings in organizational performance, that is, those that reduce the risk in the organizational portfolio or otherwise keep organizational performance satisfactory. These are diversification, divisionalization, divestment, and directors.

Adaptations May Be Confounded

Organizational portfolio theory seeks to explain when adaptive change will occur, but it also seeks to shed light on whether such changes are seen as adaptive or not. Adaptation necessarily implies that the changes are beneficial for the organization, but some changes purported to be adaptive appear not to be. When a firm makes an adaptive change, this sometimes fails to produce the expected positive results. The reorganization intends to move the firm from misfit to fit in order to raise performance. Although firm performance may rise after the reorganization, it sometimes remains constant and other times falls. Such mixed outcomes lead to querying the value of the reorganization. However, even where the reorganization is genuinely an adaptive move from misfit to fit that is producing benefits, these may be masked on occasions, leading to the mixed outcomes being observed. There is reason to believe that a portfolio effect is once again in operation, and so the rising performance from the adaptation can be offset by performance being depressed by other causes.

Adaptation occurs at a particular time because then there is a temporary association between misfit, which is depressing performance, and the other causes that are also depressing organizational performance. At this time, the effects on performance of misfit and these other causes are positively correlated, reinforcing each other. This conjunction drives performance down to become unsatisfactory, leading to adaptive organizational change. However, the association between misfit and the other causes of performance is just a happenstance, so it falls apart with the passage of time. After adaptation, the positive correlation may break down and could even reverse and become a negative correlation. In this latter case, the positive effect of the new fit is masked by the negative effect of the other causes. The new fit causes the performance to rise, whereas the other causes depress the performance and are stronger than fit, so performance decreases. Relative to fit, the stronger effect of the other causes means that they contribute more variance to performance— that is, they are a higher risk in the organizational portfolio than fit is. Thus their correlation with fit shifting from positive to negative more than offsets the effect of fit, leading to a false impression that adaptive fit is counterproductive.

A Causal Model of
Corporate-Level Change

The organizational portfolio theory explanation of change at the corporate level, that is, at the level of the whole organization, may be drawn together in a causal diagram. The eight portfolio factors and their effects are shown in

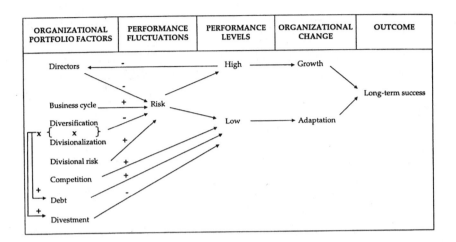

Figure 1.5 Organizational Portfolio Factors as Causes of Risk, Performance, and Organizational Change

Figure 1.5. Each factor affects firm performance, either its risk (i.e., fluctuation) or level. Greater firm risk makes it more probable that its performance will fluctuate down to low and up to high levels. Low firm performance leads to organizational adaptation, whereas high performance leads to organizational growth.

Five organizational portfolio factors affect firm risk: two positively—the business cycle and divisional risk, and three negatively—non-executive directors, diversification, and divisionalization, the last two in interaction. High-risk causes performance to fluctuate between high and low recurrently, creating large growth, elaborate structure and systems, and long-term success. Business cycles increase risk and so lead to adaptation, growth, and success. Similarly, higher-risk divisions fluctuate highly in their performance, and this contributes to the fluctuation in overall firm performance and hence to higher firm risk and adaptation, growth, and success. Conversely, non-executive directors reduce risk, and the resulting avoidance of high performance helps prevent their replacement by executives (shown as the negative feedback from performance to non-executive directors). Diversification spreads the firm across a number of business cycles, and divisionalization intensifies this effect by further reducing the correlation between the performances of divisions so that corporate risk is decreased. The risk reduction from non-executive directors, diversification, and divisionalization reduces organizational growth, adaptation, and success.

Three organizational portfolio factors directly affect the performance level, leading to low performance levels: competition, debt, and divestment. (The positive signs on the causal arrows from these variables to low firm performance level signify that the factor increases the probability of low performance; a negative sign signifies that the factor decreases the probability of low performance.) Competition lowers the performance of the firm, increasing the probability that needed adaptive changes will be made. Debt also lowers firm performance, increasing the probability of adaption. In contrast, divestment decreases the probability that firm performance will become low enough to trigger adaptation. Thus competition and debt lead to growth, adaptation, and success, whereas divestment leads to chronic maladaptation and suboptimal growth and success.

Overall, the business cycle, divisional risk, competition, and debt promote adaptive change by the organization and its growth and long-term success. Non-executive directors, diversification, divisionalization, and divestment lead to lack of adaptive change, limited growth, and long-term success considerably below the potential of the firm.

These corporate-level phenomena are paralleled, and reinforced, by similar phenomena at the divisional level.

Portfolio Analysis of Divisional-Level Change

The performance level and risk of a division affect its change. Corporate performance and risk also affect divisional change. In this way, change in a division is affected by the performances of the other divisions in a corporation. Again, we need to analyze the organization as a portfolio.

Divisional adaptation is affected by the performance of the division. Most obviously, a low performance by the division makes it ripe for adaptive change. Less obviously, the probability that corporate management will intervene in a division is affected by the performances of the other divisions. Further, the risk of the division affects its probability of adapting. In turn, divisional performance and adaptation affect corporate performance and adaptation.

In a multidivisional corporation, the head office, or corporate office, disciplines the divisions to perform at a higher level than they might attain if each division was a freestanding firm. This provides a mechanism to define the level of divisional performance at a moderately high level and enforce this on divisional managers, which helps keep corporate performance at a moderately high level. However, these intended positive outcomes are undermined by several mechanisms that lower the performance of divisions and the corporation. These performance-reducing effects arise from portfolio effects.

In a multidivisional corporation, the overall performance of the corporation results from the portfolio of performances of the divisions. The high-performing divisions are offset by low-performing divisions so that there is a negative correlation between the performances of these two sets of divisions. Therefore, a satisfactory level of corporate performance may be attained even though some divisions perform below this level. As long as corporate performance remains satisfactory, there may be little impetus for the head office to intervene to improve the performance of these divisions, which may remain in misfit with limited growth. Moreover, when corporate performance becomes unsatisfactory, there may be several divisions that are unsatisfactory performers simultaneously. Given bounded rationality, the corporate center may be unable to rectify all these divisions simultaneously and so rectifies them sequentially. Corporate performance may be restored to the satisfactory level even though some divisions remain poor performers, and so corporate office ceases its interventions, thereby allowing those divisions to continue to perform poorly.

The concept of risk can be applied to each of the divisions. A high-risk division will have large fluctuations in its performance so that its performance swings over time from low to high and then low, causing adaptation and growth increments recurrently, leading it to grow large and succeed. Thus high-risk divisions contribute to the growth and success of the corporation. However, low-risk divisions tend to lack the episodes of low performance that lead to adaptation, and so they tend to become chronically maladapted and stagnate, thereby decreasing corporate performance. More exactly, the interaction of divisional risk and divisional performance levels affects divisional adaptation and growth. In terms of the familiar strategic planning matrix, the cash cow (profit-making) division has low risk and high performance. As a result, it tends to avoid episodes of low divisional performance, and, hence, it fails to make needed adaptive changes and stagnates. Its performance becomes mediocre over the long term, and this depresses the performance of the corporation substantially. Thus divisional risk affects corporate adaptation and growth. This is an effect of divisional risk on divisional performance that contributes to corporate performance, and it is distinct from the effect of divisional risk on corporate risk, discussed in a previous section. Both effects of divisional risk increase corporate adaptation, growth, and success.

The main interactions between divisions and the corporate level are shown in Figure 1.6. Low corporate performance in a divisionalized corporation implies that several divisions are performing poorly simultaneously. Interventions in these divisions to rectify their poor performance tend to be sequential rather than concurrent. When some of these divisions have their performance restored, corporate performance regains the satisficing level so that further interventions into the divisions cease. The result is that divisional adaptation is only partial, leaving some divisions maladapted and so still performing poorly, which adversely affects corporate performance. Moreover, the fact that low corporate performance is accompanied by low performance of some divisions can lead to misattribution to the divisions. Corporate management overemphasizes divisional changes, and needed corporate-level adaptations are not made, which again adversely affects corporate performance. The low risk of the cash cow division causes it also to avoid making needed adaptations so that it becomes part of the pattern of partial divisional adaptation. Hence the performance of the cash cow becomes suboptimal over the longer term, thus contributing to mediocre corporate performance.

The optimal portfolio for a corporation would be divisions that are all positively correlated with each other to ensure that the corporation experiences fluctuations in its performance that drive its adaptation and growth long term. Also, the divisions would all be of medium-level risk. However, bounded rationality and concern for survival will lead to the adoption of a portfolio that contains some lower-risk divisions.

Plan of the Book

The aim of this book is to present a new theory: organizational portfolio theory. Each chapter discusses one aspect of the new theory and distills its ideas into a number of formal theoretical propositions.

Chapter 2 formally states the idea that organizational change is driven by performance and that the organization can be seen as a portfolio. This introduces the concept of *risk* applied to organizations and shows how the *portfolio* properties of the organization arise and their effects upon risk. These are the foundational concepts used throughout later chapters.

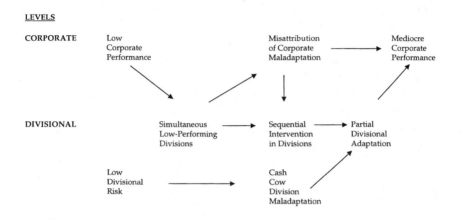

Figure 1.6 Interactions Between Divisional and Corporate Levels

Chapter 3 presents a theory of how the *business cycle* influences organizational adaptation and growth and also discusses how business cycles differ across industries, with consequences for industry structure and for the organizations therein. Further, the effects of organizational adaptation on business cycles are discussed.

Chapter 4 analyzes the effect of *competition* on the organization, including that of adaptive organizational changes by its competitors. Competition affects both the organization and the industry structure.

Chapter 5 explains why the benefits of organizational *adaptations* may often be obscured. Organizational portfolio theory is drawn upon to understand how adaptation interacts with other causes of organizational performance to produce its apparent effects.

Chapter 6 applies the concept of the portfolio to the *diversified, divisionalized* corporation. The argument is made that both its strategy and structure reduce risk and that this has detrimental long-term effects on the diversified, divisionalized corporation.

Chapter 7 examines issues in *corporate governance* from the perspective of the new theory. This sheds fresh light on some of the perplexing questions in the corporate governance arena.

Chapter 8 unbundles the organization by examining the *performances of the parts of the organization,* such as its divisions. These determine organizational performance, and this fact leads to interesting ambiguities in causal inferences by management. This in turn affects corporate adaptation.

Chapter 9 examines the *risks of divisions* and how risk affects the adaptation and growth of divisions and of the corporation. These processes tend to reinforce the processes identified in the earlier chapters. Divisional risk affects the optimal organizational portfolio.

Chapter 10 concludes the book with a *summary,* discussing *interactions* among the organizational portfolio factors. It also brings together the *new theoretical view about the defects of the diversified, divisionalized corporation* propounded throughout the book. The diversified, divisionalized corporation has hitherto been seen as the solution to many problems in organizational theory literature, but our analysis reveals negative aspects that have so far received little systematic attention. Thus an *agenda for future research* is presented as a call to arms for our colleagues.

Conclusions

Organizational change is affected by organizational performance. Therefore, to better understand why organizational change occurs, and fails to occur, we need to understand organizational performance in greater depth. It is widely acknowledged that a crisis of poor performance is needed to trigger organizational change, yet there is a lack of systematic theory about how organizational performance varies over time. The aim of this book is to offer such a theory. It draws on ideas from economics and finance. In particular, portfolio theory is used to model the organization as a portfolio. Each element of the portfolio has a certain risk and correlates with each other element in ways that determine overall organizational performance and its fluctuations over time. Organizational portfolio theory seeks to identify major causes of organizational performance and the mechanisms that amplify or dampen fluctuations in the performance of the organization. In this way, hopefully, we can gain new insight into why needed organizational changes occur or are prevented.

Performance-Driven
Organizational Change

Organizational change is driven by organizational performance. The different effects of high and low organizational performance can be distinguished, with low performance causing organizational adaptation and high performance fostering organizational growth. Fluctuations in organizational performance are shown to be affected by the portfolio properties of the organization. This chapter lays down the framework that is used in the rest of the book.

Throughout this book, we analyze two aspects of organizational change: organizational adaptation and organizational growth. Organizational adaptation occurs whenever an organization alters some attribute of itself to bring it into a better fit with its situation, so improving organizational performance. The situation may be thought of as consisting of characteristics of the external environment and also of intraorganizational or contingency factors (e.g., size or diversification). For example, organizational adaptation occurs when a diversified firm with a functional structure that is a misfit adopts instead a divisional structure that is a fit, thereby raising performance.

Organizational growth refers to an increase in organizational size or scale, such as number of employees, sales, or number of branches (Fligstein 1990b). These various attributes of size or scale are not identical but tend to correlate highly (Donaldson 1996a). Moreover, they tend to have similar effects (Donaldson 1996a). Organizational size affects many aspects of organizational structure (Pugh, Hickson, Hinings, and Turner 1968, 1969; Blau 1970, 1972; Blau and Schoenherr 1971; Grinyer and Yasai-Ardekani 1981). Further, organizational size or scale tend also to be associated with the degree of strategic diversification of a corporation (Grinyer and Yasai-Ardekani 1981). Diversification has effects separate from or additional to those of organizational size (Rumelt 1974). However, because diversification and size tend to be associated, an increase in size is often accompanied by diversification. Again, increasing organizational size is associated with greater geographic extensiveness and use of more advanced technology of production (Utterback and Abernathy 1975). Thus, for many purposes, we can conceive of a unidimensional construct of organizational growth that encompasses not only increasing size but also strategic diversification, increasing geographical extensiveness and more advanced technology.

In interpreting the present theory, organizational adaptation and organizational growth should be understood as having these broad, inclusive meanings unless specified as having narrower meanings. Throughout this book, the term organizational change is used to refer to both organizational adaptation and *organizational growth*. Organizational portfolio theory is a theory of the effects of organizational performance on organizational change in this sense. The theory states the effect of organizational performance on organizational adaptation and on organizational growth.

We begin by examining why low performance is necessary to cause organizational adaptation. Then the role of high organizational performance fostering organizational growth is briefly established. Given that variations in performance are so crucial for organizational change, this forces attention on variations in performance over time. To understand such performance variations, we need to adopt the concept of risk and the theory of the organization as a portfolio.

Low Performance Triggers
Organizational Adaptation

The sociological theory of functionalism holds that each structure has a particular functional value and that, over time, structures are adopted that exhibit greater functionality (Merton 1949). The performance of the existing structure feeds back to alter the structure to permit greater functionality, that is, higher performance. Where the structure presently existing is not highly functional, the low performance feeds back, causing structural change by adopting a more suitable structure. Structural-functional theories of organization explain structural change as occurring in this way (e.g., Burns and Stalker 1961; Woodward 1965).

According to structural contingency theory, a structure misfitted to the contingencies causes low performance that triggers structural change (Chandler 1962; Williamson 1964; Child 1972). Thus the intervening process between structural misfit and structural adaptation is low performance. Organizational performance mediates the effect of structural misfit on structural change, in the sense that an organization in misfit can nevertheless have a range of organizational performance with structural adaptation triggered only when performance is low. This mediating role of organizational performance is due to two reasons. First, there are more causes of organizational performance than just structural misfit. Second, organizational performance needs to drop below the satisficing level before structural change occurs. These two factors loosen the connection between structural misfit and structural change, thereby strengthening the mediating role of organizational performance. Each is considered in turn.

Multiple Causes of
Organizational Performance

If organizational performance is wholly determined by structure, a misfitting structure will always produce low performance and so trigger structural adaptation quickly and reliably. However, it seems extremely unlikely that organizational performance has only a single cause—organizational structure. There seem to be many other causes of organizational performance, such as strategy, human resources, product, marketing, production, logistics, and procurement. Given that organizational performance is affected by many other variables besides organizational structure, it also seems plausible that these other variables together have more effect on organizational performance than does structure (Child 1972). Therefore, the level of organizational performance at any time is conditioned by many variables. Thus structural misfit might be offset by positive effects of some other causes of performance so that performance is not low (Child 1972).

Given that organizational performance mediates the effect of structural misfit on structural adaptation, structural adaptation is affected by all the variables that affect performance. Therefore, structural adaptation is jointly determined by structural misfit and the other causes of performance. Organizational performance will be low only when structural misfit is accompanied by depressive values on the other causes of performance; only then will structural adaptation occur. Thus the multiple determination of performance means that structural adaptation will not always occur when there is structural misfit. The theoretical analysis of structural adaptation has to consider a much wider set of causes than just structural misfit. The question becomes the values taken by all the causes of performance simultaneously. There is a portfolio of causes of organizational performance that affect the probability of structural adaptation. It is the overall state of the portfolio that determines whether structural adaptation occurs or not.

The mediating role of organizational performance is due not only to multiple causes of organizational performance but also to another theoretical mechanism: the need for performance to become low before organizational change occurs.

Performance Must Drop
Below the Satisficing Level

Organizational performance gains added importance as a factor that determines whether organizational adaptation occurs, because organizational performance must drop substantially before it triggers organizational adaptation. This is a further reason why organizational performance mediates the effect of organizational maladaptation on organizational adaptation. The simple occurrence of organizational maladaptation is not enough to cause organizational adaptation because organizational maladaptation does not necessarily cause the level of organizational performance to fall low enough to cause organizational adaptation. Therefore, causality does not flow through directly from organizational maladaptation to organizational adaptation. Other factors have to affect organizational performance before it reaches the level that is required to trigger organizational change.

If structural adaptation is caused by *any* drop in performance below the maximum, it will occur readily. Indeed, structural misfit alone will produce less than maximum performance, and so structural adaptation will occur rapidly and reliably as soon as structure is in misfit. However, organizational theory embraces the idea that for change to occur performance needs to drop substantially below the maximum. The idea is that there is a satisficing or satisfactory level of performance that is quite modest, that is, considerably below the maximum possible performance level, but sufficient for organizational managers not to make changes because the situation is not a problem (Simon 1976). Thus organizational change occurs only when performance drops below this satisficing level, which means that organizational performance has to become low before organizational adaptation occurs.

The basic idea that informs the new theory is that organizational adaptation occurs only when organizational performance is low. This idea is widely accepted in organizational theory. It is found within numerous theoretical and empirical contributions. Moreover, it is advanced by several of the leading organization theorists and researchers, as now seen.

Simon (1976) and March and Simon (1958) state the point highly generally in their theory that administrative decision making is problemistic. According to them, decision makers do not maximize but rather satisfice, that is, strive to maintain outcomes, including performance, at a satisfactory or acceptable level. Simon (1976) writes, "Administrative theory is peculiarly the theory of intended and bounded rationality—of the behavior of human beings who *satisfice* because they have not the wits to *maximize*" (p. xxviii, emphasis in original). He draws the distinction between satisficing and maximizing in the following way:

> Whereas economic man maximizes—selects the best alternative from among all those available to him, his cousin, administrative man, satisfices—looks for a course of action that is satisfactory or "good enough." Examples of satisficing criteria, familiar enough to businessmen if unfamiliar to most economists, are "share of market," "adequate profit," [and] "fair price." (p. xxix)

Bounded rationality, and with it satisficing rather than maximizing administrative behavior, arises for several reasons to do with the inherent limitations of human decision making, including limited knowledge of cause and effect that prevents the selection of the best possible course of action (Simon 1976).

Similarly, March and Simon (1958) write,

> An alternative is *satisfactory* if: (1) there exists a set of criteria that describes minimally satisfactory alternatives, and (2) the alternative in question meets or exceeds all these criteria.

Most human decision-making, whether individual or organizational, is concerned with the discovery and selection of satisfactory alternatives; only in exceptional cases is it concerned with the discovery and selection of optimal alternatives. . . . To optimize requires processes several orders of magnitude more complex than those required to satisfice. An example is the difference between searching a haystack to find the sharpest needle in it and searching the haystack to find a needle sharp enough to sew with. (p. 140, emphasis in original)

Thus managers satisfice rather than maximize, and so rather than acting to restore performance as soon as organizational performance drops below its maximum, action is taken only when performance drops below the satisficing level. Hence organizational performance needs to fall considerably down from the maximum before adaptive organizational change is undertaken. Only when organizational performance falls below the satisficing level is adaptive organizational change triggered. Human decision making consists of solving problems, and in the absence of a problem, that is, unsatisfactory performance, the *status quo* is maintained.

When organizational performance is above the satisficing level, managers tend to avoid taking risks, and so their organizations tend not to change. Hence success leads to relatively conservative organizational practices, whereas the stimulus of poor performance leads to organizational risk taking and change. This theory is supported by empirical research that shows that firms with lower levels of performance take larger risks than firms with higher levels of performance; that is, high performers are more conservative (Bowman 1980; Figenbaum and Thomas 1986; Bromiley 1991a, 1991b; Wiseman and Bromiley 1991). Theory and research lead to the view that there is a target level of performance that, if exceeded, leads to conservatism, and if not attained, leads to risk taking to try to attain the target (March 1988; March and Shapira 1987; Lant and Montgomery 1987; Wiseman and Bromiley 1996). The target level constitutes the satisficing level. The satisficing level is set by prior experience rather than by the ideal aspirations that would constitute maximizing. The satisficing level is a function of the performance levels attained in the prior periods and how far targets were missed in prior periods, which is to say it is subject to adaptive aspirations (March 1988; March and Shapira 1987; Lant and Montgomery 1987).

The level of organizational performance deemed to be satisficing for an organization can change over time. Recent successes may shift the satisficing level upward, in that managers or other stakeholders may revise their expectations upward in the light of increases in performance (Cyert and March 1963; Bromiley 1991a). However, the satisficing level can also be revised downward, in the light of decreases in performance. Such downward movements in satisficing level may offset any upward movements so that over the long run the satisficing level could remain fairly constant.

The idea that only organizational performance below the satisficing level leads to organizational change has been foundational in theories of organizational structural change. Williamson (1964) argues that firms fail to adopt optimal structures because their managers build empires where the firm is not subject to competition and so has slack resources. Again, Williamson (1985) states the M-form theory: that large corporations adopt the M-form (i.e., multidivisional) structure to obviate control loss, but he makes the caveat that this happens only under competitive conditions in which performance decrements become serious. Similarly, Child (1972) argues that the presence of organizational slack allows managements to persist with structures that are ill-suited to their situational contingencies and so are suboptimal in effectiveness:

> If performance exceeds this "satisficing" level . . . the decision-making group *may* take the view that the margin of surplus permits them to adopt structural arrangements which accord the better with their own preferences, even at some extra administrative cost to the organization. (p. 11, emphasis in original)

Thus an organization in misfit between its structure and its contingencies may continue in this state rather than make adaptive change because of the presence of slack that keeps its performance at least at the satisficing level.

Hence organizational scholars have, in these ways, made the general theoretical proposition that poor organizational performance is a necessary cause of organizational adaptation (Simon 1976; March and Simon 1958; Williamson 1964, 1985; Child 1972, 1997).

Empirical research supports the idea that organizations make needed changes only when their performance becomes poor. In his seminal studies of business history, Chandler (1962) records the decisive role of performance crisis in bringing about needed organizational change. For example, at Du Pont, managers had identified the need to change from a functional to a multidivisional structure as a result of the diversification by their company, but this structural change was not implemented until the company's performance declined. Chandler (1962) writes that a crisis of poor performance led to the acceptance of the multidivisional structure:

> The company's financial statement for the first half of 1921 provided the shock that finally precipitated a major reorganization. In those six months, as the postwar recession became increasingly severe, the company had lost money on every product except explosives. At the end of the first six months, the profits from explosives had been close to $2,500,000, but the losses for the other products had been over $3,800,000. The largest deficit, over a million, came from the Dyestuffs Department. Paints added a loss of $717,356; cellulose products $746,360; and Fabrikoid $863,904. When other items, such as interest, were taken into account, the total net loss for the six-month period was $2,433,491. (p. 104)

At General Motors, the multidivisional form again was adopted only when the CEO confronted a crisis of slumping sales and massive excessive inventories that threatened the financial well-being of the company. As Chandler (1962) writes,

> While [the division managers] continued to buy supplies, the demand for their completed products fell off precipitously. . . . With fewer sales, inventories continued to grow, and at the end of October [1920], their value had reached a total of close to $210 million and, as the 1922 Annual Report added, "exceeding by $60 million the allotments of the Executive and Finance Committees. . . . This excess accounted for about 70% of the borrowing at that time."
>
> By then, too, the automobile market had collapsed. . . . [B]y the end of October, the situation had become so serious that many General Motors managers were having difficulty in finding cash to cover such immediate needs as invoices and payrolls. For November, sales dropped below 13,000, one-fourth of what they had been in early summer, and by the next January, production reached a record low of 6,151 vehicles for the month. Before the dust settled, $84 million in inventories and other commitments had to be written off as a dead loss.
>
> During the crisis, the price of General Motors stock plummeted. Then came Durant's disastrous attempt to sustain the price by buying General Motors stock on credit, which led to his financial difficulties and to his retirement as President on November 20, 1920. Ten days later, Pierre du Pont took over the presidency. . . . [O]ne of his very first acts was to approve the plan worked out by Alfred Sloan which defined an organizational structure for General Motors. (p. 129)

The case-based findings of Chandler receive confirmation in a statistical study of large U.S. corporations (Donaldson 1987). The study found that corporations that were in misfit between strategy and structure, in that they had diversified but still retained a functional structure, suffered reduced performance as a result. Despite this reduced performance, corporations failed to make the adaptation to a multidivisional structure until their performance became low (Donaldson 1987, pp. 17-18). Specifically, the corporations that made a structural adaptation by adopting the multidivisional structure did so when their sales, profit, and earnings per share became low. More exactly, the lower their performance on these measures at the start of the decade, the higher the probability that a corporation in misfit would structurally adapt during that decade. Thus structural adaptation followed low performance, providing evidence that low performance was a cause of the structural adaptation.

For organizational structural change, the underlying cause is the change in the contingency variable to a new level (e.g., diversifying from low to higher diversification). But the ensuing misfit, while adversely affecting performance, does not directly cause structural change. Only when the organizational performance declines to low performance does the change occur. Hence low performance is the direct cause of structural change, which intervenes between contingency change and structural change (Donaldson 1987).

A similar pattern has been found for adaptive change in corporate strategy. Needed changes in strategy tend not to occur until performance declines sufficiently to impel management to act. In their study of a retail chain, Mintzberg and Waters (1982) found that poor performance caused the owner to adopt a new strategy. Similarly, in a study of a clothing company, Johnson (1987) showed that declining performance induced the company to make strategic change. Further, in their study of a large confectionary firm, Smith, Child, and Rowlinson (1990) found that poor performance impelled management toward adopting a more economically rational strategy.

Thus adaptive change in both organizational structure and strategy has been shown to have low performance as its immediate cause. In his empirical case studies of the restructurings of a number of large U.S. corporations, Gordon Donaldson (1994) used the metaphor of the supertanker to capture the way in which large corporations tend to continue with existing courses of action:

> The leadership of a large, diverse, and dispersed organization is an immensely challenging assignment. . . . Once in motion, the chosen course of action takes on a force of its own, the forward momentum of which is, like a supertanker,

most difficult to deflect. It takes a massive counterforce to produce radical change in direction—or to avoid a destructive collision. (p. 39)

He goes on to find in his case studies that crisis triggered by poor organizational performance is typically the massive counterforce that is required to produce a radical change in direction for the corporation.

Similarly, Cibin and Grant (1996) studied the restructurings of large oil corporations that included changes in both strategy and structure. They found that restructurings were triggered by low financial performance. A drop in profitability caused the strategic changes, which in turn led to structural changes (Cibin and Grant 1996). For example, combining data for the three companies, Amoco, Arco, and Mobil, and taking the averages, profitability declined each year over the 6-year period 1980-1985 from an ROE (return on equity) of 21.7 percent to 9.7 percent (Cibin and Grant 1996, p. 293; Robert Grant, personal communication). As a result of this declining profitability, a corporate strategic change was announced by each of these companies during 1984 or 1985, typically involving downscoping, that is, selling off some non-core businesses. For instance, Mobil divested itself of the Container Corporation, W. F. Hall Printing, Mobil Atlas (paints), and other non-core businesses (Cibin and Grant 1996, p. 295). These restructurings took some time to implement and improve profitability, so profit continued to decline during 1986 to 6.7 percent ROE. However, the fruits of the restructurings then started to show, and profitability increased to 14 percent ROE in 1987 and then rose to 19 percent by 1990. Thus, over the decade of the 1980s, profitability declined and then rebounded after the performance crisis in the middle of the decade induced substantial change in the corporate strategy (Cibin and Grant 1996). Other factors such as trading conditions would, of course, play a role contributing to the decline and to the recovery (Grant 1993). The key initiative of corporate management was to decide to change strategy (Cibin and Grant 1996). This was triggered by the decline in profit, and the strategic change led to subsequent profit recovery. The new strategy and altered set of corporate assets in turn led to a subsequent adjustment to the organizational structure to bring about a new fit (Cibin and Grant 1996).

Thus the proposition that performance needs to drop below the satisficing level and become poor before adaptive change occurs is well established in organizational theory and is endorsed authoritatively and empirically.

Given that adaptation is problem driven, a level of performance above satisficing precludes the search for, and adoption of, alternatives to the status quo. This problemistic model of administrative behavior leads to the view that performance has to become low before change occurs and adaptation ensues. Hence, for structural adaptation to occur in a situation of structural misfit, the other causes of organizational performance need, on average, to be depressing performance for overall organizational performance to be low enough that it drops below the satisficing level. Under this model, an organization in misfit can remain this way for a long time while the other causes of performance produce a satisfactory level of performance. Thus, given that only a satisficing level of performance needs to be maintained to avoid adaptive change, change may be delayed for a long time. Hence the concept of satisficing means that performance strongly mediates the effect of structural misfit on structural adaptation.

The two ideas of performance being multiply determined and of satisficing together mean that performance is crucial as the intervening variable between structural maladaptation and structural adaptation. This model implies that the effect of structural misfit on performance is mediated by the many other causes of performance. It also implies that the effect of performance on structural adaptation is direct and that performance is the decisive cause of change.

This insight means that the functionalist theory of structural adaptation has to be modified substantially. The occurrence or absence of structural adaptation is crucially dependent on organizational performance. Therefore, adaptation is determined by the aggregate level of the causes of organizational performance, and these in turn are affected by the sources of each cause of organizational performance. Thus attention moves to the set of causes of organizational performance that are within the organization as to whether they hold similar or dissimilar values, that is, to their simultaneity and correlation as a portfolio. Also, attention moves outward from the organization to the environmental factors that also affect organizational performance, such as the business cycle and competition. How does variation over time in the business cycle affect the organizational portfolio? For both sets of factors, the interest is on how they change over time and whether they correlate to simultaneously produce the downturn in overall organizational performance that is necessary for structural adaptive change to occur when the organization is in misfit.

Although the foregoing discussed adaptation of organizational structure, there are implications for aspects of organization other than just structure. The theory that decision making is problemistic applies to many decisions and covers many different aspects of organization (Simon 1976). This includes strategy, human resource policies, marketing, logistics, and so on. For all aspects of the organization, management will retain existing approaches until they prove unsatisfactory, that is, until performance drops below the satisficing level. Given that performance is caused by multiple factors, the same conclusion holds as above: that change in any aspect of the organization will occur only when the combined values of all causes produce performance below the satisficing level. Thus the explanation of change in any aspect of the organization lies in the interactions among the multiple causes of organizational performance, that is, in the organizational portfolio. Thus organizational portfolio theory is a potentially wide-ranging and general theory of organizational adaptation. It is, however, convenient in expositing the theory to begin with organizational structural adaptation. As the theoretical argument unfolds, it is elaborated to state where there are differences among the various aspects of organization, such as distinguishing propositions about structure from those about strategy.

The fundamental propositions thus are the following:

2.1 For a maladapted organization, low organizational performance (i.e., below the satisficing level) leads to organizational adaptation.

2.2 For a maladapted organization, medium to high organizational performance (i.e., above the satisficing level) leads it to continue in maladaptation.

High Performance as a
Cause of Organizational Growth

As we have seen, low performance drives organizational adaptation. Medium to high levels of organizational performance prevent adaptation of an organization that is in misfit. However, these higher levels of performance encourage growth of an organization that is in fit, by making additional resources available. An organization in fit will have a structure and other attributes that are well suited to its situation (e.g., its size, strategy, and environment) so that it operates effectively and can make correct and timely decisions. Therefore, the organization can grow and will do so, as long as this is the strategic intent of its managers. When the organization also simultaneously enjoys high performance, it will have surplus resources. These include internally generated profits and cash flow, enhanced debt capacity, and a higher share price that allows cheap equity financing. These resources are surplus in that they are additional to the resources already committed to present operations. Surplus resources are therefore available to fund growth in the organization, such as hiring new employees, opening new geographic branches, launching new products or services, purchasing more advanced technology, and acquiring other firms. Therefore, the higher the performance of an organization in fit, the greater its resulting growth rate is likely to be.

The proposition thus is the following:

> 2.3 For a well-adapted organization, the higher its performance, the higher its growth rate tends to be.

Hence low performance for an organization in misfit leads to adaptation, and medium to high performance for an organization in fit leads to growth. Thus an organization that is adapting and then growing will experience wide performance fluctuations. Fluctuations in performance are captured by the concept of risk. Risk is in turn affected by portfolio effects. To better understand organizational change, we need to examine organizational risk and the organization as a portfolio. This involves drawing on ideas from finance and bringing them into organizational theory. We first discuss risk and then the portfolio concept.

Risk and the Organizational Portfolio

Defining Risk

Conventionally, organizational theory conceives of organizational performance as the level of some variable, usually the degree to which the organizational goals are attained (Parsons 1961). For a profit-oriented organization such as a firm, performance is the level of profit. Empirical studies reflect this conceptualization by operationally measuring performance in terms of profitability, such as return on investment, return on assets, return on equity, profit margin, and growth in profits (e.g., Child 1975). However, this thinking does not fully accord with financial economics because it neglects the phenomenon of risk.

The concept of risk refers to a different dimension of performance, that is, to the degree of variation in the level of performance from one time period to another. The level of performance may be, for example, profit in 1980. Risk refers to the fluctuation in level over time (e.g., from year to year). For example, consider two corporations with the same average profit over five years of $10 million per annum. Corporation A actually makes $10 million profit for each of the 5 years. This company has no fluctuation in profit from year to year, and thus its risk is zero. Corporation B returns profits over the 5 years of $17, $7, $12, $10 and $4 million. Thus, in the case of B, there is some substantial fluctuation around the average, and so its risk is substantial. Thus two corporations can have the same average level of performance but differ markedly in their risk. There is a general preference among investors in the economy for lower risk. This is revealed by the fact that investments that are riskier, if they are to be taken up, have to offer expectations of higher returns than less risky investments (Sharpe 1970).

In financial economics, the mean-variance model is used (Brealey and Myers 1996). The average profit of a company is captured by the mean. The variance records the year-to-year variations in profit around that mean. Risk is measured by this variance around the mean. In an influential article, Bowman (1980) states, "Research and professional practice accept this measure of risk" (p. 18).

Risk here is an objective characteristic of the organization, the variation over time in its performance. This performance variation may or may not be intended by organizational managers. Some performance variation would typically be unintended by managers, for example, a decline in performance. Risk in this sense of an objective performance characteristic is to be distinguished from managers' subjective assessment of the degree to which they are gambling or being "risky" (Singh 1986). Similarly, the objective risk is to be distinguished from the issue of whether organizational personnel make accurate subjective assessments of objective risk (McNamara and Bromiley 1997). The objective and subjective senses of risk sometimes go together and sometimes differ empirically, but the theory herein is about objective risk, that is, variance about mean performance.

This variance concept of risk is to be distinguished also from the use of the word *risk* to refer to the probability of a large loss. Some organizational researchers conceptualize risk in terms of loss—for example, the downside risk measure used by Miller and Leiblein (1996). They contrast this concept of risk with the variance-based concept used here. Their definition of risk is appropriate to the theory that they examine, but the variance view of risk is consistent with financial economics and appropriate to the theory being propounded here.

Wiseman and Catanach (1997) disaggregate the risk of an organization into risks attached to various aspects of the operations, which they term operational risks, such as liquidity risk. In contrast, we are interested in the risk of the overall organization because this drives adaptive change at the overall organizational level. Thus the analysis here principally focuses on overall organizational risk rather than operational risks.

The concept of risk used here, that is, company performance variation over time, is supported empirically in a study by Miller and Bromiley (1990). In an examination of nine alternative measures of risk, they found evidence of a factor they called income stream uncertainty that reflected variance over time in company profitability. This was composed of four variables: the standard deviation of Return on Equity (ROE), the standard deviation of Return on Assets (ROA), the standard deviation of stock analysts' forecasts of earnings per share, and the coefficient of variation of stock analysts' forecasts of earnings per share (p. 762). All four variables were correlated highly with the income stream uncertainty factor (p. 775), thus giving confidence in the validity of the construct. Two other factors were found: one based on stock market measures of risk and one reflecting various accounting measures of risk—for example, debt to equity (p. 762). The three factors were robust across two time periods (p. 762). The income stream uncertainty factor records variations over time in profitability and is therefore an empirical measure of organizational risk as meant in this book.

The overall measure of the value of a firm in financial economics is the ratio of profit to risk. The theory is that higher average returns need to be generated by higher-risk projects to compensate for the higher risk entailed; otherwise, no investor would invest in risky projects. There is empirical evidence that disputes this idea of a positive correlation between risk and return (Bowman 1980), although the studies are mixed in their findings (e.g., Figenbaum and Thomas 1986). Nevertheless, the idea that higher risk requires higher return remains a cornerstone of economics so that economic value is return divided by risk. Hence to assess the value of a firm, one needs to know both its level of profit and its risk. This is captured by the mean-variance model. The economic value of a firm is the ratio of the mean profit to its variance (Brealey and Myers 1996). Thus the value of a firm considers the two dimensions simultaneously, the level of profit and its risk. A firm may increase its value either by increasing its mean performance (i.e., profit) level or by lowering its risk (i.e., reducing its variance in profit). Hence a firm may become more financially valuable, even while maintaining its mean performance level, by reducing its risk.

Now that we have the concept of risk, we can turn to altering the concept of the organization by introducing portfolio theory from finance.

Portfolio Theory

Financial portfolio theory considers how the elements making up the portfolio, that is, the stocks or shares, produce an overall level of risk for the portfolio (Sharpe 1970; Brealey and Myers 1996). The risk of the portfolio is affected by two characteristics of the stocks:

1. *The amount of risk in each stock.* Ceteris paribus, a portfolio of highly risky stocks will be highly risky.
2. *The correlation between stocks.* High positive correlations between stocks increase the risk of the overall portfolio in that variation (i.e., risk) in one stock is added to the variation in another stock. The less positively correlated the stocks the less they reinforce each other so that low positive correlations between stocks reduce portfolio risk. Where stocks are negatively correlated, as the price of one stock moves up, the other moves down so that the overall value of the portfolio remains approximately constant. The variation over time in one stock moves counter to the variation in the other. The result is little change over time in the total value of the portfolio as a whole. Thus negative correlations between stocks in a portfolio produce low risk in the portfolio. Ceteris paribus, the greater the negative the correlation between stocks, the greater the compensatory reduction in the overall risk of the portfolio.

Thus the risk of the portfolio is a function of both the risk of each element and the correlation between elements. The greater the risk of each element and the greater the positive the correlation between elements, the greater the risk of the portfolio. Conversely, the lower the risk of each element or the less positive or more negative the correlation between elements, the lower the risk of the portfolio. Thus low risk for the portfolio can result either from low-risk elements or from a low positive or negative correlation between them. Hence the risk of a set of stocks can be reduced by placing them together in a portfolio if they have low positive or negative correlations among themselves. This can be termed the *portfolio effect*.

This portfolio effect can be stronger than the risk of the elements in a portfolio, in the sense that if two elements correlate negatively, the risk of the portfolio is small even if the risk of each element is large. This is because the large upward swings in one element are offset by the large downward swings in the other element. The portfolio effect of combining negatively correlating elements is strong enough that it can nullify the risk of the elements. Conversely, for high positively correlated elements, the risk of one adds to the risk of another element to create more risk for the portfolio. Thus, where there are high positive correlations among elements, the greater the risk of each element, the greater the risk of the portfolio. Moreover, the higher the positive correlation between elements, the more that the risk of an element adds to the risk of other elements to increase the overall portfolio risk. This discussion brings out the importance of the correlation between elements in a portfolio: whether the correlation is positive or negative and its magnitude. Therefore, organizational portfolio theory is concerned not only with the risk of each element in the organizational portfolio but also with whether the correlation between elements is positive or negative.

Given that in financial economics the value of a firm is the ratio of performance level to risk, portfolios that reduce risk thereby increase value. Even though placing several assets together into a portfolio leaves their average value unaffected so that mean performance of the portfolio is unchanged, the portfolio effect lowers risk. Thus the ratio of the mean performance to risk rises, thereby increasing economic value.

Portfolio theory has the attractive property that it is true by deduction, that is, mathematically. It is also highly general, and its application is not restricted to finance, so it may be applied to organizational theory.

The initial step in the application of portfolio theory to organizational theory is to consider an organization as itself being a portfolio of elements, where each element is a cause of organizational performance. This involves unbundling the organization. This can be done along several dimensions by analytically distinguishing different aspects of the organization as the elements in the portfolio. These might be different products or services, geographic areas of operation, branches, divisions, departments, sections, or employees. Any elements of the organization whose performances sum to make up the performance of the organization as a whole can be considered to be elements of the organizational portfolio. The elements of the organizational portfolio also include causes of organizational performance that lie outside the organization but in its environment, such as business cycles and competition. The interaction between the performances of portfolio elements is additive. Therefore, high performance of an element directly contributes to raising organizational performance, and low performance of an element directly contributes to lowering organizational performance. By analyzing the organization as a portfolio, we can see whether the elements interact to produce high risk, that is, large fluctuations in organizational performance, or whether the elements cancel out fluctuations within themselves so that there is little fluctuation in organizational performance (i.e., low organizational risk). Organizational risk is important because it is the fluctuations in organizational performance that drive organizational change.

Risk and Organizational Change

Risk is typically thought of as undesirable. However, risk is necessary for an organization to adapt and grow. This is not the commonplace observation that organizational growth requires trying new things and so, in that sense, is "risky." It asserts, rather, the idea that because change is triggered by low performance (for organizational adaptation) and high performance (for growth), organizational performance must vary markedly over time for an organization that is adapting and growing. This large fluctuation in organizational performance means that organizational risk is high. We now present these arguments systematically.

Risk as Undesirable

As seen above, the concept of risk in financial economics refers to variations in performance. The greater the risk, that is, performance variation about the mean performance, the greater the probability of an abnormally low or high performance. Abnormally low performance is unwelcome because at the limit it is bankruptcy and the enterprise is ended. But high performance above the mean also counts as variation and therefore as risk. Why is such above-mean performance considered as risk and undesirable? The reason is that in economics the underlying personal utility curves are not linear but curvilinear. Utility increases at a declining rate with respect to economic returns. A person receives less utility from each additional unit of economic return—for example, from the economic performance of a firm in which they hold stocks or shares. Thus there is a basic asymmetry in utility. For any point on the utility curve, an increase in economic return above that point produces less of a gain in utility than the loss produced by a decrease of equal magnitude in economic return. Thus loss is not matched by gain. Hence variation about a point always produces less utility than that point itself. The asymmetric utility function renders variation less valuable than more constant performance, even though the variation ranges sometimes above the mean. Thus variation about a mean is less preferable than the same mean score. Hence risk is undesirable.

This might suggest that, ceteris paribus, lower organizational risk should be regarded as more positive than higher risk. Economics argues that risk is a negative aspect of performance but that it is not automatically to be shunned because risk creates the possibility of above normal economic returns to the investor. Precisely because risk is unwelcome, most economic agents seek to avoid it, thus creating less competition in riskier activities than in less risky activities. This competition reduces the returns available in lower-risk activities relative to higher-risk activities. Therefore, higher returns, that is, mean performance, are generally available in higher-risk rather than lower-risk situations. Thus an investor may knowingly embrace a riskier option because that carries the chance of above-normal returns. However, it is only a chance, for the investment may or may not deliver those superior returns and hence is risky. This suggests that, although risk is in itself unwelcome, risk must be entertained in order to have the chance of higher returns and that, on average, higher risk will yield higher returns. Risk is a negative organizational performance outcome but one that an investor or organizational manager might choose wagering on the chance of success. Risk is undesirable and so has to be compensated for by higher average returns.

This principle holds for a single investment taken in isolation. However, investors can diversify away the risk element to a degree by holding a portfolio of investments in which returns are negatively correlated, that is, the risk of one investment can be offset by holding another investment that inherently tends to move in the opposite direction. Thus the significance of risk depends on the context. For an investment opportunity taken in isolation, return for risk is crucial. However, for a portfolio of investments, the return and risk of each investment are important, but, as we have seen, so also are the correlations among the investments. A risky investment that is negatively correlated with other investments can be placed in a portfolio with those other investments, and thus the portfolio has less overall risk than the investment held in isolation (Sharpe 1970; Brealey and Myers 1996). For an investor, it is preferable to invest in risky assets in order to attain higher average returns, which are negatively correlated so that the risk of the overall portfolio is reduced. Thus portfolio investment can attain higher returns to risk than can a single investment. Nevertheless, the principle remains that returns obtained are evaluated relative to the risk entailed, so that risk is viewed negatively, as something that would not be entertained if it were not for the expected returns. Other things being equal, risk would be avoided.

In summary, financial economics takes the view that, from the standpoint of the investor, risk is undesirable. However, we now wish to examine the issue from the standpoint of the organization. This is an approach in terms of organizational theory. Now the question becomes, what is the effect of risk on the organization? More specifically, what is the feedback effect upon the organization of the risk of its own overall, financial performance? Two different types of organizational change can be distinguished: organizational adaptation and organizational growth. These are involved in low performance and high performance, respectively. Each is analyzed in turn. In each case, we establish the effect of risk on that type of organizational change. The main point is that risk is necessary for much, though not all, organizational change.

Risk Is Necessary for Organizational Change

Work on risk in organizational theory tends toward the view that risk is a "bad thing," in the sense that risk is undesirable (Hoskisson 1987). In this, organizational theory simply follows the view taken in finance from which the risk concept has been drawn. As we have seen, risk refers to variance in organizational performance around the mean level of organizational performance (e.g., variance in corporate profit). An organization that experiences a substantial variation in performance over several successive years is coded as high in risk. Because such variance is risk and is therefore undesirable, the best performance is a high mean and a low variance. This is the position taken conventionally, but we now wish to probe this assumption.

As noted above, the theory of Simon (1976) states that managerial decision making is characterized as being problemistic. Managers, rather than constantly seeking to attain the optimum possible level of performance, actually rest content with a lower level, the satisficing level. This is due to bounded rationality, that is, the knowledge about the means required to attain the end of maximal corporate profitability is lacking. Thus Simon (1976) states that managers initiate problem-solving action only if performance falls below the satisficing level and that, in such situations, they seek to take action to solve the problems sufficiently to restore performance back to the satisficing level. Thus adaptive action by organizational managers is initiated only by subsatisficing levels of organizational performance.

The implication of satisficing theory is that corporations will retain existing, suboptimal structures, systems, policies, and practices until the level of corporate performance falls below the satisficing level. Thus an organization that maintains a level of performance from year to year that is consistently at least moderate will probably not fall into the subsatisficing zone and therefore not initiate adaptive changes. However, organizations need to make changes, such as adopting a new structure, to adapt to changes in their situation in order to be effective and to grow. To make these adaptive changes, organizations must periodically have episodes of subsatisficing performance to trigger those changes. Only when performance drops below the satisficing level will the needed change be made. Thus for adaptation to occur the performance needs to drop, at the least, to some level below satisficing.

Conceivably, an organization might remain at the satisficing level indefinitely. This would mean that its risk was zero. However, such an organization would never make any adaptive changes and would tend to not grow and thus would never reach the higher levels of corporate performance levels (e.g., high profit). In practice, such stagnant organizations would, in many environments, be left behind in the competitive race, eventually falling bankrupt or being taken over by a growing corporation. To avoid stagnation, most organizations adapt. Therefore, an organization periodically goes through variation in its performance from above to below the satisficing level. This necessarily implies that there will be variation in performance over time, that is, risk (see Figure 2.1). The level of risk cannot be zero for an adapting organization.

In turn, the effect of the adaptive change will be to raise the performance level. Some adaptive changes will be so beneficial that the performance rises considerably above the satisficing level. For other changes, the benefit for the organization will be more modest so that the organization regains only the satisficing level. Some changes may be so modest that performance rises but fails to attain the satisficing level. Thus there is a range of positive performance benefits, depending on the type of adaptive change. The general point is that

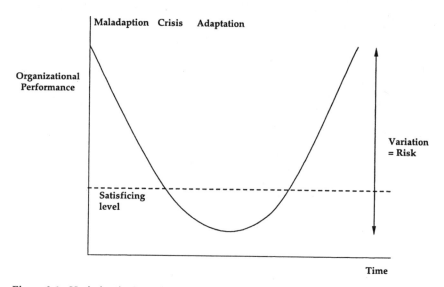

Figure 2.1 Variation in Organizational Performance Showing That Risk Accompanies Adaptive Change

performance will rise after adaptive change, and this also contributes to the variation over time in performance.

Thus organizational adaptation is preceded by a downturn in organizational performance and tends to be followed by an upturn, so that there is substantial variation over time in performance accompanying organizational adaptation. Organizational adaptation cannot be accompanied by zero risk.

The organizational adaptation into the new fit causes the organizational performance to rise, and this in turn causes organizational growth (e.g., growth in numbers of employees and branches). This growth flows from the increased performance that comes from organizational adaptation. Therefore, because risk is a necessary accompaniment of organizational adaptation, risk is necessary also for organizational growth. The low performance causes organizational adaptation, and the resulting higher performance causes growth; thus a growing organization experiences variation over time in its performance.

The repetition of this cycle of risk causing organizational adaptation and then growth increments leads to further episodes of organizational adaptation and incremental growth. These incremental changes cumulate over time into substantial organizational structural change and organizational growth. For repeated episodes of incremental adaptation and growth to occur, organizational performance must fluctuate recurrently from low to medium-high and back again; in other words, organizational risk is substantial. Thus risk is inherent in long-term structural development, organizational growth, and success.

In summary, organizational adaptation and growth imply first low and then higher organizational performance. Performance fluctuates over a substantial range, and this equates to substantial risk. This risk should not be seen as undesirable but, rather, as a healthy part of the processes of adaptation and growth. Instead of the conventional assessment in which risk is seen as undesirable, organizational theory should, rather, see some risk as a desirable attribute of an adapting organization. Of course, some performance variation will be caused by factors other than those associated with adaptive organizational change and growth—for example, extremely low performance caused by competition. This residual component of risk may be considered to be undesirable in the usual economic view.

Whether or not low performance occurs is determined not only by the fluctuation in performance, that is, the risk, but also by the mean level of performance. If the mean organizational performance is high enough, then, even though high risk leads performance to fluctuate greatly, when performance is at its minimum it would still be above the satisficing level, so change would not occur. Thus needed adaptive change will tend not to occur, even if the organization has substantial risk, if its mean performance is medium to high. It is the combination of certain levels of organizational risk and mean organizational performance that produces episodes of poor performance that trigger adaptive change. The higher the mean organizational performance, the more that performance needs to fluctuate for it to fall below the satisficing level. Thus the higher the mean organizational performance, the higher must be the organizational risk to trigger adaptive organizational change.

In summary, the satisficing theory of Simon (1976) necessarily implies that the risk of a corporation that is adapting and growing over the long run cannot be zero and must be substantially above zero. Therefore, risk should not be seen as wholly undesirable, for part of it is the engine of corporate growth.

The propositions thus are the following:

2.4 For an organization that is adapting and growing, its risk must be substantially greater than zero.

2.5 For an organization to succeed long term, its risk must be substantially greater than zero.

2.6 The higher the mean performance of an organization, the greater its risk must be for it to adapt and grow.

An Alternative View of the Effects of Low Performance

Ocasio (1995) points out that there are two different theories in the organizational literature about the effect of low performance on organizational change. The first is the theory pursued previously: that poor performance leads organizations to seek to adapt in order to raise their performance. The second theory, however, makes the opposite prediction. This alternative view is the theory of threat-rigidity (Staw, Sandelands, and Dutton 1981). This theory holds that individuals suffering poor performance experience it as a threat, which causes them to act rigidly, so failing to make needed adaptive change. Hence the response to poor performance is dysfunctional so that performance is not improved and remains poor and declines further. For organizations with poor performance, their managers may be expected, on this theory, to feel threatened so that the organization becomes rigid and fails to respond adaptively, and so its performance declines further. Under the threat-rigidity theory, the organization would not respond to an episode of poor performance by making adaptive change. Thus the theory advanced in this book would not hold. While we grant the cogency and validity of threat-rigidity theory, there are some reasons why it may be a less fruitful approach to the issues considered in this book.

The threat-rigidity theory is primarily a psychological one that applies to individuals (Staw et al. 1981). It is therefore a microlevel theory, and it becomes applicable to the macrolevel topic of organizational change by applying it to the individual managers making the decisions about the organization. To apply the threat-rigidity theory to those organizational managers assumes that they feel threatened by the low performance of their organization so that a defensive emotional mood state colors their thinking and makes them rigid. This might well be the case for disastrously poor performance that has the firm on the brink of bankruptcy, or, less drastically, for performance low enough that the manager fears reprimand, demotion, or termination. However, the low performance discussed in this book need not be that poor. Rather, low performance that induces structural (or other kinds of) adaptation is failure to attain satisfactory performance levels; that is, the profit is below target, but there may be a profit. Therefore, the low performance considered in this book is not so low that the organizational managers would be likely to go into the emotional state of threat-rigidity. The managers would perceive a performance gap and analyze the situation rationally and take corrective action (e.g., adopt a better-fitting structure). In this way, the low organizational performance may be low enough to trigger adaptation but not so low that it triggers threat-rigidity.

The case histories of organizational managements responding to low performance and making structural adaptations, such as those by Chandler (1962), display managers as rationally solving a problem rather than as being locked into threat-rigidity. This is compatible with the theory of administrative behavior as being composed of problem solving by managers (Simon 1976). Certainly, the tradition of theorizing in macro-organizational behavior has been that low performance leads to adaptive organizational change rather than to irrationality (Cyert and March 1963; Williamson 1964; Child 1972). This is the tradition being pursued here.

The theory of threat-rigidity is not the only psychological theory of human decision making in organizations. An alternative theory is of adaptive aspirations (March 1988). This argues that managers (and other people) tend to be influenced in their decision making by their context, in particular the level of performance achieved by their organization as compared with some aspired level of performance. Organizational performance that is below the aspired level tends to cause a search for remedies, including taking risks (March 1988). This theory that low performance leads organizations and their managers to take risks rather than becoming rigid and conservative receives considerable empirical support overall from studies (Bowman 1980; Figenbaum and Thomas 1986; March and Shapira 1987; Lant and Montgomery 1987; Bromiley 1991a, 1991b; Jegers 1991; Wiseman and Bromiley 1991, 1996). This model of managerial decision making is consistent with the idea that organizational performance below the satisficing level triggers organizational change. For these reasons, this book does not use the theory of threat-rigidity, although I acknowledge that it may be useful in other areas.

There is much to be said for organizational research pursuing both the organizational portfolio and the threat-rigidity theories and seeing what accomplishments can be made by following each of them. Some scholars will choose one theory to pursue and other scholars the other so that, over time, the power and limitations of each theory are more fully revealed. Ultimately, both may then be synthesized into a more complete theory of organizational change.

Factors in the Organizational Portfolio

The basic building blocks of organizational portfolio theory have now been defined. Risk is the degree of fluctuation in the performance of the organization and the constituent elements in its portfolio. For organizational adaptation and growth to occur, the organizational risk must at least be substantial so that fluctuations in organizational performance drive the adaptation and growth. Organizational risk is greater when its portfolio elements have high risk and are positively correlated. Organizational risk is lower when its portfolio elements have low risk or are negatively correlated. Misfit is one element of the organizational portfolio, and it depresses the organizational portfolio. The question is, what other factors are affecting organizational performance? What is their magnitude, that is, their risk, relative to that of organizational misfit? And what is the correlation between each of these factors and organizational misfit?

Each factor that is positively correlated with organizational misfit reinforces the depressing effect of misfit on performance, thus increasing the probability that performance will drop low enough for adaptive change to be triggered. A positive correlation means that a high level of the factor is associated with fit and a low value with misfit, so when the correlation is positive the factor reinforces the effect of fit, and when the correlation is negative the factor counters the effect of fit. The greater the effect of the factor on organizational performance, the more that the conjunction of a low level of the factor with misfit will cause low performance. Moreover, the more that the factor fluctuates, the more organizational performance fluctuates, making low performance more probable. This is to say that the higher the risk of the factor, the more that it will help trigger adaptive change when it is positively correlated with misfit.

Conversely, each factor that is negatively correlated with organizational misfit will counter the depressing effect of misfit on performance, thus decreasing the probability that performance will drop low enough for adaptive change to be triggered. The greater the effect of the factor on organizational performance, the more that a high level of the factor coexisting with misfit will cause performance to be satisfactory. Further, the more that the factor fluctuates, the more organizational performance fluctuates so that higher performance is more probable (i.e., performance above the satisficing level). This is to say that the higher the risk of the factor, the more that it will prevent adaptive change when it is negatively correlated with misfit.

The issue is to identify the factors that affect organizational performance and assess their risk and correlation with organizational misfit. This involves isolating key elements of the organizational portfolio. As stated in Chapter 1, these are the business cycle, competition, debt, divisional risk, diversification, divisionalization, divestment, and directors. These are eight factors that influence the organizational performance level or variability (i.e., its risk). Four of these can lead toward the organization experiencing low performance and so making adaptive change: the business cycle, competition, debt, and divisional risk. The other four factors tend to keep organizational performance at least satisfactory and so prevent needed adaptive change: diversification, divisionalization, divestment, and directors. Whether the organization adapts or not is the result of the balance between the factors encouraging or frustrating adaptive change through the overall level of organizational performance and its fluctuation (i.e., risk). The ensuing chapters examine these eight factors, explicating their significance for organizational performance and their correlation with organizational misfit. The order in which they are dealt with is the business cycle, competition, diversification, divisionalization, debt, divestment, directors, and divisional risk.

Conclusions

This chapter argued that organizational change is driven by organizational performance. An organization in misfit needs to experience low performance to trigger adaptive change. An organization in fit needs to experience medium to high performance to grow. Thus an organization needs to have its performance fluctuating considerably if it is to adapt and grow. Therefore, the organization cannot have low risk and must have at least a moderate level of risk (i.e., variation in performance over time). Although risk is undesirable from the point of view of economics, it is a necessary accompaniment of the cycle of adaptive change that allows the organization to prosper and grow long term.

To understand organizational change, we must examine the level of organizational performance together with its variation over time (i.e., risk). Organizational performance and risk are the result of the organizational portfolio, that is, the elements that each affect organizational performance and their mutual correlations. Our preliminary discussion in Chapter 1 identified eight factors that play a role in the organizational portfolio. These are analyzed in the chapters that follow.

The Business Cycle
and Organizational Change

One premise of this book is that contemporary organizational theory can be enriched by making it more dynamic. One of the major movements in the economic environment of organizations is the business cycle. This has been largely neglected by organization theorists to date. Yet the movements of the business cycle powerfully condition the changes that occur within the organization. Thus an analysis of the interaction between business cycles and organizational change is required. This is revealed to be an interaction between two cycles, one in the external economy and the other inside the organization. The point of connection of the two cycles is the performance of the organization, which is consistent with our theme of organizational adaptation as being performance driven.

Organizational adaptation is related to the business cycle. A firm will tend to be in misfit around the peak and in fit around the trough of the cycle. When the business cycle swings up, the firm in fit will grow and so enter misfit. This misfit depresses its performance, but this is more than offset by the buoyant economic conditions, and so its performance will be satisfactory and it will not adapt, remaining in misfit. When the business cycle swings down, the performance of the firm will be depressed enough that adaptation is triggered so that it enters fit. The firm will remain in fit through the trough until the new upswing causes it to grow into misfit, repeating the cycle of adaptation in correspondence with the business cycle. There are variations in the business cycle across industries, and these affect organizational adaptation and industry growth. Moreover, the cycle of organizational adaptation affects the business cycle. These issues are brought out in this chapter, but first we consider the need for a theory of business cycles in organizational theory.

The Need to Bring Business
Cycles Into Organizational Theory

Structural contingency theory relates organizational structure to various contingency factors such as size, technology, and strategy (Miner 1982; Pfeffer 1982). This analysis of organizational changes caused by expansion in size and diversity has been complemented by an analysis of organizational changes caused by organizational decline (Cameron, Sutton, and Whetten 1988; Freeman and Hannan 1975). Central to the theory of organizational adaptation is the idea that maladaptation or misfit between structure and contingency leads to a reduction in performance (e.g., Lawrence and Lorsch 1967; Van de Ven and Drazin 1985). As we have seen, organizational performance is an outcome but also a cause, in that when performance drops below the satisficing level, adaptation is triggered (Child 1972). Therefore, organizational performance mediates the relationship between misfit and structural adaptation.

As has been stated, organizational performance is affected both by the fit between contingency and structure and by numerous other factors, some internal to the organization and some external. The external factors affecting organizational performance include competition, level of demand, availability of consumer credit, income, taxes, and other government actions. The specific external effect of competitors on organizational performance and organizational change is analyzed in Chapter 4. This chapter examines general external economic effects on the organization. External changes affecting performance are often discussed in organizational theory under the heading of environmental munificence or environmental illiberality or environmental hostility (Child 1972; Pfeffer and Salancik 1978; Khandwalla 1977). However, these external economic conditions change over time and in patterned ways. Many of the external variables move together and are conceptualized as the business cycle. The business cycle is defined as the movement over time of total demand in the economy, as reflected in aggregate sales, consumer income, inflation, imports, employment, new business starts, and so on (Dotsey and King 1987). The business cycle typically takes about 3 to 5 years to go from upswing to downswing and back again and is more technically known as the Kitchin cycle (Van Duijn 1983; Kuczynski 1986) as distinguished from the longer cycle, the Kondratiev wave (Abrahamson 1997).

The suggestion made in this chapter is that new theoretical insight may be gained for organizational theory by considering these external economic conditions not as static but as varying in cyclical fashion. Moreover, the process of organizational adaptation to the environment is itself cyclical, and thus the organization–environment relationship can be conceptualized as a system of two interacting cycles: the cycle of organizational adaptation and the business cycle.

In his empirical studies of restructurings of large U.S. corporations, Gordon Donaldson (1994) points out the way that the profitability of these corporations is affected in many cases by the economic cycles in their industries. Adaptive organizational change is more likely to occur when ongoing deficiencies in the corporation are then aggravated by a downswing in the industry, triggering a performance crisis. In analyzing events at the Armco Steel Corporation, Gordon Donaldson (1994) identifies as the trigger the low performance brought about, in part, by downswings in the cycles of the steel industry and the oil industry, a customer of Armco. He highlights the cyclicality of these two product-market segments and their conjunction in turning downward at the same time:

> The general economic recession of 1982 had once again demonstrated the cyclicality of steel, but more ominous[ly] . . . the collapse of the OPEC-created boom in the American oil patch vividly demonstrated that the intended risk-reducing diversification into oil field machinery and equipment had a violent cycle of its own, which could, and did, coincide with that of steel. (p. 38)

This chapter builds on such empirical case insights to begin to construct a theory of the effects of business cycles on organizational adaptive change and vice versa.

Organizational form is composed of numerous aspects, such as organization structure, leadership style, and human resources. The theory proposed applies to all aspects of organizational form that affect performance, conditional upon certain contingency factors. The contingency factors covered here are all those that measure organizational size growth and increase in volume or are empirically associated with growth—employees, sales, diversification, routinization, vertical integration, and so on (Hopkins 1988). The theory proposed is for all such organizational form–size contingency relationships, broadly understood. However, to simplify the present discussion, it is couched just in terms of organizational structure and size. Structure may be thought of here as increases in structural sophistication and complexity, such as vertical differentiation, horizontal differentiation, functional specialization, formalization, decentralization, and other subdimensions of bureaucratic structure. These bureaucratic structural variables all have a linear relationship to size when size is logarithmically transformed (Blau and Schoenherr 1971; Child 1973). In the theory, the organization, once again, is taken to be a firm in a market economy.

The Cycles of Organizational Adaptation and of Business Activity

Organizational adaptation is cyclical. If an organization is in fit between its structure and size, that organization will consequently experience high performance, which will produce growth in profit, sales, and employment, thus increasing organizational size (Child 1975; Khandwalla 1973; Powell 1992). The newly enlarged organization will continue with its old structure, and this will create a size–structure misfit, which will lower performance (Child 1975). If organizational performance drops below the satisficing level, adaptation is likely to occur, changing the structure to fit the new larger size. Once at the new fit, the organization again experiences higher performance and so expands in size into misfit and again experiences a drop-off in performance and then further adaptation to attain an even newer fit. This is the cycle of organizational adaptation.

As has been stated, organizational performance is affected by factors other than the size–structure fit. It is the combined effect of size–structure fit and the other factors that determines the level of organizational performance. Thus whether the reduced performance of an organization in misfit is low enough to be below the satisficing level and so adapt into fit or not is critically affected by the other factors affecting performance. Similarly, for an organization in size–structure fit, the amount of growth that occurs is affected not only by the fit but by the other factors affecting performance. A large component of these other factors that affect organizational performance are external factors, that is, outside the organization in the wider economy. Thus the organizational cycle of adaptation and growth is to a large degree governed by these external economic factors. Organizational theory often refers to these factors under terms such as environmental munificence, noting that for an organization in misfit adaptation will not occur if slack is present to absorb the reduced performance (Pfeffer and Salancik 1978; Williamson 1970). However, the amount of slack varies from year to year in a business firm. The fluctuations over time of slack need to be explicitly brought into the model of organizational adaptation through consideration of the business cycle.

Not only is organizational adaptation cyclical but it is governed by external economic forces that are themselves cyclical, that is, by the business cycle. There are variations in the cycle across industries, but the pervasiveness and degree of synchronization of the cycle are sufficient that almost all firms in the same economy experience common effects to some degree. Our discussion of business cycles first considers the general business cycle and in a later section examines differences by sector.

The Business Cycle as a
Cause of Organizational Change

The organizational adaptation cycle is affected by the business cycle. The cycle of organizational adaptation is for firms to move from fit to misfit and then to a new fit. The timing and manner of these transitions are affected by the business cycle. A firm will tend to be in fit around the trough of the business cycle and to move into misfit during its upswing (see Figure 3.1). The firm will tend to remain in misfit around the peak of the business cycle and move into fit during its downswing. The reasons are that the business cycle affects firm growth, which leads toward misfit, and it also affects firm performance, which controls the timing of the adaptive move into fit. The upswing produces growth, whereas the downswing produces the performance decrease that causes structural adaptation. Thus the business cycle affects both dimensions of organizational change: growth and adaptation.

Let us consider a firm as it moves through the business cycle, that is, from upswing to peak to downswing to trough and then into the upswing again (i.e., moving from the left to right in Figure 3.1).

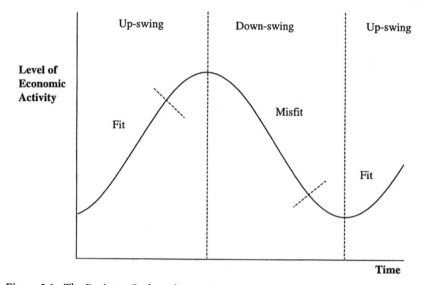

Figure 3.1   The Business Cycle and Organizational Adaptation

A firm in fit between structure and size will have, as a result, positive performance. This will be shown in high profits and sales growth, which feed back to increase firm output through fuller utilization of capacity, second-shift working, hiring new employees, and so on, thus increasing organizational size. However, this rate of increase in size is affected also by the business cycle. When the cycle is on the upswing, or at its peak, the economic factors external to the firm are strongly positive, with high consumer expenditures and demand for the products of the firm, which of themselves boost profits, sales growth, and size increase of the firm. Thus a firm in fit when the business cycle is moving upward will have a high growth rate. Its growth will quickly outstrip the existing organization structure, and so the firm soon reaches the state of misfit between size and structure (see Figure 3.1). Thus the upswing tends to cause a firm in fit to move into misfit.

For the firm, now in misfit, the movement to fit through structural adaptation is likewise conditioned by the business cycle. A firm in misfit between size and structure suffers disorganization, communications problems, poor decision making, and so on, which work to reduce its sales growth, profit and like aspects of performance (Khandwalla 1973; Child 1975; Powell 1992).

However, it tends to remain in misfit during and after the peak because the buoyant economy keeps its performance high, despite its misfit. Indeed, the strong economy tends to keep the firm growing until after the peak, after which the economy softens and firm performance begins to decrease. As the downswing continues, demand slackens and sales fall so that firm performance eventually falls below the satisficing level and structural adaptation occurs, thereby moving the firm from misfit into fit. Thus the firm approaches the trough in fit.

For the firm in fit around the trough, the rate of firm growth will be low because the demand for its products will be low. In the absence of market demand, the mere capacity for enhanced output and size growth resulting from being in fit will not produce higher output and growth. Thus the low growth rate of the firm in fit in the downswing of the business cycle means that the firm will tend not to move into misfit between size and structure, and so it will tend to remain in fit. The firm will remain in fit during and after the trough of the business cycle. Only the subsequent rise of the business cycle in a new upswing will raise organizational growth again so that it moves from fit into misfit, repeating its cycle of organizational adaptation.

Thus whether the firm moves from fit into misfit, and vice versa, and the timing are conditioned by the phases of the business cycle. Firms in fit will tend to remain there until the business cycle swings upward sufficiently, and firms in misfit will tend to remain there until the business cycle swings downward sufficiently. The cycle of organizational adaptation is affected by the business cycle.

The propositions thus are the following:

> 3.1   A firm is more likely to be in fit around the trough and to be in misfit around the peak of the business cycle.

> 3.2   The upswing of the business cycle causes a firm in fit to move into misfit.

> 3.3   The downswing of the business cycle causes a firm in misfit to move into fit.

The historical analyses by Chandler (1962) reveal the importance of the business cycle in prompting structural adaptation. In the early 1920s, both Du Pont and General Motors had structures that no longer fit their expansionary strategies, which had increased their scale and product diversity. However, both companies retained these misfitting structures until forced to change by performance crises that were caused by the post-World War I downturn in the business cycle. This combined with the inefficiencies from their misfitting structures to render organizational performance poor and so induce structural adaptation, that is, adoption of the multidivisional structure.

Thus firms subject to the same business cycle tend to move together, showing alternating periods of growth and structural adaptation and of movement and stasis in harmony with the movement of the underlying business cycle that causes them.

We can now attend to certain systematic differences within this general business cycle by industrial sector. In this way, we can appreciate that the business cycle affects not only the structure of the organization (as just seen) but also the structure of the industry.

Variations in the Business Cycle Across Industries

Business cycles differ in their amplitude, that is, in their degree of variation about their mean. Business cycles of greater amplitude have peaks that are higher and troughs that are deeper than business cycles of smaller amplitude (even with the same mean).

Business cycles are driven by differential income elasticities of different goods, that is, purchases are affected by income levels more for some goods than for others. Consumers repeatedly purchase basic items, such as groceries, despite changes in their income levels. Discretionary items such as a new automobile are purchased only when incomes are high. The aggregate demand in the economy for basic foods shows less fluctuation over time than for consumer durables and some luxuries (Amit and Livnat 1989). Fluctuations in demand for consumer durables feed back along the value-added chain, causing larger fluctuations in the capital goods industry and even greater fluctuations in basic materials such as mining products (Ball and Brown 1980). Thus, going backward along the value-added chain from consumer to primary extractive industries, the business cycles are, in general, greater in amplitude. Moreover, because demand for consumer products drives the subsequent demand for industrial goods, the business cycle in consumer products industries leads, in time, that of industrial goods industries (Van Duijn 1983).

Business cycles of greater amplitude produce more extreme cycles of organizational adaptation. The greater peaks cause a firm to face an extremely encouraging economic environment that fuels rapid growth in firm size. The momentum of this growth continues to be substantial even after the firm has entered misfit and propels the firm further into misfit, producing acute misfit. This in turn produces a pronounced reduction in performance resultant upon the extreme disorganization of the firm, although this is offset by the buoyant economy around the peak. When the cycle has turned downward, the acutely poor performance induced by structural misfit combines with the declining economic environment as the cycle turns downward to produce poor overall firm performance. This is further exacerbated, in the large-amplitude cycle, as the business cycle continues downward toward its very low trough. Firms in the trough, in large-amplitude business-cycle industries, face the worst possible performance levels of any industry. Thus the movement into fit commenced in the downturn is strongly reinforced as the firm moves toward the business-cycle trough. The response of such firms is to make massive and drastic adaptations in structure (and other aspects of their form). This means that these firms will be, in the trough, highly structurally adapted.

The propositions thus are the following:

3.4 The greater the amplitude of the business cycle in an industry, the greater the incremental size increases of the organizations in that industry.

3.5 The greater the amplitude of the business cycle in an industry, the more frequent the adaptations by the organizations in that industry.

Life in a firm in a large-amplitude business-cycle industry, such as mining, is dramatic, with rapid shifts between spurts of large growth and bouts of extremely poor performance. In the trough of depression, at the extreme, some firms will become unprofitable and some will not survive. Thus selection of the fittest through survival works most strongly in industries with large-amplitude business cycles, and so the characteristics of the population will be shaped not only by individual organizational adaptation but also by population-level adaptation as specified in population-ecology theory (Aldrich 1979; Hannan and Freeman 1989). For the survivors, the successive installments of growth increments and structural changes mean that these firms become some of the largest and most structurally sophisticated in the economy.

The proposition thus is the following:

3.6   The greater the amplitude of the business cycle in an industry, the higher the probability of bankruptcy of an organization in that industry.

For firms in an industry whose business cycle is of small amplitude, life is more placid. In the move from fit to misfit, in the upward phase of the business cycle, the growth spurt will be more modest, because market demand is not increasing much, and the resultant state of misfit less acute. The negative effect of misfit on performance will accordingly also be moderate. The reduction in performance in the downswing of the cycle will also be less acute. This will combine with the lesser structural reduction in performance to produce only a limited degree of performance loss, even after some time in misfit. Thus the probability of falling below the satisficing level is reduced in such an industry so that the firm may not structurally adapt into fit. Therefore, firms in misfit may remain in misfit throughout the full downswing of the business cycle and continue in misfit into the next or even the following business cycles. Their misfit will retard their growth rate, and their failure to make needed structural adaptations may retard their growth indefinitely. The organizations will remain small and for the most part not become socially prominent. They lack the therapeutic effect of crises whose resolution opens the door to growth. Such industries will be characterized by many small firms (e.g., small family businesses).

The differential characteristics of large- and small-amplitude business-cycle industries have significance for industry structure. The small-amplitude industries allow many firms to remain intact as modestly successful, stable small businesses that lack growth capacity because they fail to make the structural adaptations necessary for further growth. Therefore, the industry remains fragmented, and profit levels remain low due to competition. Family-owned small businesses in food retailing exemplify this type. Their low profitability might be thought to predispose them toward structural adaptation. However, the chronic nature of their low performance means that the satisficing level is set low based on past experience. The stability of their performance helps ensure that it tends to remain above the satisficing level, thus forestalling adaptation. Because these firms do not tend to make adaptations, there is no competitive effect forcing adaptations on each other. Chronic maladaptation and low performance of their many small firms become the norm in such small-amplitude business-cycle industries.

The large-amplitude business-cycle industry, in contrast, fosters the emergence over time of a few large firms out of all of the turbulence, as repeated down cycles traumatize the firms into successive structural adaptations allowing growth (Cameron, Kim, and Whetten 1987). Thus firm sizes are unequal, and concentration and oligopoly develop, reducing competition. The reduction in competition in large-cycle industries permits above-average rates of profit that provide performance slack in each of the oligopolists, cushioning them from the need to make structural adaptations. However, because cessation of competition occurs in large-amplitude industries, the amount of slack needed to keep the organization above the satisficing level in the trough of the cycle is substantial. Therefore, even oligopolists enjoying slack in these industries will experience subsatisficing performance levels in unusually severe cyclical troughs and thus will continue to display some structural adaptation, although less frequently than under competitive conditions. The Canadian nickel giant, INCO, exemplifies this process in its history, despite being a major in an oligopoly. Cyclically induced structural adaptation by oligopolists will tend to keep them somewhat adapted and allow them further growth, thus preserving their domination and the oligopolization of their industry. This helps explain why structural adaptation occurs even among large corporations whose dominance in their markets would normally be held to cushion them from having to adapt (Child 1972).

For an industry beginning as competing small firms and then concentrating, oligopoly will be reached most quickly in large-amplitude industries, at the primary end of the value-added chain, and will be most complete and enduring. Industries with more-moderate-amplitude cycles will take longer to attain oligopolistic concentration because the shallower troughs will mean that only some down phases will trigger structural adaptation and hence continued growth of the firm. However, once oligopoly has formed in these industries, the resultant slack from cessation of price competition will surpass the satisficing level on almost all down phases of the business cycle. Thus the oligopolists will remain in mild structural maladaptation and no longer grow. Hence if the market continues to grow, non-oligopolists will seize a disproportionate share, and the industry will deconcentrate. Thus, at medium levels of amplitude of the business cycle, oligopoly formation will take a long time and not be enduring. This appears to characterize developments in the steel and auto industries, where oligopoly has subsequently been disturbed by enhanced competition (Halberstam 1987).

The propositions thus are the following:

3.7 The greater the amplitude of the business cycle in an industry, the greater the growth and structural adaptations by the organizations in that industry.

3.8 The greater the amplitude of the business cycle in an industry, the higher the probability that the industry will mature into an oligopoly.

3.9 The greater the amplitude of the business cycle in an industry, the quicker the industry will mature into an oligopoly.

In summary, small-amplitude business-cycle industries yield firms with low growth rates, which remain small, leading to enduringly fragmented industry structure. Large business-cycle industries yield firms with high growth rates and poor chances of survival, and some of those that survive grow large, producing a concentrated industry. The differences in the amplitude of the business cycle across industrial sectors lead to differences in firm survival rate, size, organizational structure, and industry structure.

Diversification Spreads the Corporation Across Business Cycles

Corporations, especially large ones, frequently sell into several diverse markets, may operate in several geographic regions, and may offer multiple, unrelated products (Stopford and Wells 1972; Rumelt 1974; Egelhoff 1988). Such diversification means that the corporation is operating in several different economic segments simultaneously, each of which may have a slightly different business cycle. Thus a diversified corporation aggregates across business cycles, and this tends to neutralize the overall cyclical exposure of the corporation and is a component of the reduction in financial risk attained through diversification (Salter and Weinhold 1979). Thus the countercyclical nature of one business unit compared with others in a corporation originates in part from the fact that each division is located within an industry whose business cycle differs from the other; that is, one division is in a consumer industry that leads the cycle in the producer goods industry in which the other division is situated. The significance of diversification neutralizing cyclical fluctuations on the corporation is analyzed in Chapter 6.

So far, we have analyzed the effect of the business cycle on the structures of the organization and the industry. However, there is also an effect of the organization on the business cycle.

Organizational Adaptation
Affects the Business Cycle

The prosperity of the economy is ultimately rooted in the success of the individual firms that constitute it (Porter 1990). This principle applies also to the cycles of economic prosperity and depression in the economy. The cycles of prosperity of the economy derive from the cycles of the individual firms that constitute it. The business cycle in the economy is affected by the cycle of adaptation in the organizations that compose the economy.

As we have seen, as the economy expands during a growth phase, its constituent firms grow and tend to move into misfit with their existing structure. This organizational misfit causes the growth of the firms to slow. Because this growing-then-slowing is being experienced by other firms as they also respond to the economy, there is a general pattern of firms growing and then slowing (although firms are most affected by the cycle in their industry and, in turn, affect it most). The growth spurts of these firms happen at about the same time in many firms and mean that the economy as a whole is growing. This in turn means that each firm tends to experience the economy as booming, providing the fuel to keep the firm growing, even though the initial growth has produced some misfit. However, because growth creates and then worsens the misfit of the firm, its growth then slows—because the internal organizational structure is becoming more and more dysfunctional, leading to delays, poor decisions, and so on. Because this misfit tends to occur quite generally across the firms in the economy (because of their common recent history of growth), the result is a slowing of the economy. Moreover, those firms lagging behind, which are still somewhat well structured and so growing, will nevertheless experience the economic climate as worsening, so reducing their own growth rate. General economic growth stalls. Thus the misfit of the firms in the economy causes economic growth to slow, then stop and reverse, so the economic boom peaks and then turns downward.

The resulting recession is a period of organizational adaptation in each firm through the adoption of better-fitting structures and the like. Then the organization has regained fit and so can begin to grow again. The small initial growth of each firm compounds across the economy so that there is a general upswing in the business cycle. This reverses the decline in the economy so that it begins to rise again, commencing a new upswing in the economy. Hence the cycle of organizational fit, growth, misfit, slowing, and adaptation is initiated once again. This is accompanied by the business cycle of economic growth, boom, slowing, and recession. The cycle of adaptation by the organization feeds into and helps cause the business cycle of the economy.

The business cycle is underlaid by the discontinuities in growth and adaptation of the constituent firms. When the firms have a fitting structure, this contributes to economic growth; when the firms have misfitting structures, this contributes to economic slowdown and recession. The temporal pattern is that the period of organizational adaptation leads the period of economic growth, whereas the period of organizational maladaptation leads the period of economic stagnation. (This argument is highly general and applies not only to organizational structure but to any other organizational adaptation to a size-related contingency factor.)

The microlevel cycle of adaptation at the level of the organization helps produce the business cycle. The reciprocal causation from organizational adaptation to the business cycle sustains the existence of business cycles, thus preserving them as an ongoing feature of the environment of organizations. There are, of course, other influences upon the business cycle, such as government policy.

There is, however, a contrary opinion that the effect of organizations on the business cycle is such that business cycles are being reduced in the economy through corporate diversification. Diversified corporations have less fluctuations in their performance because the business cycle in the industry of a division is offset by that of another division. The argument is sometimes made that these reduced fluctuations in overall corporate performance dampen the business cycle in the economy. However, the performance fluctuations of each division feed into the business cycle of its industry so that the amplitudes of the cycles of industries are sustained, despite the businesses being owned by a diversified corporation. For example, if a diversified corporation owns both a sugar division and a brick division, its overall performance fluctuation will be less than that of the two divisions. However, the fluctuation in the performance of the sugar division feeds into (and is fed by) the business cycle of the sugar industry. Similarly, the fluctuation in the performance of the brick division feeds into the business cycle of its industry. It is not the case that the performance fluctuation of the sugar division is dampened by that of the brick division. Thus the amplitude of the cycles in the two industries is sustained. The business cycle of the economy is created by conjunctions between the industry cycles, and because the industry cycles are not dampened by diversified corporations, neither is the business cycle in the economy dampened. Thus corporate diversification in itself will not produce a smaller amplitude business cycle in the economy. Organizational adaptation will continue to contribute toward cycles in the economy, although for a diversified corporation much of this will be at a disaggregated level, that is, each of its divisions separately feeding their industry cycles.

For the individual manager and firm, business cycles are troublesome, preferably to be obviated. Yet they provide the dynamic that leads to organizational adaptation and growth.

Distinguishing Business-Cycle Downswing From Organizational Decline

Downswings in the business cycle may lead to reductions in organizational size, and so organization theorists might be tempted to subsume business cycle downswings under the topic of organizational decline, which has been the subject of theory and empirical research (Cameron et al. 1987; Cameron et al. 1988; Whetten 1980; Cascio 1993). However, organizational changes caused by business-cycle downswings differ from organizational decline in their scale and effects.

Students of organizational decline have distinguished decline caused by mismanagement of the firm from decline caused by a downswing in its environment, classifying them as r-type and k-type decline, respectively (Cameron et al. 1988). It is environmentally caused decline that concerns us here, with the downswing of the business cycle being a major deterioration in the economic environment of the firm.

Even within environmentally caused organizational decline, it is necessary to distinguish between secular and recurrent decline. Secular decline is a long-run organizational decline, wherein the organization shrinks from large to small and then disbands. Continuous organizational decline is the hallmark of secular decline, such as caused by the collapse of an industry. In contrast, in recurrent organizational decline, the firm has periods of shrinking interspersed with periods of growth. Thus in recurrent decline, the size of the firm fluctuates without cumulative substantial change in its size because the decrements of decline are compensated for by the increments of growth (for a discussion of fluctuation or turbulence, see Cameron et al. 1987).

Business cycles can produce recurrent decline of organizations. During downswings of the business cycle, decrements of organizational size may occur, whereas during upswings, growth increments occur so that there is little cumulative size change. Thus business cycles can lead to recurrent organizational decline rather than the large-scale, continuous organizational shrinkage of secular organizational decline. Indeed, despite any recurrent organizational decline caused by the business cycle, it can lead to a longer-term trend of growth in organizational size, such that, despite fluctuating, organizational size grows larger. Any recurrent decline notwithstanding, business cycles foster long-run organizational growth.

Some might argue that organizational decline leads the organization to move from fit into misfit because of failure to adapt to the new, smaller organizational size. This may occur in the large declines characteristic of secular decline. However, recurrent decline produces more moderate reductions in organizational size during each of its downswings, and these are insufficient to cause the organization to move from fit into misfit. Indeed, the recurrent decline in the downswing of the business cycle tends to cause the organization to move from misfit to fit. This is caused by the effect of changes in organizational performance rather than change in organizational size (or accompanying contingency factors).

Thus the theoretical model being advanced here differs from some of the work on the topic of organizational decline in both continuity of decline and effects.

Economic Depressions: A Special Case

An exception to the foregoing theory of business cycles and organizational adaptation is where the trough is so bad that it constitutes a depression. A depression may be defined as a recession that is so severe that there are three successive quarters of negative economic growth. Most troughs in the business cycle are not as severe as a depression, and so this is an exceptional case. In a depression, despite the firm being in fit, it may substantially decline so that its existing structure becomes misfitted to its new size (Cameron et al. 1988). The firm will need to adopt a new structure suited to its smaller size, so that it regains fit and so can recommence growing when the economy picks up. Because of the depression, the performance of the firm will be poor and below its satisficing level, and so such structural adaptation will be undertaken quite quickly.

The early phase of the recovery from an economic depression may be marked by those firms that have declined into misfit not recommencing growth until their reorganizations into fit are sufficiently completed. These reorganizing firms will lag behind firms that did not need to downsize in the depression and consequently emerge from it in fit and can start growing again as soon as the worst of the depression lifts.

The propositions thus are the following:

> **3.10** In an economic depression, some firms will decline in size so that they move from fit into misfit.

> **3.11** When a depression ends, firms that are in misfit need to structurally adapt and move into fit before they commence growing again.

An extreme decline by a firm may end in bankruptcy and demise for that firm. The poorer economic conditions at the trough of a business cycle increase the rate of bankruptcies among firms. The rate of bankruptcies will be higher in a depression than in the more typical business cycle trough. Therefore, some firms will not survive the depression and so will not be recommencing growth despite the onset of the economic recovery and the upswing. The population of firms exiting from a depression may be smaller than that which entered. This reduces competition (Hannan and Freeman 1989), which will tend to increase the growth rate of firms during the upswing over what it would have been if their erstwhile competitors had remained.

This depression scenario should be thought of as a special case, in that most troughs are not depressions, that is, are not as severe. It might be thought that the trough of the normal business cycle would cause the firm to enter misfit because the recession would shrink firm size so that its existing structure became a misfit. This may sometimes occur but is more likely in economic depressions because of their greater severity. More typically, the business cycle trough will only cause the firm to remain static in size or to shrink a little so that its structure remains a fit. Thus the more usual case is that firms in the trough are in fit and so can grow again as soon as the economy swings up.

Conclusions

This chapter sought to analyze a phenomenon hitherto neglected in organizational theory, the business cycle. The business cycle has been shown to interact with the cycle of individual organizational adaptation, in ways consequential for firm growth, adaptation, and survival.

The key insight is that, given that structural adaptation is mediated by organizational performance, the business cycle operates to affect the occurrence, timing, and extent of firm adaptation and growth. An organization in misfit and so suffering lower performance is more likely to suffer subsatisficing performance when the business cycle is in the downswing because then the external causes of firm performance reinforce the internally caused low performance. Hence organizational adaptation is more likely in the downswing of the business cycle. Conversely, an organization in fit is more likely to grow substantially when the business cycle is in an upswing. This in turn means that an organization is more likely to move from fit into misfit when the business cycle is in the later part of the upswing.

Reciprocally, the business cycle is caused in part by the internal organizational cycle of adaptation. When the organization is in fit and growing, this stimulates growth in the economy, so causing the business cycle to rise. When the organization is in misfit and stagnating, it depresses the economy, so contributing to the downswing in the business cycle.

Differences in the amplitude of the business cycle have been identified. These are associated with position in the value-added chain. They are argued to produce systematic differences in firm adaptation and growth leading to distinct industry structures. The greater the amplitude of the business cycle, the more frequent the cycle of organizational adaptation. Firms in industries with small-amplitude business cycles, in consequence, fail to make recurrent adaptations, and this chokes off their growth. The result for small-amplitude business-cycle industries is an industry structure of many small firms with high competition between them. Firms in industries with large-amplitude business cycles, in consequence, make recurrent adaptations, and this causes their growth, reinforced by periodic sharp upturns in the demand in their markets. Moreover, large-amplitude business cycles increase organizational mortality. The result for large-amplitude industries is an industry structure of oligopoly with few, though large, firms.

Although much of the discussion has been couched in terms of the organizational structure, the analysis generalizes across many other aspects of organization, including human resource practices, leadership style, and information technology.

In this chapter, we began the analysis of how factors that cause organizational performance affect organizational adaptation and growth. We identified the effects of the business cycle and subsequently will go further in mapping the effects of the business cycle on organizational change. In Chapter 4, however, we consider the effect on the organization of another external economic factor—competition.

Competition and Organizational Change

Competition is one of the toughest facts of economic life for a firm. It is a major source of external pressure on the firm to adapt and become more effective. Yet competition has received insufficient attention in organizational theory to date. This chapter seeks to begin an organizational theory analysis of competitive dynamics.

The approach here is to consider the interaction between competing firms. The adaptation of any one firm results in part from the effects of its competitors. This means that the adaptation of any one firm needs to be seen in the context of the degree of adaptation of its competitors. We begin to see that it is not only the adaptation of the firm that is significant but also its adaptation *relative* to the competition. This introduces a relative perspective into the analysis of organizational effectiveness. Such a perspective has been sorely lacking in organizational theory, yet it is needed for the assessment of organizational performance and of the resulting pressures on firms to adapt.

Economics has long given a central place in its theories to competition between firms (Samuelson 1980). This has been extended to the concept of the behavior between firms being modeled as a game (Saloner 1994). Business strategy has been concerned with competition in the securing for a firm of an advantageous competitive position (Porter 1985). This has been developed in industrial organizational economics into empirical analyses of the firm within its industry. In contrast, organizational theory tends to subsume competitors rather vaguely under the concept of "the environment" of the organization (e.g., Emery and Trist 1965). Resource dependence theory sees competitors as requiring to be influenced through merger or co-optation and so forth (Pfeffer and Salancik 1978). Thus competition affects the strategy and boundaries of the firm. Here we wish to analyze the impact of competition upon the internal adaptations of the firm such as its organizational structure. Moreover, in considering the overall level of competition in the environment (Khandwalla 1977), we want to explain this by the internal characteristics of the competitor firms. Thus the notion of competitive dynamics is somewhat undertheorized in contemporary organizational theory, certainly relative to economics. This chapter attempts to redress that neglect.

The structural contingency theory of organizational adaptation holds that performance feeds back to affect structure so that an organization in misfit will adopt a better-fitting structure when performance is low (Chandler 1962; Child 1972; Donaldson 1987). As we have argued, this low performance is itself partially the result of the misfit but is partially also the result of wider economic forces that govern organizational performances. Among these wider forces, competition must be included. The performance of the firm will tend to drop when it comes under pressure from competitors. Population-ecology focuses on the issue of the number of other organizations in the population affecting competition (Barnett and Carroll 1987; Barnett 1990). The internal states of these organizations are considered only briefly, mainly in terms of generalist versus specialist, which captures differences in strategy and technology (Hannan and Freeman 1989) or organizational size (Barnett and Amburgey 1990; Hannan, Ranger-Moore, and Banaszak-Holl 1990). However, a neglected issue is the internal organizational structure of these other organizations that are in the same niche as the focal organization. Being in the same niche and thus contesting for the same resources make these other firms competitors, but their internal state determines their effectiveness as competitors. A disorganized competitor will perform poorly and thus provide little competition for the firm. Stronger competition comes from the well-organized competitor. This throws the emphasis on how well the firm is organized relative to its competitors.

Comparison of one firm with another brings in processes of isomorphism of institutional theory (DiMaggio and Powell 1983). However, competition is to be distinguished from isomorphism. The opening sections will delineate competition as separate from institutional processes. After having done so, then the two theories of competition and isomorphism will be combined for a fuller model. In the ensuing discussion, we emphasize change in organizational structure, but the argument is more general and applies to organizational adaptation of any kind.

Competition Lowers Firm Performance

As we argue in this book, performance is the cause of change in the firm. Here we extend the analysis to show how the performance of competitor firms affects the performance of the firm and thereby causes organizational change. From an economics view, the stronger the competition on a firm, the lower its profitability because competition sets low prices and competitors take sales away from the firm.

The strength of competition is affected by several factors. One is the size and openness of the market. For example, increasing trade between nations has increased the competition within their economies, a trend increasing with globalization, so that markets are increasingly national rather than international (Dunning, Kogut, and Blomström 1990; D'Aveni 1994). A firm is a strong competitor if it has some competitive advantage such as lower-cost production or a superior product (Porter 1985). These advantages may in part lie in the comparative advantages of the nation in which the firm is based (e.g., lower labor costs in developing than in developed nations).

Even within one nation, competition is affected by the number of competitors. As the number of competing firms increases, this eventually raises competition to the point where the rate of new firm formation decreases and the rate of firm disbandment increases (Hannan and Freeman 1989). Competition is affected by governmental regulation and by monopoly. Some governments have deregulated some of their industries to increase the competitive pressure on firms (e.g., airlines in the United States). Monopolies have been broken up and, in some cases, moved from public to private ownership (Bishop and Kay 1988).

Whatever its source, the effect of stronger competition on a firm is to reduce its profitability so that it more readily drops below the satisficing level. Hence a maladapted firm is more likely to make adaptive changes, the stronger the competitive pressure on it.

The propositions thus are the following:

> 4.1 The stronger the competitive pressure on an organization, the more likely its performance will become unsatisfactory.

> 4.2 The stronger the competitive pressure on a maladapted organization, the more likely it will adapt.

If the firm is adapted, that is, it is in fit, it has the capacity to grow, but its rate of growth will be low when competition is strong because other firms take customers away. Conversely, when competition is weak, a firm in fit will be able to sell more, and so its growth rate will be high. The weaker the competition, the higher the growth rate of a firm in fit.

The proposition thus is the following:

> 4.3 For a firm in fit, the weaker the competition, the higher the growth rate of the firm.

Thus competition affects organizational adaptation and growth through its effect on organizational performance.

We have discussed the adaptation of the firm, but each of its competitors may be adapted or maladapted to its situation. A maladapted competitor is a weaker competitor than an adapted competitor. Therefore, the competitive pressure on a firm is stronger, the more of its competitors that are adapted. The more competitors that are adapted, the stronger the competitive pressure on the firm to adapt. Thus we need to consider the internal state of each competitor and enter this into the analysis of competition.

Competition and Relative Fit

Under structural contingency theory, a firm is well organized, that is, adapted, if it is in fit between its organizational structure and its contingency factors such as size, strategy, and so on. The question then becomes whether the focal organization is in fit or misfit *and whether each of the competitor firms is simultaneously in fit or misfit.*

If the firm is in misfit between its organizational structure and its contingencies (size, strategy, etc.), it will consequently suffer lower performance. As we have stressed, this lower performance may be low enough to cause structural adaptation, but whether it is low enough depends on the other factors affecting the performance of the firm. One such external factor is competition. If competition is strong, the performance of the firm in misfit is liable to become poor, thus triggering structural adaptation. However, for competition to be strong, the competitor firms need to be in fit because if they are in misfit their performance would be lowered and there would be less competitive pressure placed on the firm. Where competition is low because of the competitor firms being in misfit, then the performance of the firm may be good enough, despite its being in misfit, that it can persist in misfit and avoid adaptation. Thus the adaptation of the firm is affected by its fit or misfit *relative to competitors,* so the cornerstone of the analysis is the fit of the firm relative to firms that compete with it. The fit of the competitor firm affects the performance of the firm, and this interacts with the misfit of the firm to affect its structural adaptation.

The fit of the competitor firm raises its performance, lowering the performance of the firm, which then leads a firm in misfit to move into fit. Thus the fit of the competitor influences the firm to make adaptive change. This process is through the financial performance of the firm. As we have stated, the effect of the competitor firm upon the firm is mediated by the financial performance of the firm and hence also by the other causes of the performance of the firm. Many of these other causes are addressed in the other chapters of this book. In this chapter, the focus is on obtaining a systematic understanding of the effect of competitors upon fit in the firm, and so the other causes of the performance of the firm are ignored.

The concept of *relative fit* is defined as the degree to which the firm is in fit relative to its competitors. If a firm is in fit, then the more of its competitors that are in misfit, the higher the relative fit of the firm. Conversely, if a firm is in misfit, then the more of its competitors that are in fit, the higher the relative misfit of the firm. Relative fit positively affects the financial performance of the firm, and relative misfit negatively affects its financial performance. If the competitor is in fit and the firm is in misfit, then the competitor is better organized and so will compete more effectively. The competitor will take market share away from the firm and thus gain sales and typically also profit at the expense of the firm. If performance of the firm falls below the satisficing level, the firm is likely to structurally adapt in order to regain fit and performance.

The probability of a firm in misfit structurally adapting is positively affected by its relative misfit. The competitive pressure on a firm to adapt is stronger where competitors are in fit rather than misfit. The more competitors who are in fit rather than misfit, the stronger the competitive pressure on a firm to adapt. The higher the proportion of competitor firms that are in fit, the greater is the pressure on the firm to adapt.

The propositions thus are the following:

> 4.4 A firm that has the same degree of fit relative to competitor firms will tend to have the same performance as them, ceteris paribus.

> 4.5 The higher the ratio of fits to misfits among its competitors, the higher the probability that a firm in misfit will adapt.

Relative fit also affects organizational growth and thus propels a firm in fit into misfit. The more competitors that are in misfit, the higher the relative fit of a firm that is in fit. Thus the more competitors that are in misfit, the higher the performance of a firm in fit, causing it to be more likely to grow so that it moves into misfit.

The propositions thus are the following:

> 4.6 The higher the ratio of misfits to fits among its competitors, the higher the growth rate a firm in fit tends to have.

> 4.7 The higher the ratio of misfits to fits among its competitors, the higher the probability that a firm in fit will move into misfit through growth.

Thus the fit or misfit of competitors affects the adaptation and growth of the firm.

Competition, Diversification, and Divisionalization

Let us now use these concepts of relative fit and organizational performance to analyze the competitive dynamics involved in a firm's diversifying. The interest is on the firm relative to its other competitors, some of which also diversify.

Suppose the firm is an undiversified, single business with a single product and that it has a functional structure, so that its structure fits its strategy (cell A of Figure 4.1). Suppose its competitors are also undiversified and functionally

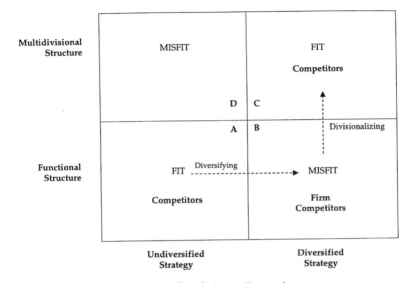

Figure 4.1 Diversified Firm in Misfit Relative to Competitors

structured and thus are also in fit. Then the firm is neither inferior nor superior to its competitors and all will perform equally well, ceteris paribus.

If the firm then diversifies, by offering a second product not related to its original product, while retaining the functional structure, it will move into misfit between its strategy and structure (cell B). However, if the competitors all remain undiversified and functionally structured, they remain in fit (in cell A). Thus the firm is in misfit relative to its competitors. The firm is internally disorganized, whereas the competitors are not and so are able to gain market share and profits at the expense of the firm. Therefore, the performance of the firm will be lower than that of the competitors. This lower performance, if continued, may eventually cause the performance of the firm to drop below its satisficing level so that it structurally adapts by divisionalizing and so regains fit and performance (cell C). Thus a lone diversified firm in an industry would be predicted to eventually structurally adapt into fit because of the effect of its undiversified competitors being in fit.

The propositions thus are the following:

4.8 A diversified, functionally structured firm will have lower performance, the more its competitors are undiversified with a functional structure.

4.9 A diversified, functionally structured firm is more likely to divisionalize, the more its competitors are undiversified with a functional structure.

If, however, the firm is diversified and in misfit and all of its competitors also diversify while retaining their functional structures, so moving into misfit, then the firm and these competitors are all in misfit together (cell B in Figure 4.1). The firm is now performing about as well as its diversified competitors because both the firm and its competitors are in misfit and so about equally disorganized. The competitors are not able to take sales away from the firm because of superior internal organization, for they suffer equally from a functional structure that misfits their diversified strategy. This means that the performance level of the firm tends to be satisfactory. Because the firm is performing above the satisficing level, there is no performance crisis and hence no pressure for it to change by reorganizing to adopt a better-fitting structure. The firm may retain its misfitted structure indefinitely. Moreover, the same is true for its competitors, so that they too may retain their misfitted structure indefinitely. There is no competitive pressure on any firm for adaptation, and so stasis results, despite this meaning that all firms remain in misfit.

The proposition thus is the following:

4.10 A diversified firm with a functional structure and whose competitors are also diversified with a functional structure will tend to retain its functional structure.

Instead of all the firms in the industry diversifying and moving into fit together, suppose that *some* firms that are competitors of the firm remain undiversified (i.e., in cell A in Figure 4.1). These undiversified firms have a functional structure, and so they are in fit between strategy and structure (cell A). Because these undiversified firms are in fit, their performance will be higher than those other firms in their industry that diversified and retained their functional structures and so are in misfit (in cell B). Thus the diversified firms are in misfit relative to the undiversified ones. Hence their performance will be low relative to that of the undiversified firms and so will lose market share to those firms. This low performance will predispose the diversified firms toward adapting their structures by adopting divisional structures to fit their diversified strategy (i.e., move from cell B to C in Figure 4.1). Thus the misfit and low performance of the diversified firms relative to their undiversified competitors will place the diversified firms under some competitive pressure to structurally adapt. So, where some firms diversify but some remain undiversified and in fit, the diversified firms will tend to move toward fit.

The competitive pressure on the diversified, functionally structured (i.e., misfitted) firm to divisionalize is, however, weaker than the competitive pressure on the lone diversified firm to divisionalize. The competitive pressure is lower on the misfitted (diversified, functional) firms to divisionalize because each of them has some competitors that are also misfitted (i.e., diversified, functional). In contrast, the lone diversified firm is in misfit, but all its competitors are in fit (i.e., undiversified, functional). Thus the increasing diversification decreases the relative misfit of the diversified firms and so reduces their probability of divisionalizing.

Competitive pressure to adapt is proportional to the ratio of competitor firms to which the firm is in relative misfit. The strength of the competitive pressure on a firm in misfit is proportional to the number of its competitors in fit relative to the number of its competitors in misfit. This competitive pressure decreases as firms in the industry diversify. As more competitors diversify into misfit, so the competitive pressure on the firm in misfit to structurally adapt decreases.

The proposition thus is the following:

> **4.11** A diversified firm with a functional structure is less likely to divisionalize, the more its competitors are diversified with a functional structure.

The Relationship of Divisionalization to Diversification

Continuing the scenario, a diversified firm will move into fit by structurally adapting, that is, by divisionalizing (i.e., by moving up into cell C in Figure 4.1). These divisionalized, diversified fits now, in turn, exert a competitive pressure on the functional, diversified misfits (cell B) to structurally adapt and become divisionalized, diversified fits (cell C). The more firms in the industry that are diversified and in fit (cell C), the greater becomes the relative misfit of the diversified firms that remain in misfit (cell B) and so the poorer their performance. Thus the more divisionalized, diversified fit firms in an industry, the higher the probability that the functional, diversified misfits will be forced to structurally adapt by divisionalizing and move into fit. The probability of a functional, diversified firm divisionalizing increases as the competitors divisionalize.

The probability that a functionally structured, diversified firm will divisionalize decreases with the diversification of its competitors and then increases as its competitors divisionalize. Thus the probability of structural adaptation into fit of a diversified misfit is curvilinear: It first decreases with increasing diversification among its competitors and then increases with more divisionalization among them.

The propositions thus are the following:

4.12   For a diversified firm with a functional structure, the probability of divisionalizing decreases as competitors diversify.

4.13   For a diversified firm with a functional structure, the probability of divisionalizing increases as diversified competitors divisionalize.

4.14   For diversified firms with functional structures, the probability of divisionalizing initially decreases as competitors diversify and then increases as those competitors divisionalize.

Overall, the probability that a diversified, functional (i.e., misfitted) firm (in cell B in Figure 4.1) will divisionalize increases the more its competitors are in fit, whether as undiversified, functional firms (cell A) or diversified, divisionalized firms (cell C). Conversely, the probability that a diversified, functional firm will divisionalize decreases the more of its competitors that are in misfit, that is, diversified, functional (cell B). Thus the probability of divisionalization of a diversified, functional firm is the ratio of cells A and C to B; this ratio measures the relative misfit of a diversified, functional firm.

Thus far we have discussed divisionalization as the adaptive response to the misfit caused by the firm diversifying, but the diversification itself is affected by competitive dynamics. For an undiversified firm, the probability that it will diversify is affected by its fit relative to its competitors. The undiversified firm with a functional structure is in fit, but those of its competitors who have diversified but retained a functional structure are in misfit, whereas its competitors who have diversified and divisionalized are in fit. The higher the ratio of misfits to fits among its competitors, the greater the relative fit and the performance of the firm so that it is more likely to grow. This growth may include diversifying, that is, using the surplus resources from its high performance to internally generate new products or services or acquire them. Thus the rate at which an undiversified firm diversifies is a positive function of the number of its competitors that have diversified but a negative function of the number of competitors that have divisionalized. Thus the initial diversification at the start of our scenario would become more frequent the more other firms that had diversified but then would become less frequent the more of those diversified competitors that had subsequently divisionalized. Thus the rate of diversifying would first increase and then decrease. This helps explain why so many firms diversify and yet, even when some firms have become highly diversified, other firms, even large ones, remain undiversified.

The propositions thus are the following:

4.15 An undiversified firm will be more likely to diversify the greater the number of its competitors that are diversified while retaining a functional structure.

4.16 An undiversified firm will be less likely to diversify the greater the number of its competitors that are diversified with a divisional structure.

4.17 The probability of an undiversified firm diversifying initially increases and then decreases with the diversification of its competitors.

Thus the probability of an undiversified firm diversifying is proportional to its relative fit, that is, the ratio of diversified, functional to undiversified, functional and diversified, divisional competitors (the ratio of cell B to A and C in Figure 4.1).

Combining the theoretical ideas about diversification and divisionalization, we see a more complete picture of the dynamics. Diversification initially has a low probability of occurrence. However, once it starts, because an undiversified firm becomes wealthy through years of being in fit, the more firms that are diversified, the greater the rate at which the remaining firms diversify. Thus the number of diversified firms rises increasingly rapidly, and the number of undiversified firms shrinks increasingly rapidly. The probability that these diversified firms will divisionalize is low initially. This tends to keep them in misfit and thus provides the increasing numbers of misfitted functional firms that are increasing the rate of diversification. However, once divisionalization commences among these diversified firms, then the greater the number of the firms that divisionalize, the greater the rate of divisionalization among the diversified firms. This reduces the number of diversified misfits, which in turn reduces the rate of diversification. Also the more divisionalized firms, the lower the rate of diversification. Thus two causal influences work together to reduce the rate of diversification so that it slows to a trickle, leaving a number of firms undiversified long term. Thus the model explains the tendency for diversification to first increase and then decrease so that there are many diversified firms that are in misfit for a while and then divisionalize so that at the endpoint most firms are divisionalized but some are functionally structured, with both being in fit and there being few diversified misfits. This theoretical model seems to accord with the pattern of diversification and divisionalization over time in empirical studies (e.g., Rumelt 1974; Dyas and Thanheiser 1976).

The Emergence of Industry
Structure Through Competition

As the diversified firms one by one move from misfit into fit by divisionalizing, their performance is no longer inferior relative to the undiversified firms that have remained in fit throughout. This places increasing pressure on the undiversified firms because they no longer benefit from the disorganization of the diversified firms. When all the diversified firms have divisionalized and moved into fit, then their performance is equal to that of the undiversified firms, ceteris paribus. Both sets of firms, diversified and undiversified, are now in fit, so there is no longer any performance advantage resulting from difference in fit. This similarity of performance will make it difficult for the undiversified firms to grow other than as part of a general increase in the market; that is, they will not be able to gain market share at the expense of their competitors. This may help explain the continuance in an industry of smaller, specialist, functionally structured firms alongside larger, diversified, divisionally structured firms.

Further, among the diversified firms, one firm has been the first to move into fit by adopting the divisional structure. This means that it enjoyed a performance advantage relative to the other diversified firms. This superiority may be sufficient to allow the firm to make some further expansionary moves.

These may amount to additional diversification moves. In the extreme, these diversification moves could be sufficient to lead to a new misfit. However, when other diversified firms moved into fit, the firm would lose its temporary advantage and would be forced to cease expansionary moves and also to regain fit. At this point, the industry would contain a highly diversified firm plus the moderately diversified firms and the undiversified firms. This account shows how industry structures of a range of degrees of diversification could emerge over time and be quite stable as a result of the competitive process and relative fit.

In theorizing the effect of competition, we have discussed the effects of competitor firms. However, economics has a broader concept of competition, that is, of a contestable market (Baumol, Panzar, and Willig 1982). In a contestable market, the behavior of firms is constrained by the threat posed by the possibility of firms entering the market. This contestability concept is cogent for many questions in economics, such as constraints on excessive profit-making by monopolists or oligopolists by limiting the prices they charge. However, for the issue examined here, the internal organizational adaptation of a firm being driven by unsatisfactory profitability, this is more likely to be caused by the actions of actual competitors rather than by potential competitors. Actual competitors can take away sales from the firm and reduce its profit below the satisficing level. Potential competitors that do not yet operate in the market cannot. Thus analyzing competition principally in terms of actual competitors, as done here, seems sensible, at least for an initial attempt at theory construction within organizational theory. Later, more refined efforts at theorizing competition effects on organizations may make use of the broader concept of contestability.

In summary, part of the understanding of competition and the ensuing organizational and industry dynamics is through the concept of the fit of an organization relative to its competitors. This is a causal factor that directly affects organizational performance, which in turn causes the organization to move into misfit and then into fit through growth and structural adaptation.

Support From Empirical Research

Some support for the effect of competition on organizational structure comes from the study by Armour and Teece (1978) of companies in the oil industry.

They found that divisionally structured companies outperform functionally structured companies, but only in the early years, as in the later years the performance of the two structures is similar. Armour and Teece (1978) referred to the role played by competition so that the greater effectiveness of the divisionalized companies pressures the other companies to adopt the divisional structure. Thus divisionalization spreads through the industry, becoming more common over time.

In terms of the present theory, companies attain advantage economically through adopting the divisional structure only if it is a fit with their strategy. It is fit rather than structure per se that affects organizational performance. Over time, as companies divisionalized they moved into fit with their diversified strategy; thus fewer of the functionally structured companies would be in misfit (by having retained that structure while being diversified). However, empirical research shows that there are substantial time lags for many companies in their divisionalization after having diversified, so many diversified companies remain functionally structured and in misfit for years (Rumelt 1974; Dyas and Thanheiser 1976). Therefore, in the earlier period, the comparison would be of functional structures, some in fit but some in misfit, versus divisional structures that would be almost wholly fits. Therefore, the divisional category would show higher performance than the functional category because the divisionalized companies would be in relative fit. In contrast, later there would be fewer misfits among the functionally structured companies because they had divisionalized and so moved into fit. Hence the comparison of divisional structures with functional structures in the later period is likely to be between structures that are both in fit, leading to no difference in performance, as Armour and Teece (1978) found. However, this change in outcomes would not be due to the superiority of divisional over functional structure being only temporary but, rather, to shifts in the ratio of fits to misfits in each category as structural adaptation occurs over time.

The dynamics of structural adaptation are predictable from theory: that structural change over time is expected to be associated with changes in the pattern of misfits. As companies diversify, the proportion of misfits first rises and then decreases as subsequent divisionalization leads to structural adaptation. Competitive pressure among companies in the industry causes the rate of diversification to rise initially and then decrease, and competition causes the diversified companies in misfit to divisionalize. This leads to companies diversifying into structural misfit and then fit so that the number of diversified companies with a functional structure first rises and then falls, leaving a group of undiversified, functionally structured companies in fit alongside the diversified, divisionalized companies in fit. The findings of Armour and Teece (1978) are consistent with this model and therefore lend it some empirical support. However, whether the underlying dynamics in the oil industry companies are as postulated here is unknown because the authors did not examine their data with the present model in mind. It is a task for future research to see whether the dynamics of structural adaptation occur according to the model sketched here. The consistency of the Armour and Teece results with the derivations from the present theory is at least encouraging.

Relationship to Institutional Theory

Distinction From Institutional Theory

The processes theorized herein are distinct from the processes stated by institutional theory, although both may be present to some degree. *Institutional theory* holds that firms come to resemble others in their field through coercive, mimetic, and normative isomorphism (DiMaggio and Powell 1983; Scott 1987). This has been held to apply to firms copying the structures of other firms in their industry, for example, the divisional structure (Fligstein 1985; see also Fligstein 1991). However, Kraatz and Zajac (1996) have argued that some organizational changes attributed to mimetic isomorphism by institutional theory may be caused by the pressure of economic necessity. The analysis developed here is kindred to their line of argument rather than to institutional theory.

A difference from institutional theory is that it usually deals with universals, whereas the present theory deals with contingent states. In institutional theory, firms mimic each other by copying the form of the other firm (e.g., firm B copies the divisional structure of firm A), or the government or professions influence the firm to adopt a particular structure (DiMaggio and Powell 1983; Fligstein 1985). However, in the present theory the issue is whether the firm moves from a structure that does not fit its contingency to a structure that is in fit with the strategy. For example, the firm has a functional structure that misfits its diversified strategy and then adopts the divisional form that fits its diversified strategy.

In contrast, in institutional theory, one structure leads to a like structure, whereas in the present theory one structure can cause a dissimilar structure. In the process of mimetic isomorphism in institutional theory, firm B adopts the same structure that firm A already possesses. However, in the present theory, the fit of firm A leads to the fit of firm B but not necessarily to the *same* fit. The contingency factors may have a different value between the two firms, leading to different structures fitting them. If undiversified firm A is in fit by having a functional structure, its superior organization will pressure diversified firm B to move into fit by adopting a divisional structure. Thus firm A influences firm B without the structure adopted by firm B being the same as the structure adopted by firm A.

Again, for institutional theory, firm B copies the structure adopted by firm A because the structure is a norm or confers legitimacy or support from powerful third parties, like funding bodies (DiMaggio and Powell 1983). In contrast, in the present theory, the competitor, firm A, influences firm B to structurally adapt because firm A, having already adopted a structure that fits itself, enjoys superior performance that reduces the performance of firm B by taking away business from B. The crucial intervening variable is the depressed performance of firm B due to its competitor, firm A, being better organized and so winning away customers and making more profit than firm B. The emphasis is thus on instrumental adaptation and not on conformity to the institutional environment.

Further, it is essential in the present theory that firm A be a competitor of firm B, that is, competing for the same customers by offering the same goods or services. Only then does the superior organization of firm A relative to B lead to performance loss for firm B, which is the trigger for the structural adaptation of B. This again distinguishes the present theory from institutional theory where firm B is influenced by any firms in the organizational field, for example, the same industry (Fligstein 1985, 1990a), so that firm A need not be a competitor of firm B to influence B. Thus the range of organizations that may affect the firm is far larger in institutional theory than in the present theory.

The range of firms against which the firm compares itself could be large in institutional theory, whereas in the present theory causation lies only with competitors. Not all comparators are competitors—for example, a manager in General Motors might compare GM and IBM without them being competitors. Moreover, a competitor can affect the firm without that competitor being a comparator. For instance, firm A is in fit, and this lowers the performance of firm B so that B moves into fit. However, firm B may not use firm A as a comparator and may not even know the identity of A, let alone whether A is in misfit or not. For example, in international competition, a U.S. manufacturer might be forced to adapt its structure into fit in response to loss of market share caused by a Chinese firm that is in fit. Yet the identity and nature of that Chinese firm might be unknown to the U.S. firm. This is a somewhat extreme case, but it illustrates that the present theory is not based on social causation in the manner of institutional theory but, instead, stresses economic processes. Being economic, the emphasis is on causality that can work through markets in an impersonal, asocial way, on occasion, between economic actors who are anonymous to each other.

Thus, in contrast to the direct influence of one organization upon another through mimetic isomorphism, we are arguing for a more indirect causal path. The fit of the competitor firm directly affects the performance of the firm, and this combines with its misfit to produce poor performance, causing structural adaptation. Thus the impact of competitors on the firm is indirect through relative fit and the performance of the firm. Therefore, the impact of the competitor on the firm is mediated by whether the firm is in fit or misfit. A competitor in fit influences the firm toward changing its structure only if in misfit because only then is the performance of the firm inferior to that of the competitor.

Fligstein (1985) draws on institutional theory for the proposition that the probability of a firm changing structure from functional to divisional is proportional to the number of other firms in the same industry with divisional structure. The proposition from *competition theory* would be that the probability of a diversified firm changing structure from functional to divisional is proportional to the number of competitor firms in the same industry that are in fit. Moreover, as has been seen above, those competitors do not need to have the divisional structure. Firms in fit that have a functional structure exert competitive pressure also on the firm to move into fit. The crucial factor is the relative fit leading to performance loss of the firm. The fit of competitors can come from them having any structure (i.e., functional or divisional) as long as it fits their strategy (and other contingency factors). It is not the demonstration effect of other firms having adopted the new structure but, rather, their having prospered as a result of it being a fit that creates the competitive performance pressure on the firm to adopt a new structure.

Having distinguished the present competition theory from institutional theory, it may be, nevertheless, that both causal processes play a role.

Synthesis of Organizational Portfolio and Institutional Theories

In this section, both organizational portfolio and institutional theories are drawn on to give a more comprehensive explanation of the effects of competition on organizational adaptation.

It is possible that the organizational portfolio theory effect of relative fit on the firm's performance may combine with some isomorphism process from institutional theory so that both push the firm toward adopting a certain structure sooner or more completely than it would have with either force alone. Relative fit impacts on the performance of the firm, and so the firm searches for better-fitting structures by looking at other firms that are successful. The institutional effect is that inspection of other firms, either competitors or noncompetitors, through the network of contacts of the firm in its social structural environment may suggest a new structure and bestow legitimacy on that option, leading to adaptive change in the firm (Davis 1991). In institutional theory, there may also be an imperative for the firm to adopt a particular structure because of the pressure from governments, funding providers, or professions.

Social comparison processes may also enter into competitive dynamics in another way. Social comparison may affect the satisficing level. The level of performance deemed the minimum that is acceptable for a firm may well be affected by social processes. The power holders who influence decisions in the firm include owners, managers, directors, bankers, consultants, and others (Cyert and March 1963; Child 1972). In assessing whether the performance level of the firm is satisfactory, they might look at the performance of competitors. If the competitors are in misfit relative to the firm (which is in fit), then the performance of the competitors will be lower than that of the firm (ceteris paribus), leading these observers to conclude that the performance of the firm is satisfactory. However, if the competitors are in fit relative to the firm (which is in misfit), then the performance of the competitors will be higher than that of the firm (ceteris paribus), leading the observers to conclude that the performance of the firm is unsatisfactory. Thus the level of performance that constitutes satisficing will be affected by the relative fit of the competitors. This, in turn, affects the probability of the firm's performance dropping below the satisficing level, so triggering structural adaptation.

Drawing all these theoretical ideas together, there are three causal paths that connect relative fit to structural adaptation, that is, three mechanisms whereby competition leads the firm to move from misfit into fit. The performance of the firm is one route: Relative fit places competitive pressure on a firm in misfit through lowering its performance so that it becomes subsatisficing, which leads to structural adaptation (from misfit into fit). The second route is the social comparison: Relative fit of competitors raises the level of performance regarded as satisficing for the firm, and this means that its declining performance is viewed as subsatisficing sooner rather than later, thus triggering structural adaptation. The third route is the institutional effect: Managers in the firm observe other firms and copy their structures or are pressured to adopt a certain structure by governments or professions.

Each of the three mechanisms operates at a different point in the causal chain. The causal chain runs from the relative fit of competitors to the performance of the firm, which is then assessed against the satisficing level and when subsatisficing triggers structural adaptation. The first route is the effect of relative fit on performance (see Figure 4.2). The second route is the social comparison effect of relative fit on the satisficing level. The third route is the institutional effect on the selection of a fitting new structure. By positing three different independent variables in the same model, the three theories are being combined in synthesis, that is, each contributes part of the explanation of the adaptation by the focal organization (i.e., an additive synthesis).

Competition Through Differentiated Strategy

The prevailing treatments of the effect of one organization on another in organizational theory tend to be of the focal organization following along with others by adopting their strategy and structure (e.g., Chandler 1962). This is seen clearly in institutional theory with its postulate of mimetic isomorphism so that the focal organization conforms to norms and becomes more like other organizations over time (DiMaggio and Powell 1983). The organizational portfolio theory of competition makes no such assumption about mimetic or isomorphic processes but nevertheless has painted organizations as moving in similar trajectories to each other as they develop over time in their strategy and structure in response to competition. However, competition may also lead to divergence in organizational strategy and structure over time.

A firm may seek competitive advantage by avoiding head-to-head competition with the other firms in its industry. This might be done by focusing on offering a narrow product range and becoming the lowest-cost producer

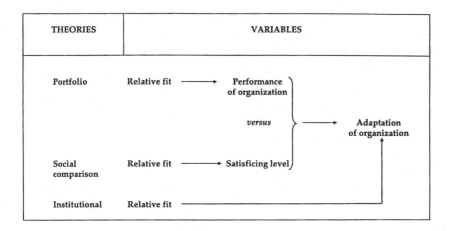

Figure 4.2   Effects of Competition on Organizational Adaptation Synthesis of Three Theories

through mass production and thus the lowest-price seller of relatively standardized products or services (Porter 1985). The key is cost control of homogeneous offerings, and so a functional structure would fit this strategy (Donaldson 1979, 1985b). Other companies in the same industry might eschew this strategy and instead opt to offer a fuller range of products that contain novel features but that sell at a higher price to more discerning and wealthier customers (Porter 1985). The key is innovation of heterogeneous offerings, so a divisional structure would fit this strategy (Donaldson 1979, 1985b).

Thus if a firm followed this differentiation strategy and diversified its products, leading it eventually to adopt a divisional structure, another firm following the former, low-cost strategy might not. The second firm might elect to remain undiversified and functionally structured, and this would not be temporary until it caught up with the diversifying firm; rather, it might be deliberate and enduring. The comparison by the firm of itself with its competitors might lead the firm to consciously reject conformity and diverge in strategy and structure in order to seek financial benefit. Whereas institutional theory speaks of conformity, norm following, and unconscious following of the taken-for-granteds (Powell and DiMaggio 1991), competition theory allows for nonconformity and norm breaking caused by pursuit of the corporate economic interest. An implication is that some organizations may remain undiversified with a fitting functional structure even after competitor organizations have diversified and adopted a fitting divisional structure.

Conclusions

Competition is an economic phenomenon that has been somewhat neglected in organizational theory. This chapter attempted to fill the gap by offering elements of a theory of how competition affects organizational change.

The stronger the competition, the lower the performance of a firm and so the more likely it is to make adaptive change. The weaker the competition, the greater the growth rate of a well-adapted firm.

Competition is stronger where competitors are adapted to their situations. Better adapted competitors have higher performance and so decrease the performance of the firm so that it is more likely to make needed adaptive changes. A maladapted firm is more likely to adapt, the greater the number of its competitors that are adapted, because it has lower performance. Thus the internal organizational adaptation of a firm needs to be analyzed relative to competitors.

This analysis has been pursued here in terms of the dynamics among a set of competing firms as they diversify over time. At each stage, the impetus, or lack thereof, for adaptation into fit by each firm is determined by the proportion of competitors in fit. This means that the pressure on each firm to adopt a fitting structure is not constant over time but, rather, changes in predictable ways as the competitors diversify and adapt. For a diversified, functionally structured firm, its probability of divisionalizing decreases with the diversification of its competitors but increases with their subsequent divisionalization.

Similarly, the probability that a firm will diversify is also affected by competition. A firm in fit is more likely to grow and so move into misfit, the more of its competitors that are in misfit because the firm is in fit relative to those competitors. Thus the diversification of a firm is affected by the diversification and structural adaptation of its competitors. For an undiversified, functionally structured firm, its probability of diversifying increases with the diversification of its competitors but decreases with their subsequent divisionalization.

Organizational portfolio theory holds that the adaptation of the firm is driven by its performance. Thus the effect of competitors is through their effect on the performance of the firm. Institutional theory, however, suggests an isomorphic effect of other firms on the firm. Such mimetic and social comparison effects are distinguished here from organizational portfolio effects. Nevertheless, these other effects may well also be operative and so are combined with the organizational portfolio effect to give a fuller model of the effect of competition on the adaptation of the firm.

Moreover, unlike the isomorphic effect of institutional theory, some adaptation by a firm involves differentiating itself from competitors by adopting a different strategy rather than copying competitors.

Thus this chapter presented an analysis of a major component of the economic environment of a firm—its competitors. In Chapter 5, we consider the significance of external economic causes of organizational performance for the outcomes of organizational adaptation.

Adaptation Confounds

Organizational adaptations are intended to be beneficial but sometimes appear not to be. In this chapter, we consider organizational adaptation and show why the usual expectation about its benefits often fails to hold. Organizational portfolio theory reveals adaptation effects to be more subtle than supposed under existing theory. The chapter develops an analysis of how adaptation relates to organizational performance. The role of other factors that affect organizational performance is revealed to be crucial. These other factors often confound the benefits that flow from adaptation, leading to false conclusions that many organizational changes are in fact not adaptive.

In previous chapters, we discussed adaptations—that is, changes to organizational structure and the like—as being caused by low performance. By definition an adaptation is something that improves the fit of the organization to its situation and thereby improves its performance. This chapter pursues the issue of adaptation by considering performance after adaptation and contrasting it with performance before the adaptation. The usual expectation is that performance is low before adaptation and rises to a higher level after the adaptation. This improvement is the intention of management in making changes that it believes will be adaptive for the organization. This may seem eminently rational, but the pattern is not so simple. There are sometimes quite contrary occurrences in which organizational performance declines after the change. To understand the relationship between firm performance and adaptation, we need, once again, to consider the organization as a portfolio. This enables us to appreciate that the perceived effects of organizational adaptations will often be contrary to their true effects.

As we have stressed, firm performance is caused by a combination of internal and external factors. These factors act together over time. They may be tightly coupled or loosely coupled. Moreover, the internal and external causes of firm performance may be tightly coupled at one time and loosely coupled at another. This is the key to understanding the relationship between firm adaptation and performance.

We begin by briefly reviewing the relationship between adaptation and performance as received from the traditional organizational theory. We then expound the new view from organizational portfolio theory.

Traditional Organizational Theory

Traditional organizational theory holds that organizational adaptation improves performance. The adaptation moves the organization from a misfit between the contingencies and the structure to a fit between them (Chandler 1962). The misfit reduces performance, and this eventually becomes low enough that it is below the satisficing level, thus triggering the adoption of the new structure and thereby regaining fit. The attainment of a new fit causes performance to rise. Therefore a decline in performance causes the adaptation, which feeds back, thus causing performance to rise subsequently. Thus performance declines before the adaptation and then rises after the adaptation.

The hypothesis would be that, in a regression analysis of firm performance over time, the slope of performance measured each year of the "after" years would be more positive than the slope of the "before" years. More specifically, the slope of the "before" would be negative, and the slope of the "after" would be positive. These hypotheses would hold for corporations in general and therefore would be revealed by taking the average annual level of performance for a sample of organizations and examining the slopes for each several year period, and then comparing the period before with the period after adaptation.

Harris (1983) empirically studied corporations among the largest 250 industrial firms that adopted a multidivisional structure in place of another organizational structure. He hypothesized that they would show improvement in performance after their adaptation. However, his examination of firm performance (rate of return) failed to find any significant difference after adaptation. Such failure to confirm the prevailing theory prompts its reexamination here and its replacement by a more adequate theory.

Adaptation as Temporary Tight Coupling

Organizational portfolio theory recognizes that although misfit reduces performance, other factors also reduce performance, and it is their combined effect that reduces performance low enough to trigger adaptation. Misfit is a necessary but not a sufficient cause of adaptation. Misfit causes lower performance, but whether it is low enough to trigger adaptation depends on whether the other causes of performance are low or high. It is the happenstance of misfit occurring together with the other causes depressing performance that triggers adaptation. This conjunction between misfit and the other causes may be only temporary. After adaptation, the conjunction can break down so that the other causes of performance may remain depressing performance, or may shift to become even more depressive. Depending on what happens to the other causes of performance, the positive performance effect from the adaptation may be truly revealed, reinforced, or masked. Thus, after adaptation, performance may rise or sink. Hence performance after adaptation is variable and may not move in the way predicted by traditional organizational theory.

More formally, there are two sorts of causes of organizational performance. One factor is the fit between the contingency and the organizational structure; this factor is internal to the organization. The other factors include causes external to the organization such as competition, the business cycle, and so on. The insight of organizational portfolio theory is that fit, the internal cause of firm performance, is only loosely coupled with the other causes of performance that together compose the organizational portfolio (Weick 1976). Before adaptation, the other causes of performance temporarily come into synchronization with the internal misfit, both of which depress corporate performance, and an adaptation is triggered. Adaptation occurs because the organizational portfolio factors are positively correlated—that is, both misfit and the other causes of performance are lowering organizational performance. However, the positive correlation is only temporary and so can turn from positive to negative after the adaptation. After adaptation, the new fit causes performance to rise, but whether a firm's performance does in fact rise is affected by the other causes.

If, after adaptation, the other factors remain synchronized with fit, they will also turn positive and reinforce the positive effect of fit on performance so that overall effects are positive and firm performance rises. This means that performance after adaptation will be higher than performance before adaptation. However, if the synchronization breaks down between fit and the other factors, overall firm performance may not rise and could fall. If, after adaptation, the association between fit and the other factors becomes negative, overall firm performance can drop. In that case, the result is that overall firm performance declines and is lower than firm performance before adaptation.

If the positive correlation between fit and the other factors of organizational performance is maintained after adaptation, much of the rise in performance will be due to those other factors. In that situation, the reinforcing effect of the other factors can lead to an overestimation of the benefits from adaptation. Only if the other factors retain the same levels after adaptation as before will the rise in performance all be correctly attributable to the adaptation. Thus a correct estimate of the degree of benefit from the adaptation will be made most exactly when the positive correlation between the adaptation and the other factors breaks down and turns negative. Of course, if the correlation becomes even more negative, then the other factors will so depress performance that they can nullify the positive effect of the adaptation. If the correlation becomes even more negative again, the other factors can mask the benefits of the adaptation so that performance falls after adaptation.

There may be nothing ensuring a long-run positive association between misfit and the other factors. Indeed, the long-run association between misfit and the other factors is unknown and may approximate zero. Fit and the other factors are separate causes of performance, reflecting the nature of organizational performance as produced by a portfolio of fluctuating variables whose associations can change over time. The other factors, such as competition, the business cycle, and governmental regulation, can be independent of each other. For this reason, they may not all move simultaneously, so their coming together to all depress firm performance at the same time may be a rare event. In that sense, the low performance that triggers structural adaptation is to some degree an accident. Correspondingly, these different factors tend subsequently to break apart from each other and resume fluctuating independently of each other so that firm performance rises after adaptation for some firms but remains static for other firms and may decline for still others. Hence the synchronization, that is, the temporary positive association between misfit and the internal factors that triggers reorganization, is liable to decay over time.

After adaptation, the situation will tend to revert toward the long-run situation of low or nil correlation between fit and other causes of performance. Any sample of organizations will vary about this mean, and so their performance after adaptation will be, at random, higher or lower than their performance before adaptation. Therefore, the results of empirical comparisons of firms will display variation between finding that performance improves after adaptation to finding nil effect or that performance declines after adaptation.

There is variation not only between samples but also between individual organizations within a sample. For some organizations, the synchronization is maintained for years after the adaptation, whereas for others, the synchronization decays rapidly so that the association breaks down or, in some cases, turns negative. Hence, even if all the organizations are benefiting from their recent adaptation, their performances after adaptation can vary markedly because of the confounding effect of the other causes so that some may rise but some may fall. Thus, for the set of firms in a study, their average performance after adaptation will be determined by the relative number of firms in which synchronization remains positive relative to those in which it becomes nil or negative. The higher the proportion of firms in which the association turns negative after adaptation, the greater the probability that average firm performance will decline after adaptation.

The propositions thus are the following:

5.1 Firm performance declines before an organizational adaptation.

5.2 At the time of organizational adaptation, lower firm performance from the maladaptation will be positively correlated with the other causes of firm performance.

5.3 After an organizational adaptation, the other causes of firm performance may remain depressive or may rise, so firm performance may rise, remain constant, or fall.

5.4 After an organizational adaptation, the correlation between the effects on firm performance from the adaptation and the effects of the other causes may be positive, nil, or negative.

Thus empirical studies will tend to find the expected decline in performance before organizational adaptation but often not the expected rise after adaptation. For a sample of firms, their average postadaptation performance may rise, remain static, or fall. It may be linear or nonlinear, representing the fluctuations in the other variables. Therefore, firm performance after adaptation will often fail to show the rise that organizational theory predicts. This may lead to the conclusion that adaptation fails to raise performance, but this could be erroneous, reflecting the confounding effect of the other factors.

Furthermore, for the period before the adaptation, firm performance will usually show decline, as organizational theory predicts, because without a decline adaptation will not occur. This may lead to the inference that declines trigger adaptation but that adaptation does not raise performance, its intended effect. Thus analysts may conclude falsely that adaptation is irrational, being caused by panic when performance declines but not leading to any restitution of performance. As we have tried to show, such conclusions would be a misunderstanding, based on a failure to appreciate the underlying role of the other causes of performance.

Increases in Performance Variation After Adaptation

As has been stated, in the years after the adaptation, the other causes could change to raise firm performance or continue depressed or become even more depressive. Therefore, the component of firm performance that is caused by the other factors will vary markedly in the postadaptation period and more so than in the before-adaptation period when it would have to be depressive for the adaptation to occur. Thus the hypothesis is that firm performance would show more variation from firm to firm in the years immediately after adaptation than in the years immediately before adaptation. This reflects the operation of the other factors on performance that are uniformly tending to depress firm performance and thereby triggering the adaptation in the years before the actual adaptation, but tend then to fluctuate in different ways to each other from firm to firm in the years after adaptation. The implication is that the variation in performance of firms that make adaptive changes will be greater after adaptation than before.

The proposition thus is the following:

> 5.5 Variation in performance between organizations is greater after than before an organizational adaptation.

Some support for the idea of substantial variation between organizations in their performance postadaptation comes from the empirical study of Hoskisson and Galbraith (1985). They studied the adoption of the M-form (i.e., multidivisional structure) among large U.S. corporations and distinguished between quantum (relatively radical) and incremental (minor) structural change. Hoskisson and Galbraith found that the effects of adaptation were generally positive on firm profitability and that the effect of quantum adaptation was greater than that of incremental adaptation. However, whereas the quantum adaptations mostly were statistically significant, the incremental adaptations mostly were not, which renders their benefit questionable. There was considerable variation from corporation to corporation. Using their measure of the total impact of the adaptation on firm profitability, Hoskisson and Galbraith found that for quantum adaptations the mean effect was 2.31 but the range varied from −4.60 to 5.36 and that for incremental adaptations the mean effect was 0.82 but the range varied from −2.24 to 2.41 (p. 68). Thus, for each type of adaptation, there was a wide variation in performances after adaptation, including negative values. In fact, the magnitudes of the most extreme negative performances were almost equal to that of the most extreme positive performances. This supports the expectation from organizational portfolio theory that the performances of organizations after adaptation vary widely, producing cases both of improvement and of decline. This wide variation in performance after adaptation across corporations could be due to the influence of the other factors that affect organizational performance, as the temporary correlation between structural misfit and these other factors breaks down after the adaptation.

Thus, on theoretical grounds, we would expect wide postadaptation performance variations between corporations. This can mislead us into believing that benefits from organizational change are situationally specific, in that some corporations benefit while other corporations are harmed. The true effect of radical M-form reorganization is positive, as estimated by Hoskisson and Galbraith (1985) through the mean effect sizes that control for case variation. However, the case variation is strong, rendering some cases negative, so calling into doubt the general efficacy of radical M-form reorganizations. This opens the door to the idea that its effects are highly situationally specific, in that some corporations gain from them but others lose.

Yet the perception that the radical M-form reorganization benefits some corporations but harms others may be to a considerable extent illusory. The effects of the other causes of performance can vary widely from case to case, in some cases adding to the benefits of the reorganization and in other cases more than masking them. Thus the high positive results are probably an overestimate of the true effect, and the negative results are probably also misleading. The average will tend to nullify the spurious effects of the other causes of performance, leading to a better estimate of the true value. For this reason, the effect of radical M-form reorganization is probably more generalizable and less situationally variable than the widely varying results suggest. Thus the insight of organizational portfolio theory that the results of organizational adaptations are likely to be strongly confounded by other factors may help caution us from falsely rejecting adaptations as not beneficial or from falsely seeing the benefits of adaptation as highly situationally variable.

Risk, Adaptation, and Confounds

What is the significance of the confound idea for the association between organizational adaptation and risk that was argued in Chapter 2? Preadaptation organizational performance tends to decline, and this was earlier argued to contribute to organizational risk (i.e., performance fluctuation) so that risk is non-zero for an adapting organization. Earlier, postadaptation organizational performance was held to rise and so also contributes to organizational risk. However, in this chapter we have established that postadaptation organizational performance not only could rise but also could remain static or fall due to the effect of confounding variables. Nevertheless, postadaptation organizational performance would still contribute to organizational risk, as we will now see.

If postadaptation organizational performance rises by more than the effect of the adaptation, this additional fluctuation in organizational performance contributes to organizational risk. The additional rise is, of course, due to confounds that produce a stronger association between organizational adaptation and organizational risk. Similarly, if postadaptation organizational performance falls, this also contributes to organizational risk. Again, the fall is due to confounds that increase the association between organizational adaptation and organizational risk. However, if postadaptation organizational performance remains static, there is no postadaptation fluctuation in organizational performance contributing to organizational risk. In this case, the confounds reduce the association between organizational adaptation and organizational risk. Thus in most cases, the confounds increase the association between organizational adaptation and organizational risk. Thus the idea advanced in

Chapter 2 that risk is nonzero for an adapting organization holds even after allowing for confounds.

The greater variation among firms after adaptation compared to before it will tend to increase the risk of each firm associated with its adaptation. As has been seen, organizational performance declines before organizational adaptation, but after organizational adaptation, organizational performance could move in any way, ranging from sharp increase to sharp decrease, depending on the confounds. Thus there will often be substantial postadaptation fluctuation in organizational adaptation for each firm. This contributes to an association between adaptation and risk for the firm. Moreover, the association between organizational adaptation and organizational risk will be stronger at the firm level than for a sample of firms, because taking sample averages will cancel out much of the variation between firms in postadaptation organizational performance. This averaging controls for much of the confounds and so yields results more in conformity with our earlier theoretical expectation that organizational performance declines before adaptation and rises after. Thus the idea that organizational adaptation is associated with organizational risk remains sound, even recognizing that there will often be considerable variation between organizations in postadaptation performance.

Conclusions

The relationship between adaptation and performance is more complex than might appear at first glance. Organizational theory holds that performance decline triggers the adaptation whereby the organization moves from misfit to fit. The new fit then raises performance. This theoretical expectation accords with the intent of management and its reason for reorganizing. However, the relationship between adaptation and performance is not quite so simple. Organizational portfolio theory helps us appreciate its subtleties.

To better understand adaptation, the overall performance of the firm has been conceptualized into two parts: (a) the effect on performance caused by misfit and (b) the effect on performance caused by other causes. These other causes of performance depress it in the years before the adaptation because the adaptation occurs due to the simultaneous occurrence of misfit and these other, depressive causes of performance. If these other causes of performance had been not depressive, there would have been no adaptation. However, there is no such necessary conjunction between fit and these other factors after adaptation. For some organizations, these other factors reinforce the effect of fit, so firm performance rises. In other organizations, these other factors are depressive and oppose the effect of fit, and so firm performance declines after adaptation. An implication is that empirical assessments of the effect of adaptation on subsequent performance can be strongly confounded, leading to erroneous inferences. Another implication is that the variations in performance across firms are greater after than before adaptation.

This chapter focused on the way other causes of organizational performance interact with organizational adaptation to affect overall performance and the perception of whether adaptation is successful. In Chapter 6, we focus on the internal factors that affect organizational performance and the ways they mostly work to inhibit organizational change.

6

The Corporation and Risk

In Chapters 3 and 4, we focused on factors external to the organization that affect organizational risk. Now we want to examine factors internal to the organization that affect organizational risk. We focus on the large corporation because it is in this type of firm that the issues being discussed are seen most strongly. Large corporations are typically diversified and divisionalized. The multiple divisions in such corporations constitute a portfolio, in that the performances of these divisions interact to affect the overall corporate performance. Thus the concepts of risk and portfolio effects can be applied within the corporation. Moreover, debt and divestment are other frequently found features of the large diversified, divisionalized corporation that affect the organizational portfolio. Therefore, this chapter discusses the portfolio factors of diversification, divisionalization, debt, and divestment and their effects on organizational adaptation and growth.

Traditionally, diversification has been argued to affect corporate performance (e.g., Rumelt 1982), and the fit of divisionalization to diversification has also been argued to affect corporate performance (e.g., Hill et al. 1992). However, the interest here is on how diversification and divisionalization affect corporate risk, that is, the fluctuation of corporate performance. We argue that both diversification and divisionalization tend to reduce the risk of the corporation. This has a number of implications. There is a positive effect of risk reduction on the economic value of the corporation. There is a negative effect on adaptation and growth. Divestment affects corporate performance and also tends to inhibit adaptation and growth. However, debt tends to increase the chance of poor corporate performance and so of organizational adaptation. Thus diversification, divisionalization, and divestment reduce organizational adaptation, whereas debt increases it.

We begin by defining terms and then analyze, in turn, the effect of diversification, divisionalization, debt, and divestment on organizational performance.

Definitions of Diversification and Divisional Structure

Diversification refers to a firm offering more than one product or service. A firm is more diversified the more products or services that it offers and the more they differ from each other, that is, the more they are unrelated (Rumelt 1974). At medium diversification, the corporation is composed of two or more products or services that are related. At high diversification, the corporation is composed of two or more products or services that are unrelated.

Divisional structure refers to a multidivisional structure. This is a decentralized form of organizational structure in which the main organizational subunits are divisions (Chandler 1962). These divisions are differentiated from each other on the basis of each being a different product or service or customer or geographic area (Davis 1972). A division contains a wide range of operating functions (e.g., sales and manufacturing) and so is to a considerable extent a self-sufficient business and is a profit center (Galbraith 1973). A division enjoys autonomy from the head office in operational decision making (Dyas and Thanheiser 1976; Chenhall 1979). The head office, or corporate-level management, monitors divisional profitability and makes strategic decisions (Chandler 1962). This broadly is what is meant in this book by the term *multidivisional structure*, which here is often abbreviated to divisional structure, the more usual term.

Within the broad divisional structural form, there are substantial variations. The exact degree of autonomy of the division and hence of organizational decentralization, the type of corporate control systems, and the nature and composition of the head office all vary substantially across divisional structures (Pitts 1976; Allen 1978; Chandler 1994). These differences are caused in part by variations in the contingency factors, such as strategy—in other words, degrees of diversification and vertical integration (Lorsch and Allen 1973; Pitts 1976). The more diversified the corporation, the more it is decentralized and the more autonomous its divisions are (Lorsch and Allen 1973). The variations in divisional structure are also caused by the degree to which the organization is in fit with its contingencies and by time lags in adaptation (Williamson and Bhargava 1972; Lorsch and Allen 1973; Dyas and Thanheiser 1976; Pitts 1976; Hill 1985a, 1985b, 1988).

Empirically, the diversified, divisionalized corporation is the dominant, modern form of large corporation across the advanced industrial world—in Australia, Canada, France, Germany, Italy, Japan, New Zealand, the United Kingdom, and the United States (Channon 1973, 1978; Rumelt 1974; Khandwalla 1977; Dyas and Thanheiser 1976; Pavan 1976; Chenhall 1979; Suzuki 1980; Capon, Christodolou, Farley, and Hulbert 1987; Palmer, Friedland, Jennings, and Powers 1987; Mahoney 1992; Palmer, Jennings, and Zhou 1993; Hamilton and Shergill 1992, 1993). Hence the large corporation is typically diversified and divisionalized, so analyzing these properties is important for understanding the large corporation.

Diversification Strategy Reduces Corporate Risk

Strategy is discussed in terms of diversification from one product to more than one product (a similar logic applies to diversification of services). Diversification reduces the risk of the corporation. For an undiversified corporation consisting of a single business, that is, a single product, corporate performance (e.g., profit) will completely reflect any variations over time in the performance of that product. Initial diversification will add products that are related to the original product, so their performances will be positively correlated. However, further diversification will add products less closely related to each other, so their performances will be less positively correlated. The greater the diversification, the less positive and then the more negative the correlations among the performances of the products. For a corporation consisting of unrelated products, where the performance of each product is negatively correlated with other products, downward swings in the performance of one product will be offset to some degree by upward swings in the other products (Salter and Weinhold 1979). Therefore, negative correlations between any two products lower the fluctuation of the overall organizational portfolio. Thus the resultant corporate performance fluctuates less than that of the constituent products.

If a corporation is composed of two divisions, A and B, and the business cycle of industry B is counter to that of industry A, the fluctuations in the performance (e.g., profit) of division B cancel out the fluctuations in A, leaving the overall corporate performance constant (see Figure 6.1). In contrast, because the performance of each division fluctuates strongly, it periodically drops below the satisficing level of the division (Figure 6.1). Thus corporate performance fluctuates less than divisional performance so that the risk of the corporation is less than its divisions. Hence the risk of a diversified, multiproduct corporation is less than that of an undiversified, single-product firm (i.e., division A if it was a freestanding firm).

As shown in Figure 6.1, the performance fluctuations of these two divisions, A and B, are perfectly negatively correlated, producing the portfolio effect of reducing the risk of the corporation. If the divisions composing a corporation are negatively correlated to any degree or have a low positive correlation, this reduces the risk of the corporation. The higher the level of diversification and thus the less positive and more negative the correlations among divisional performances, the greater the corporate risk reduction. Hence diversified corporations will have less risk than undiversified corporations. This idea is a familiar one in finance and business policy (for a critical discussion of the empirical evidence, see Hoskisson 1987).

The reduction in risk from diversification in turn reduces the probability of the corporation making a needed adaptive change. If the two divisions are negatively correlated, as in Figure 6.1, the overall corporate performance will not fluctuate down below the satisficing level, and so corporate-level adaptive changes that are required will not be made. More moderate diversification, such as by low negative or positive correlations between the performances of divisions, will nevertheless also reduce corporate risk and thereby reduce the probability of corporate performance dropping below the satisficing level, though by a moderate degree. The weaker the degree of diversification, the less the risk reduction and so the higher the probability of corporate performance dropping below the satisficing level and thus of needed corporate adaptation occurring. The key is the correlations between the divisions: the more negative the greater, the risk reduction; the more positive, the lesser the risk reduction.

In contrast, if each of divisions A or B was still an independent firm, each would periodically experience performance falling below the satisficing level. Therefore, as independent firms, A and B would periodically experience a crisis

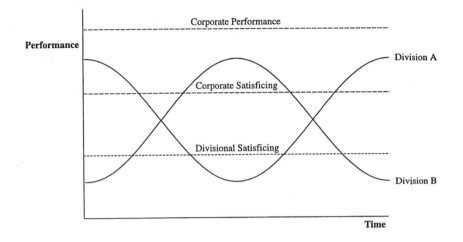

Figure 6.1 The Portfolio Effect: Counteracting Fluctuations in Divisions Smoothing Corporate Performance

of poor performance that would trigger them to make whatever adaptive changes they needed. Hence the diversification of the corporation leads it to be less adaptive than its divisions would have been had they remained as independent firms. Moreover, as divisions of the corporation, A and B still experience periodic crises of poor divisional performance such that they drop below their satisficing level (Figure 6.1), which will tend to trigger divisional adaptation. Hence the divisions are more likely to adapt than the corporate-level organization is. Thus the diversification by a corporation reduces its risk and so makes it less adaptive at the corporate level.

As just seen, the episodes of low corporate performance that are required to trigger adaptive change have lower probability of occurring after diversification. Therefore, the diversified corporation will often persist with its existing functional structure after it has diversified, despite this no longer being a fit. The misfit lowers corporate performance, and if it were still a single product, a downturn in the business cycle of its product market might be sufficient to depress performance below the satisficing level, causing adaptive change (i.e., adoption of the divisional structure). However, now that the corporation is diversified, the cyclical downturn in the performance of one division will tend to be offset to a degree by the cyclical upturn in another division. Therefore, despite the misfit lowering its performance, the corporation may remain in misfit for a considerable period before divisionalizing. Empirical research shows that there is often a lag of many years between diversifying and divisionalizing (Rumelt 1974; Dyas and Thanheiser 1976) and that many corporations remain in misfit before a financial crisis eventually causes them to divisionalize (Donaldson 1987; Hamilton and Shergill 1992, 1993). Thus the risk reduction from diversification helps account for the lag in structural adaptation after diversifying.

The propositions thus are the following:

6.1   Diversification reduces organizational risk.

6.2   Diversification reduces the probability of organizational adaptation.

Eventually, the functionally structured, diversified corporation adopts the divisional structure that it needs because its misfit combines with other performance causes that become depressive enough that the corporation experiences poor performance. This divisional structure is brought about by the earlier diversification but may itself affect further diversification in the future. Divisionalization has been argued to increase diversification, so that once a divisional structure is in place it feeds back to increase the level of diversification (e.g., from medium to high). The idea is that divisionalization allows new businesses, unrelated to the core, to be acquired and simply slotted on as additional units with little disruption to the existing divisions (Scott 1971). Moreover, divisionalization can foster innovation that increases diversification (Scott 1971). Further, divisionalization fosters a strategic assessment of opportunities beyond the existing core business (Rumelt 1974). The empirical evidence is mixed (Rumelt 1974; Donaldson 1982; Amburgey and Dacin 1994). However, any such feedback effect provides a way in which divisionalization affects risk through increasing the level of diversification.

Apart from a feedback effect of divisionalization boosting diversification, there may also be a direct effect of divisionalization on risk reduction. Although it is a commonplace that diversification reduces risk, it may do so in part through an effect of divisional structure on risk. Diversification leads to divisionalization, and so some part of the reduction in risk attributed to diversification may result from divisionalization. In this way, divisionalization may intervene between diversification and risk so that some of the causal connection between diversification and risk flows through divisionalization. We shall develop this idea in the following section by arguing how divisionalization could affect risk. This involves extending the portfolio theory to the organizational structure, a domain to which the portfolio concept has not previously been applied.

Do different organizational structures have different consequences in terms of risk? We will consider the different effect upon risk of functional versus divisional structures. When diversified corporations replace their functional structure with a divisional structure, what effect does this have on organizational risk? How does any such structural effect on risk interact with the risk-reduction effect of diversification just discussed?

Divisional Structure
Reduces Corporate Risk

Structure is discussed in terms of the distinction between a functional and a divisional structure. In a functional structure, the major subunits of the organization are functional departments, such as manufacturing, marketing, and research and development. These elements are highly interdependent in that marketing sells what manufacturing makes. Each functional department is a cost center. The total costs and revenues are brought together in an accounting sense only for the whole organization, which is a single profit center. The decision making is relatively centralized in that the CEO is involved in the operational coordination of the functional departments. This functional, centralized structure is appropriate for a firm with a single product because it is simple and inexpensive (Chandler 1962; Mintzberg 1979).

In contrast, in a divisional structure, the major subunits are usually built around the different products, each of which is organized as a division. The operational coordination of the functions in each division is handled by the general managers of that division (Chandler 1962). These divisions are less interdependent than are the departments in a functional structure and operate more as separate businesses. Each division acts to a degree autonomously and is a profit center (Chenhall 1979; Grinyer and Yasai-Ardekani 1981). Divisional structures are more loosely coupled systems (Weick 1976; Orton and Weick 1990) than are functional structures.

Applying portfolio theory to the issue of risk reduction and divisionalization implies examining risk both within and between divisions. For a divisionalized corporation, each division is considered an element of the total organizational portfolio. Total portfolio fluctuation is determined by the fluctuation in the performance of each division and the correlations between the performance of the divisions. For example, for high corporate performance fluctuation, the fluctuation of each divisional performance is high, and the correlation between the divisional performances is highly positive. Equally, for low corporate performance fluctuation, the fluctuation of each divisional performance is low, or the correlation between the divisional performances is highly negative. In contrast, for a functionally structured corporation, the only profit center is the corporation itself. Thus the fluctuation in the total profit performance is the fluctuation of corporate profit. Because in the functional structure, unlike the divisional structure, there are not multiple divisional profit centers, there is no opportunity in functional systems for corporate performance fluctuation to be dampened at the divisional level. Nor is there the possibility for corporate performance fluctuation to be curbed by negative correlations, that is, through portfolio effects, because there is no portfolio, that is, separate elements (e.g., divisions) the performances of which sum to make corporate profit.

Fluctuation in organizational performance will be lower in the divisional structure if the average fluctuation of the performance of the divisions is lower than the performance would be of the same corporation structured functionally. Also, fluctuation in organizational performance will be lower if the correlation between the performances of the divisions is low positive or negative. Both mechanisms operate to some degree so that, in combination, corporate risk is reduced by divisionalization. The reduction in fluctuation of the divisions is achieved through "smoothing," which is applied within each division prior to aggregation into the corporate profit account. Also, negative correlations between the performances (i.e., profits) of divisions can occur in the following way. The negative correlations are based on the phenomenon of the autonomy enjoyed by divisions in the divisional structure, relative to the functional structure. Autonomy allows independence of action of one division relative to others, which makes the decisions of one division independent of the decisions of the other division, so the decisions are loosely coupled. They can thereby become disjoint so that they may become negatively correlated.

Thus a divisional structure, in contrast to a functional structure, produces smoothing and loose coupling of divisional performances, which lead to lower risk of the corporation. Each of these two mechanisms is further explained below.

Divisional Managers Smooth Performance

Divisional managers tend to manipulate their reports of the profit of their divisions to smooth out variations across time. For managers responsible for divisional profit centers, there are incentives to reduce the fluctuation in the profit figure from one time period to the next. The divisional managers smooth reported profits for three reasons: to avoid poor performance, to be reliable, and to keep expectations low.

First, divisional managers want to avoid poor performance, as in a time period in which the profit drops below the level their superordinates deem adequate. This suggests that in periods when profit is unusually high, not all of it should be reported; some should be stored to provide a cushion to boost poor profit in a future period. In other words, some part of very high profit performance is stored in the profit center as slack to help ride out bad times in the future. This can be done in many ways, such as by incurring costs in the present time period that are not strictly necessary at present—for example, making accelerated payments on new equipment or purchasing extra raw materials. Bowman (1980) refers to practices of these sort as " 'real' income smoothing," as distinct from " 'artificial' income smoothing," which merely disguises reported fluctuations through accounting practices (p. 26). Either sort of manipulation of a division's performance by its divisional manager tends to reduce the severity of the peaks and troughs over time in the results for that profit center.

Second, divisional managers whose profits fluctuate only moderately over time will be seen as producing more consistent results than those whose profits fluctuate wildly between bonanzas and losses. These latter managers constitute a problem for superordinates due to the unpredictability of their divisions' performances. This is enshrined in the legendary words of the CEO to subordinates: "I hate surprises!" Each divisional manager wants to turn in a profit performance that is reliable and so produces a fairly constant set of yearly profits, each of which is below the maximum that could be attained in the best year. Divisional managers trade off the occasional peak profitability in return for reliability. In some firms, this emphasis on reliability is formalized in that the personnel appraisal and bonus systems explicitly include conformance to budgeted targets as one of the criteria that are rewarded.

Third, divisional managers do not want to report an unusually high profit to avoid having that record-high figure used as the benchmark in ensuing years. As Cyert and March (1963) state, prior performance sets the organization's level of aspiration for performance for the next period (see also Miller and Leiblein 1996). Thus keeping divisional profit more moderate from year to year keeps the benchmark budget figure lower and more attainable. This helps maintain the reputation of the divisional managers for reliably attaining budgeted profit targets for their divisions.

For these three reasons, divisional managers seek to manipulate the profits reported for their divisions to the head office. They underreport high profits and overreport low profits, thereby smoothing out the profit fluctuations of their divisions. It reflects a fundamental insight of organizational behavior: Whenever a control system seeks to control people by measuring their performance on some variable, those people will seek to manipulate that variable so as to regain some control of their lives (Argyris 1964).

In contrast, the functionally structured corporation is the profit center and has no subordinate units reporting profits to the head office; thus there can be no manipulation of the profit figure by operating units. Hence, unlike the functional structure, the divisional structure provides a filter for reducing profit fluctuation. This lowers the risk of each division and therefore of the corporation.

The proposition thus is the following:

6.3   In a divisional structure, the divisional managers smooth out fluctuations in profits reported to the corporate level, so the risk in corporate performance is lower than in functional structures.

Williamson (1970, 1985) argues that the divisional structure has a superior capacity to monitor and control its divisions because of its elite staff—accountants and other personnel in the corporate office who audit the performance of each division and establish its true level. In contrast, the functional structure has fewer elite personnel and so less capacity to accurately audit its operating units, the functional departments. This enhanced capacity offsets the efforts by divisional managers to manipulate reports of divisional performance, so providing a truer picture, and it threatens to expose such manipulators to corporate sanction for their deceit. Such structures and processes in the divisional structure work to offset the smoothing of divisional performance. The superior auditing capacity of the divisional structure places limits on the frequency and severity of performance smoothing by the divisions.

Nevertheless, the incentives for divisional managers to smooth performance reports are so strong that, on balance, more smoothing will occur in divisional than functional structures. Moreover, information asymmetry exists between the corporate staff and the divisional managers who have much more detailed knowledge of their own divisions. Corporate auditors are seldom able to attain data completely independently of divisional management so that these auditors must rely to a degree on information supplied by the divisions. Further, corporate managers have some incentives to collude with the divisional managers and allow the latter to smooth the reported divisional performances. The corporate managers positively value predictability of performance, and this is assisted by allowing divisional managers to smooth divisional performance so that unexpected deviations are removed and budgets attained. Thus corporate managers will allow divisional managers to exercise some smoothing of the results of their divisions. Hence the theory about the divisional smoothing of reported profits that has been advanced here is likely to enjoy some validity notwithstanding the auditing capacity of divisional structures.

Loose Coupling of Divisions
Facilitates Negative Correlations

There is a second mechanism of risk reduction in the divisional structure that comes into play due to the disaggregation into divisions. There is a tendency toward a negative correlation between portfolio elements, that is, the profits of divisions.

In a functional structure, the different products are managed together so that they are treated in a common fashion. For example, all the products come under the common manufacturing department, and so decisions about the manufacture of one product are made in concert with decisions about the manufacture of other products. All products report to the same superordinate manager (e.g., the head of the manufacturing function), so decisions about the products will display some consistency. Given similarities in strategic and operational decisions across products, their performances will tend to covary together so that they are positively correlated.

In contrast, in the divisional system, these decisions are decentralized and taken by each division separately. This is structurally facilitated and encouraged by the autonomy granted to divisions (Chandler 1962; Chenhall 1979; Grinyer and Yasai-Ardekani 1981; Lorsch and Allen 1973; Pitts 1974). Thus divisions each pursue their own strategies and operational tactics. In this way, the decision making is disaggregated and varies across divisions, which can be termed decisional disaggregation. The result is that the performances of divisions tend to be less positively correlated than are the performances of different products in a functionally structured corporation.

As the corporation progressively diversifies further and decentralizes more over time, the divisions become more loosely coupled, and correlations between the performances of divisions may become negative. Hence the fluctuations in performance of the divisions offset each other to a degree. Thus overall corporate performance fluctuation (i.e., risk) will be lower in divisional structures than in functional structures because of the structurally induced, reduced correlation between the products.

The proposition thus is the following:

> 6.4 Decentralization of decision making in divisional structures leads to lower positive correlations and may lead to negative correlations among performances of divisions so that risk is lower for divisional structures relative to functional structures.

In summary, organizational portfolio theory postulates that divisional structure leads to lower risk through reduced fluctuation in the performance of divisions and negative correlations between divisional performances.

It is possible that risk reduction in divisional structures may also be achieved by central decisions. Hoskisson (1987) notes that divisional structures feature a central corporate office that can emphasize strategic management and that this may extend to orchestrating risk reduction through deliberate planning.

Empirical Support

In a study of U.S. corporations, Hoskisson (1987) finds that the shift from a functional to a divisional structure leads to a reduction in the risk of return on assets. Similarly, in their study of German corporations, Buhner and Möller (1985) find that the disclosure that a firm has adopted the divisional structure in place of the functional structure leads to a reduction in the risk of the stock price of that firm. Thus a similar conclusion is reached using both accounting and stock price indicators of financial performance. Moreover, both studies use longitudinal, before-and-after research designs, adding confidence to the inference that structure affects risk level. Hence there is empirical evidence that divisionalization leads to risk reduction.

Diversification and Divisionalization Interact to Reduce Corporate Risk

As has been seen, the risk reduction effect of divisionalization is analytically distinct from the reduction in risk that occurs through diversification. To this point, the portfolio effect has been considered here as composed of two distinct sources: strategic diversification and divisional structure, each of which contributes to reduction in the risk of the organizational portfolio. However, the reduction in performance fluctuation due to diversification is only fully realized when the divisional structure is adopted so that the full potential for risk reduction through a filtered, uncorrelated portfolio is realized. Thus diversification and divisionalization interact to affect risk reduction.

The interactive model of the effects of diversification and divisionalization on corporate risk is shown in Figure 6.2. We first explain the meaning of the two solid lines in the figure and then describe the actual trajectory of an organization (the dashed line) through this conceptual space as it moves along and between those lines. Diversification reduces risk—hence the two lines slope downward from left to right. The line for the divisional structure is below that for the functional structure, signifying that a divisional structure produces less risk at each level of diversification.

When diversification is zero, then in theory, divisionalization, by splitting the homogeneous product market activities into several divisions, would still create divisional filtering of profit performance and hence some lower corporate risk relative to the same corporation organized functionally (Figure 6.2). Greater diversification affords more scope for divisional filtering of profit performance and also for negative correlation to arise between divisions as the activities in these divisions become inherently more different from each other. This diversity of activities constitutes a potential for negatively correlated action across the corporation that is fully realized only under divisionalization because it structurally facilitates fuller expression of disaggregated action through divisional autonomy. Thus the risk reduction from divisionalization will be larger for greater degrees of diversification.

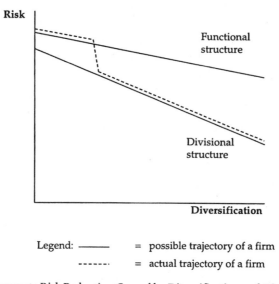

Figure 6.2 Corporate Risk Reduction Caused by Diversification and Divisionalization

Of course, in reality, corporations divisionalize after they have diversified somewhat (Chandler 1962; Rumelt 1974). Therefore, the actual trajectory of an organization in Figure 6.2 is to be first on the top line, that is, to have a functional structure, and to retain that while initially diversifying (i.e., moving along the top line toward the right). This increase in diversification causes the corporation to divisionalize; thus it moves down to the lower line in Figure 6.2. As the corporation then diversifies further, it moves along the lower line and toward the bottom right in Figure 6.2.

Diversification, however, has more than a one-time effect in the life of a corporation. If it diversifies further, the divisionalized corporation decentralizes its structure further (Lorsch and Allen 1973). A corporation that has diversified to the medium degree possesses a set of related products (Rumelt 1974). There will be some decentralization and divisional autonomy, but these are limited, however, by substantial head office involvement seeking to maximize the operational synergies between the divisions (Lorsch and Allen 1973; Pitts 1976, 1977; Chandler 1994). Some corporations will diversify further, attaining a high degree of diversification—that is, unrelated products—and becoming a conglomerate in the extreme (Rumelt 1974). The highly diversified corporation has no operating synergies to reap between divisions, so the head office tends toward minimal operational involvement in the divisions (Lorsch and Allen 1973; Pitts 1976, 1977; Chandler 1994). Decentralization and divisional autonomy are at a maximum in the highly diversified corporation. Hence the meaning of divisionalization changes as the corporation becomes more and more diversified.

As diversification increases, the divisions become less interdependent on each other and more autonomous, so they become more loosely coupled and decisional disaggregation can become more complete. Therefore, the risk reduction from divisional autonomy is greater the more the corporation diversifies. Hence increasing diversification from medium to high not only increases the risk reduction from diversification but also increases the risk reduction from the increasing decentralization. For both strategic and structural reasons, risk reduction is greater for the unrelated than for the related product corporation. Risk reduction is low for the undiversified, functionally structured corporation, medium for the related-diversified, divisionalized corporation, and high for the unrelated-diversified, divisionalized corporation.

In causal model terms, diversification has both a direct and an indirect effect on risk, both causing lower risk. Diversification and divisionalization interact to reduce risk, as has just been shown, so diversification has a direct effect on risk. However, diversification also causes divisionalization. Thus diversification has an indirect effect on risk reduction through its effect on divisionalization. Diversification is the underlying cause of risk reduction in the model. However, divisionalization both moderates and mediates the effect of diversification on risk. The interactive effect of diversification and divisionalization on risk means that divisionalization moderates the effect of diversification on risk; that is, the degree of risk that results from a level of diversification depends on divisionalization (Hill et al. 1992). Similarly, because some of the effect of diversification on risk flows through divisionalization, divisionalization mediates some of the effect of diversification on risk.

Economic Implications

Recognition of the risk reduction benefits of diversification and divisionalization is important for an appreciation of the economic gains from the divisional structure. The diversified–divisionalized and undiversified–functionalized combinations both constitute fits of structure to strategy, so both would be expected to produce similar levels of mean performance. However, as already seen, diversification and divisionalization interact to reduce risk. By lowering risk, they raise the ratio of performance to risk, which we saw in Chapter 2 is the measure of economic value. Thus, even if the diversified, divisionalized corporation has the same mean performance as the undiversified, functionalized corporation, the diversified, divisionalized corporation has superior economic value because of its risk reduction.

Notwithstanding this advantage, divisionalization reinforces the effect of diversification of reducing risk, which reduces adaptation and so causes growth to decline below its optimum, leading to mediocre long-term profitability, as is argued below. Therefore, the short-run advantages of diversification and divisionalization coexist with long-term disadvantages.

Less Risk Causes Less Corporate Adaptation

As seen above, the diversified, divisionalized corporation experiences less fluctuation in performance than an undiversified, functional firm. If the limited fluctuations in performance were around a low mean level of organizational performance, performance would sometimes drop below the satisficing level, triggering adaptation. However, the mean performance of the diversified, divisionalized corporation will tend not to be low because the divisional structure fits the diversified strategy and so has a positive effect on organizational performance (Donaldson 1987; Hill et al. 1992). Thus the diversified, divisionalized corporation tends to have the low risk and at least moderate mean performance that combine to produce lack of adaptation. This implies that the probability of the overall financial performance of a diversified, divisionalized corporation dropping below the satisficing level is low and is lower than the probability for an undiversified, functional firm that tends to have greater performance fluctuations.

Thus diversified, divisionalized corporations tend to be pathologically stable and to avoid adaptive change relative to undiversified, functionally structured corporations. The needed corporate-level adaptive changes could be of any kind, such as organizational structure, strategy, information technology, or human resources. The diversified, divisionalized corporations become suboptimal performers, and their performance tends to drift downward over time as their failure to adapt becomes more acute because of their changing situation. Eventually, their maladaptation and consequent performance loss become great enough (in conjunction with other causes of organizational performance) that their performance drops below the satisficing level and adaptive change is triggered. The diversified, divisionalized corporations will not thereby remain maladapted indefinitely but may nevertheless be maladapted and suboptimal for long periods, harming their long-term success.

Large, diversified, divisionalized corporations have achieved partial insulation from financial crises but thereby also from the therapeutic effects of crisis. The low-risk, stable performance that seems on the surface to be an attractive feature of the diversified, divisionalized corporation is revealed on closer inquiry to be a disadvantage for the longer-run prosperity of that corporation because it blocks whatever future changes are required. Moreover, the reduced risk of the diversified, divisionalized corporation makes bankruptcy less likely, and so these corporations are more likely than less diversified firms to survive. Hence despite their lack of adaptiveness, they are liable to endure as features on the economic landscape.

The propositions thus are the following:

6.5　The low risk of the diversified, divisionalized corporation causes it to avoid making needed adaptations.

6.6　The low risk of the diversified, divisionalized corporation causes its performance to become suboptimal.

This is not to deny that divisionalization is a sound move for diversified corporations, for it moves their structure into fit with their strategy and thus leads to higher performance (Donaldson 1987; Hamilton and Shergill 1992, 1993). Moreover, divisionalization can fit with larger organizational size (Williamson 1970; Grinyer and Yasai-Ardekani 1981). Also, the divisional structure has other advantages, such as creating a corporate office that focuses on strategic management issues (Williamson 1985). For all these reasons, divisionalization is a rational move by corporations and their managers. The advantageousness of the divisional form is reflected in the way it has become the dominant form among large corporations in many countries and remains so; in other words, it has passed the test of survival rather well. However, in structural-functional theory, structures that have functions can also have dysfunctions (Merton 1949). These dysfunctions are often unintended by the people who create them (Merton 1949). In the present case, corporate managers intend that the divisional structures will be effective when they adopt them, but the risk reduction of the divisional structure has the unintended and unapparent dysfunction of inhibiting corporate adaptation longer term.

Debt Increases Adaptation

Debt tends to increase the likelihood of organizational adaptation. Thus its effect is opposite to diversification and divisionalization and reduces their impacts. Moreover, debt tends to follow diversification and divisionalization. Thus debt works to reduce to a degree the pathological stability of the corporation that results from its earlier diversification and divisionalization.

Debt, through requiring large, recurrent interest payments, raises the satisficing level. This in turn means that organizational performance has less far to drop before it reaches the level at which adaptation must occur. Gordon Donaldson (1994) documents how CPC International increased its debt in 1986 and, in doing so, eliminated its historically positive liquidity so that its management lost the "corporate risk-relieving function of such ready reserves" (p. 64). Here Donaldson is referring to downside risk, the probability of low performance, and acknowledging that this probability is increased by debt. Thus the greater the debt of the corporation, the more readily adaptation occurs. Hence the higher the leverage—that is, the debt to equity ratio—the greater the probability of adaptation.

Even in the diversified, divisionalized corporation, which therefore has low risk (i.e., performance fluctuation), adaptation tends to occur more frequently for high leverage because debt increases the satisficing level. Thus high leverage tends to work against the low-risk and long-term pathological stability of the large corporation. Debt thus tends to offset the pathology of the stable performance of the large corporation by rendering smaller-amplitude downward turns in performance sufficient to cause adaptation.

The propositions thus are the following:

6.7   Debt raises the satisficing level.

6.8   Debt increases the probability of organizational adaptation.

Debt also fosters organizational growth. As we have just seen, debt increases the probability of organizational adaptation into fit; this gives the organization the capacity to grow. Debt also increases the financial resources to fund organizational growth and so increases the rate of growth. Debt, then, serves to lead the organization toward greater long-term success.

The proposition thus is the following:

6.9   Debt increases the rate of organizational growth.

The enhanced organizational adaptation and growth are benefits of debt that are distinct from any reduction of agency loss through the reduction of the free cash flow available to managers (Jensen 1986). Even if the agency theory of the benefits of debt is false, there may still be a positive benefit resulting from the greater propensity to adapt and grow under organizational portfolio theory. Equally, if agency theory is valid regarding the debt discipline on free cash flow, this would add to the benefits from enhanced organizational adaptation and growth.

The low risk of the large, diversified, divisionalized corporation makes it a safe borrower, and so banks are willing to lend to such corporations, thereby increasing their debt to equity ratio (i.e., higher leverage). Thus the lowered risk of the large corporation, resulting from its diversification and divisionalization, fosters debt financing, in that lenders are more comfortable making the loan and at lower rates of interest. Thus debt becomes a cheaper mode of finance for the large, diversified, divisionalized corporation than for the small, undiversified, functionalized corporation. Hence the large corporation that has diversified and divisionalized may be somewhat more likely to use a large amount of debt financing.

Thus diversification and divisionalization reduce risk but also increase debt. The reduction in risk reduces adaptation, but the increase in debt increases it. Hence diversification and divisionalization have a direct negative effect on adaptation and then also a longer-run, indirect positive effect on adaptation through increasing debt. Being only indirect, the magnitude of this positive effect would be expected to be lower than that of the direct, negative effect, so the net effect of diversification and divisionalization on adaptation is expected to still be negative.

There may well be a sequence here. The diversification and then division-alization of the large corporation decreased its probability of adaptation. However, the increased indebtedness common among many large corporations heightened the probability of adaptation. Insofar as indebtedness increases significantly *after* the corporation has diversified and then divisionalized, so, then, the decrease in adaptive propensity is followed by an increase. The net effect is that the pathological stability of the large corporation remains but at a more moderate level after taking on substantial debt. Thus the sequence is that adaptation first declines because of the diversification and then declines further after the ensuing divisionalization, the increasing debt causes adaptation propensity to rise somewhat, but it still remains lower than it was before the diversification and divisionalization.

Debt also increases the risk of failure for the corporation, in that debt may force the corporation into bankruptcy. The large, regular interest payments may exceed the operating profit, creating loss and insolvency, which, at the extreme, produce bankruptcy. Thus debt under adverse conditions forces profit performance not only below the satisficing level but also below zero. Thus, by increasing risk, debt increases the chance of corporate failure and disbandment (i.e., mortality; Hannan and Freeman 1989). Hence, although debt generally increases organizational adaptation, at the extreme it may cause some organizations to exit the population. Therefore, in examining the effect of debt on a population of organizations, it needs to be borne in mind that the proportion of the population that is maladapted falls when debt causes some maladapted corporations to die. This population effect needs to be separated out to reveal the effect of debt causing a corporation to make adaptive changes.

Over the broad historical period from the 1950s and 1960s into the 1970s, there was a tendency for debt to increase. Large corporations became more leveraged, increasing their ratio of debt to equity capital. However, sub-sequently, there has been some trend among some corporations to decrease their debt. Wary of its risk, or recoiling from high interest on debt, or frustrated by covenants on the debt that constrained managerial autonomy, some corpo-rations (e.g., Union Carbide) have replaced portions of their debt by equity (Eccles and Crane 1988). There is some tendency for firms taken over by debt-financed moves, such as leveraged buyouts or management buyouts, to subsequently have their high levels of leverage reduced by raising fresh equity capital. Thus the trend in earlier decades toward higher debt shows some signs of having been halted or reversed in certain quarters. Therefore, where debt is reduced, its effect is lessened so that the level of organizational performance that is satisfactory declines and organizational adaptation becomes less probable again.

Divestment Postpones Adaptation

As we have just seen, debt increases the likelihood of organizational adaptation, whereas diversification and divisionalization reduce it. However, the tendency of large corporations to resist making needed adaptive changes is reinforced by another factor. Where corporate performance drops severely, the corporation may make the radical response of divestment (G. Donaldson 1994). Given the diversified nature of many large corporations, divestment often takes the form of selling non-core divisions created or acquired previously in diversifying, so the corporation becomes less diversified—in other words, it downscopes (Hoskisson and Hitt 1994). The sale of these non-core assets generates cash that restores corporate performance and wealth, leading to a surplus. The replenished finances of the corporation could keep its performance above the satisficing level for a lengthy period because of the large amounts of cash raised by selling a substantial-size division. This could forestall organizational adaptation to the existing situation or to the new, less diversified strategy.

Depending on the magnitude of the new organizational slack created by divestments, it may be some time before performance drops low enough to once again trigger organizational adaptation. This period will be longer than that between diversifying and divisionalizing, the structural adaptation to diversifying (Rumelt 1974; Donaldson 1987), because diversification spends corporate resources whereas divestment replenishes them. Thus the delay in structurally adapting to downscoping could last decades, during which the maladapted structure causes performance to be suboptimal. Similarly, any other needed adaptation could be delayed because of the slack present after the corporation has divested.

A divestment can be followed by a subsequent, further divestment or by a series of divestments so that the wealth surplus is constantly refreshed. This means that organizational adaptation can be delayed for a very long period. Poor corporate performance triggering needed adaptations by the corporation will occur only after all the peripheral assets are liquidated one by one and the money spent, which can take a very long time for a large, highly diversified corporation.

Divisionalization facilitates divestment in that a division is a self-sufficient business that can be sold without disrupting the remainder of the corporation. Similarly, diversification facilitates divestment, because the more diversified the corporation, the more that it would have non-core assets to shed over a longer time. Thus conglomerates that sequentially downscope over time will be particularly able to avoid organizational adaptation for a lengthy period. Hence conglomerates that have commenced downscoping are prone to chronic maladaptation and financial suboptimality.

There may be a sequence visible in a number of corporations whereby divestment follows in time after diversification, divisionalization, and debt. As argued above, the diversified, divisionalized corporation has lower risk that facilitates taking on debt. The debt increases the vulnerability of the corporation to experience poor performance. However, as just seen, diversified, divisionalized corporations are also well placed to respond to poor performance by divestment, so that divestment may often follow the increased debt that, in turn, followed after diversification and divisionalization. Thus in some corporations there may be a historical sequence of diversification, divisionalization, debt, and divestment. In such cases, the diversification and divisionalization reduce the probability of organizational adaptation, then debt raises it, and then divestment reduces it again.

The propositions thus are the following:

6.10   Divestment generates organizational slack that keeps organizational performance above the satisficing level.

6.11   Divestment reduces the probability of an organization making needed adaptations.

6.12   The more diversified the corporation, the longer that divestments can forestall adaptation.

Conclusions

Organizational portfolio theory has been used to generate propositions about the effects of diversification and divisionalization on risk reduction. Diversification and divisionalization both reduce risk. Diversification spreads the corporation over different business cycles that tend to offset each other, thereby reducing corporate risk. The effect of divisionalization is analytically separate from the reduction of risk caused by diversification. However, diversification and divisionalization interact to determine risk. The effect of diversification on risk reduction is greater with divisionalization.

Risk reduction results from divisionalization through two mechanisms. The first is the reduction in the level of risk of the division through smoothing fluctuations in its profits. This is a response by divisional managers to the profit accountability to which divisionalization subjects them. The second mechanism is the loose coupling between divisions that produces decisional disaggregation across the corporation and fosters the emergence of negative correlations between the performances of divisions. Thus organizational portfolio theory illuminates ways in which risk is reduced through diversification and divisionalization.

The reduced risk of the diversified, divisionalized corporation raises the ratio of its mean performance to risk and so increases its economic value. However, the risk reduction also has the disadvantage that it makes less probable the episodes of poor performance necessary for the organization to make adaptive changes. Thus there will be some tendency for the diversified, divisionalized corporation to drift over time into maladaptation and suboptimal performance. Moreover, if an episode of low performance occurs, the corporation may divest a business, which restores its performance so that it may avoid making needed adaptive changes. Divestment may allow a corporation to remain maladapted for a long time. The diversified, divisionalized corporation may in this way possess a disadvantage, lack of corporate adaptation, that deserves to be taken into consideration along with its advantages.

Debt tends to lead toward organizational adaptation and growth. Thus, insofar as the diversification and divisionalization of the corporation lead toward greater debt financing, this will offset to a degree the large corporation's pathological stability. However, subsequent divestment may restore it.

Whereas Chapters 3 and 4 examined external factors that lead to organizational change, this chapter examined factors internal to the corporation that mostly lead to the retardation of organizational change. In Chapter 7, we combine both sets of factors to analyze corporate governance.

Risk and Corporate Governance

Corporate governance is a topic receiving much popular and academic attention today. Popular commentaries highlight as anomalous the number of CEOs who are also chairs of their boards, thus reducing the control over management by an independent board. Weak corporate governance is perceived, and much abuse is held to result. Stern prescriptions to toughen corporate governance are made. Academically, the prevailing theories map managerial aggrandizement and specify the structures to curtail it. Several disciplines upon management are conventionally depicted. However, the organizational portfolio theory offers a new perspective upon corporate governance and makes visible different causal mechanisms.

Corporate governance is affected by corporate performance. Therefore, in order to explain corporate governance and its changing nature, we need to see it as the outcome of the various factors in the organizational portfolio. Earlier, Chapters 3 and 4 analyzed the effects of external factors, including the business cycle, on organizational performance, and Chapter 6 analyzed the way factors internal to the organization affect its performance. This chapter combines the effects of internal and external factors on corporate performance, specifically diversification, divisionalization, debt, divestment, and the business cycle, to better understand corporate governance.

Overview

The phenomena of corporate governance provide a fertile area for the application of organizational portfolio theory. Agency and transaction theories hold that boards that are independent of management produce higher levels of corporate profitability and returns to shareholders (Jensen and Meckling 1976; Williamson 1985). Agency and transaction theories also hold that because of the superiority of independent boards, corporations adopt them (Jensen and Meckling 1976; Williamson 1985). However, the evidence disconfirms the theory that independent boards are superior. Moreover, many companies have not had independent boards for long periods of time. Thus the theories of agency and transaction costs fail to explain corporate governance, prompting the need for a new theoretical explanation. Organizational portfolio theory offers an alternative perspective on corporate governance that sheds light on its changing nature. The key is to analyze the way organizational performance has changed over time under the impact of shifts in the levels of its external and internal causes.

Boards of directors of large corporations have gone through three periods: boards dependent on management, boards more independent, and then return to the more dependent boards. The immediate proximate cause is organizational performance. When organizational performance is high, executives are seen as capable and trustworthy and are allowed to control the corporation relatively unfettered, so they are allowed to chair the board and compose the majority of its directors (i.e., the dependent board). Thus the three-period shift, from less to more then less independence, is caused by the organizational performance being satisfactory, then unsatisfactory, and then more satisfactory.

The period of satisfactory performance of large corporations followed their adoption of the diversified, divisionalized form with its low risk and consequent above-satisficing performance. This allowed executives to chair the board and compose a virtual de facto majority of directors. The main offsetting force was when such corporations went on to increase their debt. This would have the effect of increasing somewhat the propensity for the occurrence of low performance that might lead to the adoption of a more independent board. However, the net risk level was still quite low and this combined with the large size of corporations to yield performance that allowed most of them to retain a dependent board. Thus the internal factors, that is, the effects on organizational performance from within the organization itself, were tending to produce satisfactory performance and hence a dependent board.

The systematic push toward boards independent of management was caused by the shift in the external factors influencing performance. Starting around the early 1980s and gathering force thereafter, a series of changes in environmental economic conditions pushed organizational performance in a downward direction. These changes included economic recessions and stock and real estate market crashes. Such events forced the performance of many organizations down to an unsatisfactory level, leading to changes in corporate governance. The increasing power of institutional investors coupled with their increasing dependence on large corporations produced a reform movement. This movement resulted in shifts in the boards of some large corporations toward greater independence from management.

Subsequently, boards in some large corporations have shifted toward being more dependent again. The underlying cause has been the rise in performance of those large corporations. The economy has emerged from the recession of the early 1990s, thus lifting corporate profits. So, once more, managers are perceived as capable and trustworthy.

Overall, we see how the organizational portfolio theory can illuminate corporate governance and explain phenomena that are unexplained by the theories usually deployed on that topic, such as agency and transaction costs theories. The key is to understand that corporate governance is primarily driven by organizational performance and that this, in turn, is driven by the portfolio properties of the organization in its interaction with the economic environment.

The Development of Corporate Governance

Corporate governance refers to the structures and processes that provide the ultimate governing mechanisms of corporations (Tricker 1984). More concretely, this includes the board of directors and top management.

Classically, the company was governed by its owner, who also managed the enterprise (Chandler 1977). As the company grows it tends to require additional capital, leading to increasing outside ownership. With the passage of time, the founding entrepreneur tends to be replaced by family descendants and then by professional managers (Chandler 1962, 1977, 1994). In the large modern corporation, ownership is widely dispersed among outsiders, and the managers may own little or none of the corporation. Thus ownership is separated from control, which creates a situation in which managers may act to further their interests at the expense of the outside shareholders (Berle and Means 1932).

Agency theory states that managers will on occasion use their discretion to benefit themselves so that there is a loss of value to owners (Jensen and Meckling 1976). Transaction cost theory, similarly, sees a market failure in which lack of discipline on managers allows them to gain at cost to shareholders (Williamson 1985). Both agency and transaction cost theories see the board of directors as a means of reasserting control over managers, by monitoring and sanctioning management on behalf of outside owners. For this to occur, the board must be substantially independent, such as by having a majority of directors who are independent of management (Jensen and Meckling 1976; Williamson 1985). Also, the board needs to be chaired by an independent outsider; otherwise, board independence is compromised. Agency theory holds that corporations tend to adopt efficient means of governance (Jensen and Meckling 1976), which leads to the expectation that large corporations will have adopted boards that are independent of management.

There are presently widespread calls for boards to be more vigilant and active in the monitoring of management so that problems are avoided, in particular failures to adequately protect the interests of outside shareholders (Eisenberg et al. 1994; Cadbury 1992). As seen above, these populist views receive support from prevailing organization theories of agency and transaction costs that are established in academic circles.

Thus both academic organizational theory and conventional wisdom hold that large corporations should have boards that are able to assert control over management by being composed mostly of independent, non-executive directors and being chaired by an independent, non-executive director. However, empirically, large corporations in countries such as the United States have not typically had such independent boards. Instead, their boards have tended to be chaired by the CEO, a major violation of the ideal of the board being an independent control over the managers (Kesner and Dalton 1986). In addition, it has been estimated that only a minority of directors are truly independent. Many boards of large U.S. corporations contain only a minority of executives among the directors; however, about half of the outside or non-executive directors are related to management in ways that reduce their independence and render them somewhat dependent on management (e.g., retired executives, family connections, and suppliers to the corporation), so that genuinely independent directors are in a minority (Kesner and Dalton 1986). Thus the composition of boards of large U.S. corporations typically contradicts the normative prescriptions for "good governance" advanced by theorists and widely supported in the community.

Because boards are visible and their membership open to inspection by outside shareholders and commentators, the lack of board independence has been apparent and subject to critical commentary. There have been some moves to make boards more independent, by appointing an independent outsider to chair the board and by increasing the proportion of directors who are independent outsiders. However, recently there has also been some reversion to less independent boards—for example, CEOs being appointed as chair.

Having the CEO also hold the chair is referred to as CEO duality and is seen as a particularly shocking transgression of the principle of board independence (Kesner and Dalton 1986). How has this and other violations of the ideals of strong corporate governance come about? Why have they only recently been subject to changes to make boards more independent? And why are these changes now being reversed in some corporations?

Organizational Performance as a Cause of Corporate Governance

Organizational portfolio theory holds that poor corporate performance provides a shock to the status quo that triggers adaptive change. At the board level, this leads to the establishment of boards independent of management, in order to control them. Low performance leads to the appointment of more directors who are non-executives and to the appointment of a non-executive to chair the board in place of the CEO or other executive. The performance of the corporation is interpreted as an indicator of whether the executives are capable and trustworthy or whether they lack the ability or motivation to be trusted to act autonomously (Mayer, Davis, and Schoorman 1995). Therefore, when corporate performance is poor, the autonomy of their executives is reduced by having non-executives placed over them on the board. This is consistent with research that shows that low-performing individuals or organizational units are granted less autonomy than high-performing individuals or organizational units and vice versa (Graen and Schiemann 1978; Yukl 1994). Conversely, high corporate performance results in executives being viewed as capable and trustworthy by shareholders, so executives are appointed as directors and board chair in place of non-executives. High corporate performance also feeds back to produce growth in organizational size and diversification, which raises the complexity of the corporation and encourages the professionalization of its management to be extended up to the board.

The propositions thus are the following:

7.1 Low organizational performance leads to an independent board of directors (e.g., non-executive chair and high proportion of non-executive directors).

7.2 High organizational performance leads to a nonindependent board of directors (e.g., executive chair and high proportion of executive directors).

Thus the motor of change in corporate governance is organizational performance. This is driven, in turn, by factors internal and external to the organization.

Diversification and Divisionalization Lead to Executive Directors

As we have seen, the large corporation is diversified and divisionalized, and these two characteristics jointly interact to lower its risk (see Chapter 6). This reduces the probability that its performance will drop below the satisficing level. Thus the large corporation will tend to remain stable in its performance and not suffer crises of poor performance. Therefore, the performance of the large corporation will tend to be seen as acceptable. Given acceptability of performance, executives are seen as trustworthy, and because corporate governance is now not considered a critical issue, boards are allowed to be dominated by the executives of the corporation. Thus arises the typical board structure that is dependent on management: The board chair is the CEO (board duality), about a third of the directors are executives, and about another third are affiliates (e.g., retired company executives, suppliers), so only a minority of directors are truly independent (Kesner and Dalton 1986). While performance is high or acceptable, such a dependent board can continue to exist.

The period in which corporations performed satisfactorily produced the dependent board. The satisfactoriness of performance was assisted by the low risk that followed from diversification and divisionalization. Hence arose the typical pattern of the large corporation as simultaneously diversified and divisionalized, with a dependent board and CEO duality (i.e., CEO as chair).

The propositions thus are the following:

7.3 Low organizational risk leads to a nonindependent board of directors (e.g., executive chair and high proportion of executive directors).

7.4 The diversified, divisionalized corporation leads to a non-independent board of directors (e.g., executive chair and high proportion of executive directors).

Economic Downturns Lead to Non-Executive Directors

In organizational portfolio theory, because the precondition for the non-independent board is satisfactory performance, when the performance of corporations turns down, dependence of the board upon management becomes unacceptable and more independent boards are created. A decline in the performance of the corporations arises for both external and internal reasons.

In particular, external causes have a substantial downward pressure on corporate performance. The stock market crash of 1987 produced a general decline in the share values of corporations. The collapse of real estate values in the late 1980s adversely affected banks and other corporations that had invested in real estate or loaned money to real estate investors, producing substantial "nonperforming loans" (Carew 1997). In general, high-risk strategies that produced good returns in booming markets produced financial crises as market prices collapsed. A number of entrepreneurs had built up large corporations by pursuing high-risk strategies. When the markets turned downward, these high-risk strategies produced massive failures. Some governments had created banks that embarked on risky loan-making in an effort to build market share and stimulate the economy; some of these banks collapsed or suffered massive losses as economic conditions deteriorated.

More widespread, the recessions of the early 1980s and 1990s produced a decline in corporate profits. The business cycles turned downward, creating crises of poor corporate performance or even insolvency. This in turn lowered the returns to shareholders or created losses borne by shareholders or other stakeholders such as governments, depositors, or employees (through redundancy or loss of their pension funds). Also, intensifying competition, often from international competitors, led to losses of market share, sales revenue, and profits for some corporations—for example, General Motors lost a share of the U.S. domestic automobile market to the Japanese during the 1980s.

To these external causes of low organizational performance can be added factors internal to some corporations that worked to reduce performance and so reinforced the trend toward low performance for those corporations. Some large corporations increased their debt, and this increased their financial vulnerability, occasioning episodes of low performance that sapped investor confidence in management.

When corporate performance turned unacceptably low, questioning of corporate governance ensued, leading to criticism of boards for having failed in their duties to protect shareholders and so forth. This in turn led to demands from shareholders to reform boards to make them more independent of management and therefore more able to discipline management. The previously fragmented, outside shareholders of large corporations began to combine and become powerful through the growth of shareholdings by institutional investors, including pension funds. In the United States, these funds (e.g., CALPERS) were active in promoting more independent boards (Davis and Thompson 1994). Previously, institutional investors tended either to support incumbent management against critics or sell their shareholdings ("the Wall Street walk"; Kesner and Dalton 1986). However, the size of institutional funds means that selling is less of an option because they need to place their funds, and so continuing to hold stocks of the large corporations becomes unavoidable. Denied the option of "exit," institutional investors have recourse to "voice" when dissatisfied with incumbent management, thus aligning them with the critics against management.

The 1980s and 1990s witnessed a movement to reform boards in which outside owners became active, with institutional investors being prominent (Davis and Thompson 1994). The process included demands on specific corporations that they adopt more independent boards. Some of these demands were voiced at annual general meetings of shareholders and through proxy fights, which produced conflict at traditionally harmonious annual general meetings. The result was that some large corporations changed their boards to become more independent of management. These structural changes included appointing an independent director as board chair instead of the CEO and appointing more independent directors. Another widespread structural change was to create committees of the board for audit, nomination, compensation, and other purposes (Clifford and Evans 1996). These committees of the main board were often filled by the independent directors, providing a further check on management (Clifford and Evans 1996). Corporations were required to disclose any affiliations between directors and management that might compromise their independence (e.g., acting as a supplier). In these and other ways, boards became more independent of management than they had been in the earlier period.

The propositions thus are the following:

7.5   Downward turns in financial markets lead to independent boards of directors (e.g., non-executive chair and high proportion of non-executive directors).

7.6   Troughs in the business cycle lead to independent boards of directors (e.g., non-executive chair and high proportion of non-executive directors).

7.7   Increased competition leads to independent boards of directors (e.g., non-executive chair and high proportion of non-executive directors).

As the early 1990s moved toward the mid-1990s, the economic recession eased, and many corporations enjoyed a return to high profits and in some cases record profits. The stock market boomed, also attaining record levels. For many corporations, their performance in profit, share value, and so on was restored to high levels. In this situation of renewed high performance, some corporations began to move back toward the nonindependent board. The direction of change was not always uniform, however, because some ongoing changes to the board were still attempting to increase board independence in this period. Nevertheless, some structural changes were to make the board less independent once more, such as by making the CEO the board chair again (Daily and Dalton 1997)—for example, American Express in 1993 ("That's Chairman Golub to You" 1993:35). The restoration of CEO duality is a particularly definite and visible departure from the ideals of "strong corporate governance." However, the new higher corporate performance was interpreted as indicating that senior managers were indeed able and willing to serve shareholder interests. Thus the upswing in the business cycle led to some restoration of the dependent board and, specifically, of CEO duality.

The propositions thus are the following:

7.8   Upward turns in financial markets lead to nonindependent boards of directors (e.g., executive chair and high proportion of executive directors).

7.9   Peaks in the business cycle lead to nonindependent boards of directors (e.g., executive chair and high proportion of executive directors).

Thus portfolio theory explains the growth of nonindependent boards, by the reasonably high and stable performance that eventuated from large corporations becoming diversified and divisionalized. The growth of the independent board is then explained by the downward turns in the economic cycles, particularly as they interacted with risky strategies adopted by some organizations in the 1980s. Similarly, the return back toward dependent boards is explicable in terms of the upward turn in the business cycle causing an external lifting of corporate performance.

Performance Unaffected
by Non-Executive Directors

Academic theories and popular beliefs about the necessity for a board to be independent of management hold that board structure has definite consequences feeding back to affect performance. According to agency and transaction costs theories, the dependent board lowers corporate performance and the independent board raises it (Jensen and Meckling 1976; Williamson 1985). This means that organizational performance would be expected to be lower for organizations with dependent boards.

Research studies to date, however, fail to support the generalization that dependent boards cause lower performance. This holds for the effects of both non-executive directors and non-executive board chair on firm performance (for a review, see Donaldson and Davis 1994). Some studies show a negative effect on performance of dependent boards; that is, executives on boards or as board chair reduce firm performance (e.g., Baysinger and Butler 1985; Ezzamel and Watson 1993). However, other studies show the opposite: namely, a *positive* effect on performance of dependent boards; that is, executives on boards or as board chair raise firm performance (e.g., Kesner 1987; Donaldson and Davis 1991). A review has shown the average effect of CEO duality on firm performance to be practically nil (Boyd 1995). Another review of studies of CEO duality effects on firm performance and related outcomes finds them to be overall mixed and inconclusive (Daily and Dalton 1997). Therefore, at the present time, there is no reason to hold that there is a feedback effect from board structure to organizational performance.

Non-Executive Directors Reduce Risk

Although board structure has no effect on the level of mean organizational performance, it may have an effect on fluctuations in performance over time (i.e., risk). Thus, board structure may not affect the mean performance of a firm but may affect the variation over time in performance around the mean. Non-executive directors and chairperson reduce performance variations so that they are less likely to fluctuate up to high levels or down to low levels. The board plays the role of providing a check and balance upon management.

Grossly foolish or incompetent actions by management are visible to the board. The board is required to act to curb managerial actions detrimental to the corporation, and its non-executive directors, being independent of management, are in a position to rein in management and prevent very low corporate performance. Empirical research shows that the probability of bankruptcy is reduced by non-executive directors (Daily and Dalton 1994a, 1994b; but Chaganti, Mahajan, and Sharma [1985] failed to find such an effect). Thus a non-executive board reduces the chance of corporate performance fluctuating down to a low level.

Similarly, the board may question riskier strategies being proposed by management and generally inhibits management from taking unorthodox actions the board cannot readily comprehend or that are not readily justifiable to outsiders. Empirical studies show that the non-executive directors reduce the risky strategy of investing in research and development and also pursue the risk-reducing strategy of corporate diversification (Hill and Snell 1988; Baysinger, Kosnik, and Turk 1991). Therefore, more non-executives on the board may unintentionally tend to limit corporate performance from becoming extremely high, despite that being desirable for the corporation.

By contrast, in a corporation with a board that predominantly consists of executives, management is less restrained and checked. While most managers will no doubt seek to act responsibly, they can pursue strategies that are risky. Moreover, some managements may lack competence, thus producing poor decisions. Therefore, the higher the proportion of executive board members, the higher the risk of corporate performance—that is, the more its performance fluctuates over time.

Clearly, the risk reduction effect of non-executives on the board is positive on the downside in preventing bankruptcy and negative on the upside in preventing very high performance. Moreover, it has the effects identified by organizational portfolio theory. Namely, by reducing the probability of low performance, the non-executive directors tend to prevent needed adaptation from occurring. Also, by preventing high performance, the rate of growth is kept at a more moderate level.

The risk reduction effect of non-executive directors is contrary to the basic axiom of finance theory, which holds that corporations should take risks in order to maximize their returns to shareholders, who can reduce their personal risk through holding a personal portfolio of investments in risky corporations (Brealey and Myers 1996). Thus it is suboptimal from the viewpoint of the investor. Nevertheless, the risk reduction effect of non-executive directors is likely to be increasing over time. The modern trend is for directors to be held strongly accountable to the outside shareholders for any downside performance of the corporation, with strong public criticism and the threat of legal action for failure in their fiduciary responsibility (Davis and Thompson 1994). This is a pressure on non-executive directors to become more risk averse and also to be more activist so that they, in turn, pressure management to take less risk.

The propositions thus are the following:

7.10   The higher the proportion of non-executive directors, the lower the corporate risk.

7.11   A non-executive board chairperson leads to lower corporate risk.

The greater risk from boards composed predominantly of executives leads to more episodes of low performance that lead to the proportion of executives being reduced. Thus, although diversification, divisionalization, and other factors that reduce risk cause a period in which many corporate boards gained executives as directors and chair, this, in turn, raised risk. The enhanced risk from the executive-oriented boards leads to some poorly performing corporations that install more independent boards (i.e., non-executives replace the executive directors and chair). The new board, independent of management with a high proportion of non-executives, leads to the risk reduction that works to prevent episodes of high performance and so tends to prevent a less independent board from being installed. In this way, the higher risk from executives tends to keep them off an independent board, and the risk reduction from non-executives helps keep them on the board. Thus the risk reduction from non-executive directors works toward prolonging the period of board independence from management and shortening the periods of the managerially dependent board. The actual duration of the independent board, of course, is the result of all the internal and external factors discussed herein.

Debt Leads to Non-Executive Directors

Agency theorists have pointed out another discipline on management, additional to the board of directors, that reduces the magnitude of agency loss. This is debt. According to agency theory, a large free cash flow in a corporation allows its managers to squander the wealth of the outside owners through costly acts such as diversification, perquisites, or research and development that destroy shareholder value (Jensen 1986). Debt needs to be serviced, and this means that much of the corporate cash flow is already assigned to make interest payments to borrowers, thus reducing the amount of cash flow that is free to be squandered by managers, according to agency theory. Thus replacing equity by debt reduces agency problems (Jensen 1986). Within the agency theory framework, by providing an alternative discipline on management, debt might reduce the need for the board to be independent of management.

Organizational portfolio theory identifies another effect of debt that affects corporate governance by affecting board structure. As was argued in Chapter 6, debt increases the likelihood of the organization experiencing poor performance and thus of adapting. As part of the organizational adaptation this triggers, shareholders may press for the board to become more independent of management. The poor performance reduces the credibility and perceived trustworthiness of the management, leading to the replacement on the board of executives by non-executives. Thus debt increases the non-executive directors and the likelihood of a non-executive board chair.

In this way, debt works the opposite to diversification and divisionalization, which both reduce risk and so increase executive directors. Whereas
diversification and divisionalization stabilize corporate performance, debt
destabilizes it and so leads toward a more non-executive board. Thus if debt
comes after diversification and divisionalization in time, it tends to reverse to
a degree their effects on board composition.

The propositions thus are the following:

7.12   Debt increases the proportion of non-executive directors.

7.13   Debt increases the probability of a non-executive chair of the
board.

Divestment Leads to Executive Directors

As was argued in Chapter 6, divestment provides new liquid financial resources
for the corporation that increase its organizational slack. This works to keep
corporate performance above the satisficing level so that crises of poor performance are avoided. In particular, the share price of the corporation is likely to
rise considerably above the market average so that shareholders view performance as satisfactory. For example, General Dynamics divested many of its
divisions, which led to a tripling of its share value during the years 1992–1993
(Murphy and Dial 1994). The resulting satisfactory corporate performance
leads to more confidence in the executives so that they are allowed to take more
directorships and act as board chair in place of non-executives. For a corporation that divests one division after another over a period of years, it will have
sustained satisfactory performance so that executives can become well en-
trenched on the board. Hence divestment is a factor that works to increase the
representation of executives on the board instead of non-executives.

Divestment joins with diversification and divisionalization in tending to
increase the executives on the board by keeping corporate performance satisfactory. As was noted in Chapter 6, diversified, divisionalized corporations are
well placed to make divestments in response to downward turns in their
performance. Therefore, divestment will often come after diversification and
divisionalization in time and reinforce their effect of increasing executives on
the board.

The propositions thus are the following:

7.14   Divestment increases the proportion of executive directors.

7.15   Divestment increases the probability of an executive chair of the board.

As stated above, diversification and divisionalization may also lead to increasing debt before divestment. In such cases, diversification and divisionalization tend to increase the executive directors on the board, debt tends to reduce them, and then divestment tends to increase them again.

Conclusions

Corporate governance has been a strange phenomenon in that boards of many companies have long been structured in ways that contravene theoretical and normative definitions of effective structures. In boards of many large corporations, an executive chairs the board and executives (or their affiliates) dominate the remaining directorships. Thus the role of the board, to provide an independent monitor and sanctioner of management, has been compromised. However, organizational portfolio theory helps resolve this apparent puzzle.

Board structures have been driven by the level of organizational performance. When organizational performance has been high, boards dependent on management have resulted. When organizational performance has been low, independent boards have resulted. Thus changes in board structures have been affected by changes in organizational performance. As is typical in organizational portfolio theory, the performance of the organization is analyzed in terms of internal and external causes of organizational performance. The internal causes refer to diversification, divisionalization, debt, and divestment. The external causes refer to the cycles in the economy and competition. Using this framework, it is possible to understand why corporate governance has moved through three periods: boards dependent on management, then more independent boards, and then more dependent boards again.

The diversification and divisionalization of the large corporation lowered its risk and thus led to stable performance of an acceptable level. This allowed the board dependent on management to become established in many large corporations. The increasing use of debt undermined this stability to a degree, but performance remained acceptable in many large corporations, and so dependent boards were maintained. However, this pattern was disturbed by downward shifts in economic cycles. The ensuing low corporate performance produced a movement to reform corporate boards. Thus boards in many large corporations became somewhat more independent. Then the cycles in the economy moved upward, producing economic expansion and booming stock markets that led to restored corporate fortunes. This led to some corporations reverting to more dependent boards. When their performance declines again, some diversified, divisionalized corporations divest divisions, boosting performance, and so maintaining or increasing the executives on the board.

Empirical evidence to date suggests that board structure has almost no general effect on the mean level of organizational performance, but it may have an effect on organizational risk (i.e., the fluctuation in performance). Non-executive directors and non-executive board chairpersons reduce risk, which works to prevent adaptive change and reduce growth. In contrast, executives tend to increase risk, leading to greater fluctuations in organizational performance that foster adaptation and growth. However, the effect of non-executive directors also feeds back to avoid the high performance that leads to their replacement by executive directors. Thus boards independent of management are somewhat more likely to remain so, whereas executives tend to produce the performance fluctuations that lead to their replacement, thereby working to shorten the periods in which the board is executive dominated.

Sense may be made of corporate governance by looking beneath the surface, which excites so much adverse commentary, to the underlying causes in the organizational portfolio.

This chapter completes our analysis of the corporate level, that is, the overall organization. However, we can also apply organizational portfolio theory to analyze parts of the corporation, such as the divisions of a corporation, to explain changes in the parts and their implications for the overall organization.

Divisional Performance and Change

In previous chapters, we discussed the effect of corporate performance on the corporation as a whole. However, a corporation can be considered to be composed of several different parts, such as its divisions. We now need to discuss the relationship between overall organizational performance and the performances of these parts. In particular, we need to analyze change of a division as driven by the performance of that division and also by performance of the corporation. Corporate performance is, in turn, affected by divisional performance; thus we need also to analyze change in a division as affected by other divisions. It also is likely that focusing on the divisions could lead to the neglect of corporate-level adaptation. These issues are examined in this chapter.

We have argued that organizational change is affected by the performance of the whole organization. The performance of the corporation is, in turn, determined by the performance of its parts (e.g., each of its divisions). What then is occurring at the level of the parts when the corporate performance becomes low? Obviously, the performance of some or all of the parts themselves must be low, but what more exactly is occurring?

Because organizational performance is the sum of the performances of its parts, several of those parts will need to be suffering poor performance before adaptive change occurs. For overall organizational performance to be restored, adaptive changes must be made to most of these parts. This means that adaptive changes in an organization will often occur at about the same time. This heightens the difficulty, drama, and vulnerability of the change period.

Organizational Change From the Additive Effects of Divisions

In the organizational portfolio, the performance of each part independently affects organizational performance. A major case is the different divisions of a multidivisional corporation. Most large corporations are multidivisional structures (Channon 1973; Rumelt 1974; Dyas and Thanheiser 1976). These divisions operate independently in a corporation that has unrelated products or services (Rumelt 1974). Interdependence between divisions reduces their independence, and this condition exists most acutely in the vertically integrated form of multidivisional structure; however, this composes a minority of corporations (Channon 1973; Rumelt 1974; Dyas and Thanheiser 1976). Many corporations have related products or services and so some degree of operational interdependence exists between their divisions; however, this may often be minor. Thus the divisions in a multidivisional structure can typically be considered independent and additive in their effects on overall corporate performance. How does this additive property affect organizational change? This chapter considers the significance of the additive property first on the change of divisions and then on the change at the corporate level.

Change in a division is affected by its performance. In a multidivisional structure, the corporate level monitors divisional performance and sanctions divisional management to produce satisfactory profitability (Williamson 1970; though see Hoskisson, Hill, and Kim 1993). Divisions that are performing poorly will be subject to corrective action. Such corrective action may be initiated either within the division by its management or at the corporate level through its intervening in divisional affairs. Although such rectifying moves will not always be successful, some will. The low-performing divisions will experience adaptive organizational change. The result is some tendency for the poorest-performing divisions to have their performance rise over time to bring them more into line with the other divisions.

The proposition thus is the following:

8.1   The probability of making needed divisional adaptations is greater in low-performing divisions.

Insofar as divisional performance below the divisional satisficing level triggers adaptive change, poor divisional performance will readily spur its rectification by divisional or corporate management. Moreover, the negative correlations between performances of divisions that arise from diversification and divisionalization lead to the poor performances of divisions being separated from each other in time, making attending to poor-performing divisions an easier task for corporate management. This reassuring view, however, needs to be qualified by other considerations of organizational portfolio theory. The probability that a low-performing division is rectified is affected not only by divisional performance but also by corporate performance.

Low Corporate Performance Increases
Probability of Divisional Change

The theory of Simon (1976), that adaptation is problemistic, necessarily implies that the disciplining effect of the corporate center on the divisions in the multidivisional structure is contingent upon corporate performance. The corporate center has the responsibility for supervising the divisions and has the authority to so do; therefore, it may intervene in low-performing divisions even if overall corporate performance is above the satisficing level. However, when corporate performance is satisfactory, the corporation is less impelled to make adaptive change in maladapted divisions. It is only when corporate performance is poor (i.e., subsatisficing) that the corporate center has an imperative to intervene in poorly performing divisions to try to raise their performance level. Similarly, when corporate performance is above the satisficing level, the corporate center may tolerate lower divisional performance before intervening.

The propositions thus are the following:

8.2   Intervention by the corporate center to raise low performance in a division is more probable when corporate performance is subsatisficing.

8.3   Intervention by the corporate center to raise low performance in a division occurs at lower levels of divisional performance when corporate performance is at, or above, the satisficing level.

As seen in Chapter 6, the diversified, divisionalized corporation tends to have lower risk. Hence, its overall performance tends to remain at least satisfactory, and so there is often little impetus for the corporate center to intervene in low-performing divisions. The more diversified and divisionalized (i.e., decentralized) the corporation, the lower its risk and therefore the less its impetus to intervene in a low-performing division.

The proposition thus is the following:

> 8.4   The more diversified and divisionalized the corporation, the less likely it is to intervene in a low-performing division.

Low Divisional Performances
Cause Low Corporate Performance

Corporate performance is, in turn, affected by the performances of the divisions. More specifically, corporate performance is the sum of the performances of its divisions. If a corporation consists of two divisions and the profit of the first division is $3 million and the profit of the second is $5 million, then the profit of the corporation is $8 million (ignoring the costs of the head office). Thus the effect of the performances of divisions on the performance of the corporation is additive. The performance of each division adds to the performance of the corporation separately. Therefore, if one division has low performance, the other divisions can have any level of performance from low to high. Low performance of one division can be compensated for by higher performance of other divisions, that is, the portfolio effect. Even if one division is performing very poorly, this could still lead to satisfactory corporate performance if the performances of the other divisions are medium or high. For example, if the satisficing level of profit for the corporation is $8 million but one of its two divisions makes nil profit, the other division can completely compensate for it by making a profit of $8 million.

The proposition thus is the following:

> 8.5   Independent parts (e.g., divisions) have additive effects on organizational performance and so form an organizational portfolio.

Divisions vary in their size and thus in their contribution to overall corporate profit. One division could be much larger than the other divisions and so its potential effect on corporate profit could equal that of the other divisions combined. If the large division had high profit, overall corporate profitability could be satisfactory even if the smaller divisions each had low profit. This might be the case for a corporation with only limited diversification, when its core business remains large relative to the other divisions that constitute the diversification (i.e., a single business or dominant corporation in the operational definitions of Rumelt 1974). However, this is a special case, with the more usual situation being one in which the divisions are more equal in size. For most multidivisional corporations, their degree of diversification is more substantial, being a related or unrelated corporation in the terms of Rumelt (1974). Therefore, there is no one dominating division, and the corporation is composed of several divisions of approximately equal size and, more important, equal profitability.

Low Performances of Other Divisions Are a Cause of Divisional Change

Assuming divisions of approximately equal performance, if the performance of a multidivisional corporation becomes poor, the performance of the average division must also be poor. Some divisions may decline in their performance more than others, and one or two divisions may even rise in performance, but only simultaneous decline in performance of most of the divisions will produce decline in organizational performance. Thus, for corporate performance to be poor, the performances of some substantial proportion of its divisions must be poor simultaneously. The more divisions in the corporation, the larger the number of them that typically must be poor performers for corporate performance to be poor. The exception is when one division has such very poor performance that it renders corporate performance poor despite good performance from other divisions. As we have seen, this is possible but less probable for a highly diversified corporation composed of divisions of approximately equal profits.

Usually in a highly diversified corporation, for corporate performance to be subsatisficing, the performances of several of its divisions must also be subsatisficing. The underlying assumptions are that the corporation contains considerably more than several divisions and that their performances are fairly equal. It also assumes that the satisficing level for the corporation and for the average of its divisions are about the same. This seems reasonable because the corporation sets the satisficing level for each of the divisions. No rational corporate office would set satisficing levels for its divisions that in aggregate failed to meet the corporate satisficing level. However, a corporate office could set satisficing levels for its divisions that are greater than those for the corporation. The point remains that for corporate performance to be subsatisficing, a substantial proportion of divisions must also be subsatisficing in their performance.

The propositions thus are the following:

8.6 When corporate performance becomes subsatisficing, the probability is that more than one division will be performing at the subsatisficing level simultaneously.

8.7 The more divisions in the corporation and the more equal their profits, the higher the probability that more divisions will be performing at the subsatisficing level simultaneously when corporate performance becomes subsatisficing.

If, however, corporate performance is so low that it drops below the satisficing level, this means that the performance of the average division is also below that satisficing level. Thus, adaptive change of divisions by corporate management is triggered only when there is poor performance among several divisions, yet the probability of adaptive change in a division is affected by the performance of the other divisions. Change in one poorly performing division will be associated with change in other poorly performing divisions. Hence, changes at the divisional level tend to occur together when several divisions are performing poorly simultaneously. At other times, however, poorly performing divisions will be left alone because corporate performance is at or above the satisficing level.

Given the increasingly negative correlation between the performances of the divisions as the corporation diversifies and divisionalizes, the occurrence of simultaneous subsatisficing performances by the divisions is a rare event (this is consistent with the earlier argument that the portfolio properties of diversified, divisionalized corporations lower their risk). Thus most organizations go through periods of calm with no divisional change, interspersed by periods of crisis during which several divisions must be changed.

The proposition thus is the following:

8.8   Changes in divisions to rectify low performance tend to occur at around the same time period.

However, when it occurs, such rectification will be difficult and hazardous. Having several divisions performing poorly simultaneously implies that corporate management face the task of turning around performance not just in one or two divisions but in several divisions at the same time. This will be difficult given the limited attention and problem-solving capacities of management, that is, the bounded rationality of corporate management. Given the multiplicity of demands upon corporate management, it is likely to attend sequentially—that is, deal with some divisions immediately, leaving other divisions until later, by which time their performance may have further declined. Thus rectification of poor corporate performance caused by several divisions performing poorly simultaneously will take some time. The multiplicity of tasks confronting management gives the problems an added sense of drama and crisis. The difficulty and lengthy time of the task make its resolution more problematic. If management is not able to rectify the performances of enough divisions soon enough and some of them worsen sufficiently, overall corporate performance may decline into bankruptcy. Anticipation of this possibility fuels the sense of corporate crisis when the performances of several divisions become poor simultaneously.

The proposition thus is the following:

8.9   The more divisions that are performing poorly, the higher the probability that corporate intervention into the divisions is sequential rather than simultaneous.

As seen above, poor corporate performance occurs when the average divisional performance is poor, meaning that several divisions have low performance simultaneously. However, to return to satisfactory performance the organization has only to restore performance in some of these divisions. This is obviously an easier task than resolving all the problems and can be effectuated more quickly than would be possible if all divisions had to be turned around. Thus interventions by corporate management into divisions to improve their performance tend to cease or become less intense once the satisficing level of corporate performance has been regained and therefore may cease before all poorly performing divisions have been improved.

The proposition thus is the following:

> 8.10 Corporate interventions in divisional performance tend to cease once the corporation regains its satisficing level of performance.

Divestment Avoids Change in Remaining Divisions

Thus far we have discussed the interventions by corporate management in poorly performing divisions. However, another response is to get rid of the division, usually by divestment (i.e., sale) or less usually by disbanding it. Either way the division exits from the portfolio. However, there is also an effect on the remaining portfolio. If the lowest-performing division leaves the corporation, the overall corporate performance rises—that is, the average profit of the remaining divisions is higher because it is no longer being dragged down by the lowest-performing division. Moreover, if the poorest-performing division is sold, the resulting cash increases the wealth of the corporation. Thus divestment of the lowest-performing division raises corporate profits and wealth, thereby moving its performance up to the satisficing level and so removing the imperative for the corporation to make adaptive changes. Hence, divestment of the lowest-performing division tends to stop interventions by corporate management into the remaining divisions, even into those performing poorly. The worse the performance of the divested division, the greater the profit improvement in the corporation and so the more likely that corporate management will stop intervening in the remaining divisions. Similarly, the greater the number of divisions that are divested, the better the wealth improvement in the corporation and so the more likely that corporate management will stop intervening in the remaining divisions.

The propositions thus are the following:

> 8.11 The poorer the performance of a divested division, the higher the probability that interventions by the corporate office in other poorly performing divisions will cease or be forestalled.

8.12 The more divisions that are divested, the higher the probability that interventions by the corporate office in other poorly performing divisions will cease or be forestalled.

As we have just argued, some poorly performing divisions may be rectified in a multidivisional corporation, but what if the problem is caused at the corporate level?

Corporate-Level Maladaptation
May Be Misattributed to Divisions

We have discussed how poor divisional performance may be dealt with, but what if the origin of the problem lies higher up the hierarchy—namely, deficiencies at the corporate level? How will needed changes there be brought about?

Change at the corporate level is caused, we have argued, by poor performance of the corporation overall. But this condition corresponds to poor average performance of the divisions that constitute the corporation, for corporate performance is nothing but the sum of the performances of its divisions. Thus poor corporate performance could be perceived as originating at either the corporate or the divisional level. Which level is seen to be the problem by corporate management: the corporate or the divisional? In consequence, does the corporation react to poor corporate performance in terms of changes at the corporate level or at the divisional level?

A number of psychological mechanisms encourage the perception by corporate management that the problem is caused by the division(s) rather than the corporate level. One such mechanism is the attributional bias that tends to lead humans to focus on more tangible factors, such as that the division that is making product A is faring worse than the division that is making product B—in other words, the focus is on the product. A related attributional bias is toward people, such that the focus is on the person managing the division. A second type of perceptual mechanism is problemistic search (Simon 1976), whereby the solutions to problems are sought close to the problems rather than more distantly, so that when the divisions have performance problems the solutions are sought in the divisions. A third type of perceptual mechanism is ego defense, in that blame is attributed to divisional managers rather than corporate managers questioning their own actions. The greater power of corporate managers makes it difficult for division managers to shift the attribution of causality to the corporate level. The combined effect of these perceptual mechanisms is that corporate managers are liable to focus on divisional performance when corporate performance is subsatisficing. Even if the corporate managers do not completely fixate on the division, their attention may still be somewhat distracted away from the corporate level.

Hence, corporate managers may fail to recognize that subsatisficing corporate performance has its origins in maladapted corporate arrangements, such as misfitting corporate organizational structure or corporate strategy or corporate management. Therefore, even in conditions of subsatisficing corporate performance, corporate management may fail to make needed corporate-level adaptive changes.

The proposition thus is the following:

8.13   Poor corporate performance caused by maladaptation at the corporate level tends to be misattributed to the divisions.

As we have said, corporate-level management may attend to the problem divisions sequentially so that its task becomes tractable. However, this means that corporate-level management is so absorbed in trying to change one division after another that it may be deflected from examining corporate arrangements for a long time. Moreover, as soon as organizational performance becomes satisfactory again, the theory of satisficing suggests that serious efforts to make adaptive changes will largely cease. Hence, corporate-level management may not inquire into deficiencies at its own level, and so these may go unresolved. The crisis of low corporate performance may be at an end, but a maladapted corporate-level structure may still exist. This provides a further way in which maladaptation at the corporate level can continue for a long period. Thus organizational performance may remain less than optimal.

Moreover, time may need to elapse and performance to decline further before adaptive corporate-level changes are made. This increases the chance that poor corporate performance may decline further into acute financial disaster (e.g., insolvency).

The propositions thus are the following:

8.14   Misattribution of corporate problems to the divisions tends to prevent corporate adaptation.

8.15 Misattribution of corporate problems to the divisions increases the probability of financial disaster for the corporation.

At the point when chronic, low corporate performance becomes acute, corporate management at last may see that the widespread failings in divisional performances have their common origins in a maladapted corporate structure. In such cases, corporate management will recognize that many of their divisions are performing poorly, not because the divisions and their managers are the problem but, rather, because they are the subordinates of a defective corporate-level structure or management. At this point, the depth of the performance crisis makes the organization vulnerable to failure. The key issue is whether corporate management can act quickly enough to rectify the corporate structural deficiencies that have been causing poor corporate performance. In this way, the organization may escape failure or external intervention (e.g., merger) and restore its performance to above the satisficing level.

The key here is that because corporate performance is necessarily the aggregate of the divisional performances, poor corporate performance must always be accompanied by poor performance across some of the divisions, thereby inviting the perception that the divisions are the root cause when actually their poor performances may be the product of corporate-level failings.

Seeing the way that the corporate performance is a portfolio constituted by the addition of the performances of its divisions adds depth to our appreciation of some of the dynamics that stem from poor corporate performance. This in turn leads to understanding why even subsatisficing corporate performance may often lead to the needed divisional and corporate-level adaptation only after substantial delay and further performance decline.

Conclusions

In the organizational portfolio, its parts, such as its divisions, each have an effect on organizational performance independently of the other parts (e.g., divisions). Organizational performance is the additive sum of the parts. Several of those parts need to suffer poor performance before adaptive change occurs. This means that adaptive changes in different parts of an organization will often occur somewhat close together in time. This heightens the stress and precariousness of the change period for the managers of the organization.

Applied to the divisions in a multidivisional firm, changes needed to rectify poorly performing divisions are more likely to be made when the overall corporate performance is low, that is, when several divisions are performing poorly. The risk reduction inherent in the diversified–divisionalized corporation tends to make such episodes of change rare. Nevertheless, when they do occur, the change process is liable to occur under conditions of corporate crisis. Changes in poorly performing divisions tend to occur around the same time period. However, the multiplicity of poorly performing divisions will absorb managerial attention over a lengthy time, so that delays in making divisional-level changes tend to occur. More important, there may be some tendency for the corporate management to respond to poor corporate performance in ways that fixate on the divisions and so fail to make needed adaptive change at the corporate level. Delays in making changes at the divisional and corporate levels increase the probability of the financial crisis becoming more acute. These ideas follow from treating the organization as a portfolio in which corporate performance is the additive sum of divisional performances.

This chapter considered the issue of disaggregating organizational performance into its parts that compose the portfolio, especially the divisions. The discussion concentrated mainly on divisional change as affected by the performance of not only one division but also other divisions. The focus was on the level of performance of the divisions and of the corporation. However, we need also to consider the fluctuation in performance, that is, the risk, of divisions and its effects upon changes in divisions and the corporation. This is the focus of Chapter 9.

Divisional Risk

In this chapter, we take further the analysis of the divisions that make up the corporation. Again, we are interested in their performances, their consequent propensity to make needed adaptive changes, and their resulting degree of organizational adaptation. Once more, we use the new perspective of the organization as a portfolio. We commence our discussion by developing the concepts of systematic risk and unsystematic risk as applied within an organization. Then we turn to a consideration of differences between divisions in their positions in their industries.

In previous chapters, we argued that a low-risk *corporation* tends eventually to become suboptimal in its performance. In this chapter, we argue that a low-risk *division* tends to becomes suboptimal in its performance. Thus once again, the seemingly attractive property of low risk contains a hidden disadvantage. This also indicates some generality to the idea that low risk produces suboptimal performance, in that it applies at both the corporate and the divisional levels.

Once again, the discussion focuses on the diversified, divisionalized corporation in which further disadvantages are revealed. More specifically, low-risk divisions within the diversified, divisionalized corporation are shown to become suboptimal and thus directly depress corporate performance. Moreover, these low-risk divisions also indirectly depress corporate performance through reducing corporate risk. Hence the analysis in this chapter uncovers further mechanisms that work to reduce the performance of the diversified, divisionalized corporation over time.

Risk Within the Corporation

In Chapter 6, we discussed risk in terms of the correlation between the profits of the divisions in a corporation (i.e., between the parts of the corporation). But we can also analyze risk in terms of the relationship between each division's performance and corporate performance (i.e., part and whole). The concept of systematic risk provides a framework for such an analysis.

Finance theory holds that the risk of a company can be differentiated into two parts: systematic and unsystematic (Sharpe 1970; Brealey and Myers 1996). Systematic risk refers to the variance of the company's share price that reflects the variance in the underlying share market, that is, in the wider causal system. Hence systematic risk is the variance in company performance that is associated with the variance in performance of the other companies in the market. Unsystematic risk is the variance that arises from that company itself, from factors idiosyncratic to it and not due to the market. Unsystematic risk is unassociated with the variance in performance of the other companies in the market. In finance theory, the systematic risk of each company, that is, of its stock, is assessed so that the stocks of different companies can be combined into optimal investment portfolios. The question here is to apply these concepts to better understand the composition and dynamics of the organization as a portfolio. This will be furthered by treating each division in a corporation as the unit of analysis.

The risk of any division can be thought of as composed of two components that are analogous to the concepts of systematic and unsystematic risk at the corporate level in finance theory: systematic divisional risk and unsystematic divisional risk.

Systematic Divisional Risk

The first component of divisional risk is the systematic divisional risk. This is variance in divisional performance that correlates with the total organizational performance. The higher the correlation between divisional performance and corporate performance, the more similar their risk. This also means that the fluctuations in performance levels of the division and the corporation are synchronized. When divisional performance is low, corporate performance is also low, so the division may mirror the corporation in terms of the cycle of maladaptation, subsatisficing, and adaption. The mirroring is in terms of timing rather than the content of adaptation, which will differ between corporate and divisional levels. However, performance similarities often will not cause adaptation at both the divisional and corporate levels because of the difficulties referred to in Chapter 8. The higher and more positive the correlation between corporate performance and the performance of a division, the more the division's problem may reside in problems at the corporate level, and yet the corporate level may resist such a diagnosis.

When the correlation between corporate performance and divisional performance is zero, then any problems at corporate and divisional levels are independent and are from different underlying causes. If the correlation between corporate performance and divisional performance is negative, the effect of the division is to suppress variation in performance at the corporate level, and thus it contributes to the stability and lowers the risk of the corporation.

The Degree of Systematic Risk of a Division

Finance researchers often assess the degree of systematic risk of a stock by the beta coefficient (Brealey and Myers 1996). This is the standardized coefficient of the slope of the regression line of the price of the stock of the company on the price of the stock of the companies in the stock market. A beta of 1 says that the volatility of the company's stock price is the same as the market, meaning that when the company's stock price is high, the market is also high. A beta of less than 1 says that the company is less volatile and more stable than the market. A beta of more than 1 says that the company is more volatile and less stable than the market. This mode of analysis can be applied to divisions within the corporation.

Divisional Beta

We can apply the idea of the beta coefficient inside the corporation to measure the systematic risk of each division relative to the corporation. To avoid confusion with the established use of the word *beta* in finance, we call the coefficient here the *divisional beta* to make clear that it measures divisional risk. The divisional beta is defined as *the standardized slope coefficient of the profit of a division regressed on the profit of the corporation.* Thus the divisional beta measures the volatility of the divisional profit over time relative to the fluctuations in corporate profit over the same period and makes the analysis of variations in systematic divisional risk more specific. A divisional beta of 1 says that the volatility of the divisional profit is the same as the corporation, meaning that the divisional profit over time fluctuates up and down as much as the corporate profit (see Figure 9.1). A divisional beta of less than 1 says that the divisional profit is less volatile and more stable than the corporate profit. A divisional beta of more than 1 says that the divisional profit is more volatile and less stable than the corporate profit. These differences in the divisional beta lead to differences in the relationship between the management of the division and the management of the corporation.

Divisional beta coefficients that are positive signify that the correlations between the performances of the division and the corporation are positive. Therefore, in discussing variations in divisional beta coefficients greater than zero, we are discussing divisions whose performances correlate positively with the performance of the corporation.

Unsystematic Divisional Risk

The unsystematic risk of a division is the variation in the performance of a division that is uncorrelated with the performance of the corporation. Such unsystematic divisional risk contributes to the heterogeneity of performance between divisions. It also contributes to the propensity for subsatisficing divisional performance to occur and so for divisional adaptation. This divisional adaptation will be unconnected with adaptation in most other divisions or at the corporate level because the poor performance of the focal division is unconnected with the performances of most other divisions and the corporation. Thus the higher the level of unsystematic divisional risk in a corporation, the greater will be the divisional adaptation that is unsynchronized across divisions and unsynchronized with corporate adaptation.

The performances of divisions that are high in unsystematic risk will be different from those of divisions that are high in systematic risk. High-systematic-risk divisions' performances fluctuate together in harmony with the corporation in general, whereas high-unsystematic-risk divisions' perfor-

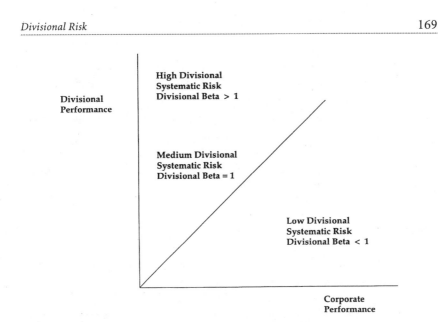

Figure 9.1 Divisional Systematic Risk: The Divisional Beta

mances may be low when the rest of the corporation is enjoying high performance, and so they will stand out. Hence the division that is high on unsystematic risk is likely to attract the attention of corporate-level management. This could be for no good reason, in that the low performance of the division may reflect inherent factors such as low performance of its industry, relative to the industries in which the corporation's other divisions are located. Nevertheless, this could distract corporate-level management from more serious matters, such as the corporate-level structure being maladapted.

Divisional systematic risk lends itself to more predictions than unsystematic risk and so is the focus of our analysis of the differences across divisions in the level of their systematic risk.

Variations in Systematic Divisional Risk

In the following discussion, it is assumed that the division being discussed contributes only a fraction of overall corporate performance. This implies that the other divisions composing the corporation have a substantial effect upon the profitability of the corporation. Thus corporate profit can, to a considerable degree, vary independently of the profit of the division. Of course, corporate profit is never completely independent of the division because some part of its profit comes from the division. In the absence of partial independence between corporate profit and the profit of the division, corporate and divisional profit become the same variable and so are completely correlated. Thus the assumption is required to allow the analysis to proceed and also helps make it less artificial and more realistic, in that most divisionalized corporations have multiple divisions with no one division completely dominating corporate profitability (Palmer et al., 1987).

Division With Low Systematic Risk

When the systematic risk of the division is low, that is, the divisional beta is less than 1, the divisional performance fluctuates less than the corporate profit. This is to say that the profit of the division fluctuates less than that of the average profits of the divisions that make up the corporation (assuming the performances of divisions are roughly similar in magnitude). Thus the profit performance of the division will be more stable than that of the corporation as a whole.

Often, divisional performance is stable and moderate. Corporate-level management thus tends to see the performance of a division that is stable as providing stability to corporate profits across the years. Thus this division is a sort of anchor for the corporation as a whole. This may predispose the corporate level to treat this division with benign neglect. The division is no problem for corporate-level management, which tends to leave the division alone. However, the lack of fluctuation in profit performance of this division means that there tend to be few episodes of poor performance that would trigger divisional adaptation. Yet the prolonged years of moderate performance tend to eventually produce growth of the division that leads it into misfit. Thus the low-risk division may frequently drift into misfit, making its performance suboptimal. This will feed back to prevent high-performance episodes and so keep its risk low. Thus the low-risk division tends toward pathological stability.

The propositions thus are the following:

9.1   A division of low systematic risk (i.e., divisional beta of less than 1) tends to gradually increase in maladaptation over time.

9.2   A division of low systematic risk (i.e., divisional beta of less than 1) tends to become mediocre in long-term performance.

The low performance variance of the division leads toward the same malaise that was identified for the diversified, divisionalized corporation as a whole. The low-risk division is the division-level parallel of the corporate-level phenomenon of pathological stability.

Division With Medium Systematic Risk

When the risk of the division is medium, that is, the divisional beta is 1, the divisional performance fluctuates to the same extent as the corporate profit. This means that the profit of the division fluctuates in proportion to the profit of the corporation. Therefore, the profit of the division fluctuates similarly to the average profit of the other divisions. Thus the fluctuations in the profit performance of the division will be typical for the corporation as a whole. Corporate-level management will therefore see that division as being normal and unexceptional.

When the profit level of the division is low, so too will the profit of the corporation be low. This could signal the need for change in the division; however, other divisions will be in the same position of low performance. Most of the divisions in the company will be low performers (assuming divisions of about equal performances), and so they are also candidates for inspection and change by their managements and also by corporate management. Therefore, corporate management may rectify performance in some of the other divisions before turning to the division with medium risk. Rectifying the performance of other divisions may be sufficient to restore corporate profitability to the satisficing level, and so the corporate center may not intervene in the medium-risk division, which means it may continue maladapted and performing poorly. Thus adaptive change may occur for the medium risk-division but sometimes be delayed considerably.

The proposition thus is the following:

9.3 A division of medium systematic risk (i.e., divisional beta of 1) has a medium probability that when maladapted it will remain so.

Moreover, because corporate performance is low when the performance of the medium-risk division is low, this may mean that at the corporate level there is maladaptation needing change. However, as was argued in Chapter 8, there is a tendency for problems to be interpreted as lying within the divisions rather than at the corporate level, so change efforts may be more concentrated at the divisional than corporate levels.

For a corporation composed of divisions all with divisional betas of 1, poor corporate performance occurs when all its divisions are performing poorly, so the corporate center is prone to attribute the problem to the divisions rather than to the corporate level, so leading to prolonged maladaptation of the corporate center when it is the problem. The more divisions in a corporation that have medium risk, the more likely that problems of the corporate center will be misattributed to the divisions.

The proposition thus is the following:

> 9.4 A division of medium systematic risk (i.e., divisional beta of 1) increases the probability that maladaptation at the corporate level will be misattributed to the division, thus delaying corporate adaptation.

Division With High Systematic Risk

When the risk of a division is high, that is, the divisional beta is more than 1, the divisional performance fluctuates more than the corporate profit. This is to say that the profit of the division fluctuates more than that of the average profits of the divisions that make up the corporation (assuming the performances of divisions are roughly similar in magnitude). Thus the profit performance of the division will be more volatile than that of the corporation as a whole. This will make its annual performance quite extreme for its own divisional management and the corporate-level management. Therefore, much attention may focus on this division. Its sharply fluctuating performance and frequent internal change are likely to command the attention of corporate-level management. Their interventions when divisional performance sinks low reinforce the impetus for divisional management to make adaptive change and restore performance. The periodic episodes of high performance boost growth and so forth so that misfit is created. However, the periodic, intervening episodes of low performance will trigger divisional adaptation to attain the required new fit. Thus there will be much ongoing change, with increases in divisional size alternating with increases in its structure.

Thus, in the high-systematic-risk division, increases in contingencies, such as size, are followed by increases in structure within a relatively short time period. Similar remarks apply to adaptations in other aspects of the division, such as its technology, human resources, and so on. This change process is repeated from one cycle to another. The alternating periods of fit and misfit increase and then decrease divisional performance, thus feeding back to keep the systematic divisional risk high. In this way, the division will grow and adapt so that it is maximizing its performance over the long run. Thus this division has the attractive property of being the one of the three levels of systematic risk (low, medium, and high) that is delivering the most increase in performance over time.

The propositions thus are the following:

9.5 The probability of making needed divisional adaptations is greater in divisions of high systematic risk (i.e., divisional beta of more than 1).

9.6 A division of high systematic risk (i.e., divisional beta of more than 1) tends to have sustained growth.

9.7 A division of high systematic risk (i.e., divisional beta of more than 1) tends to have long-term high performance.

The Effects of Unsystematic Divisional Risk

Thus far we have discussed the effect of systematic divisional risk on divisional change. However, unsystematic risk also has an effect, and this needs to be understood to comprehend fully the effects of divisional risk on the division. The full effects of divisional risk on divisional change are due to the interactions between unsystematic and systematic divisional risk. We first identify the effects of unsystematic divisional risk on divisional change and then consider the effects of the interactions between unsystematic and systematic divisional risk.

As stated above, unsystematic risk is variation over time in divisional profit that is uncorrelated with corporate profit. Low unsystematic risk implies that the profit of the division does not fluctuate independently of corporate profit. Thus divisional change will be driven by the profit fluctuations arising from the systematic divisional risk, as identified in the preceding section. Therefore, the situation in which unsystematic divisional risk is low can be ignored because the effect of risk on the division is simply the effect of systematic divisional risk. Unsystematic divisional risk adds most to the effect of systematic divisional risk when unsystematic divisional risk is high, so our focus is on that situation.

Greater unsystematic risk, like any risk, increases profit fluctuations and therefore increases the probability that a division that is maladapted will experience the low profit necessary to trigger its adaptation. Moreover, because unsystematic divisional risk is uncorrelated with corporate profit, low divisional performance often occurs while other divisions have satisfactory performance. The low-performing division will be prominent and command the attention of corporate management so that it is likely to intervene in the division and adaptation is likely to occur. Hence high unsystematic risk increases the probability of divisional adaptation when this is required, avoiding prolonged maladaptation and opening the door to divisional growth. Similarly, when the division is adapted, greater unsystematic risk increases the probability of episodes of high profit that foster higher rates of growth of the division. The fluctuations in profit over time from high unsystematic risk lead to long-term organizational growth and success. This holds regardless of whether the systematic divisional risk is low or high. Unsystematic divisional risk is uncorrelated with systematic divisional risk. Therefore, the effect of unsystematic divisional risk is independent of, and additional to, the effect of systematic divisional risk on divisional adaptation and growth.

The propositions thus are the following:

9.8 In addition to the effects of systematic divisional risk on divisional adaptation, high unsystematic divisional risk increases the probability of a division making needed adaptations.

9.9 In addition to the effects of systematic divisional risk on divisional growth, high unsystematic divisional risk increases the rate of divisional growth.

9.10 In addition to the effects of systematic divisional risk on long-term divisional performance, high unsystematic divisional risk increases long-term divisional performance.

Having analyzed the effects on divisional success of systematic and unsystematic divisional risk, we now discuss the mix of divisions forming the optimal portfolio for the corporation.

The Optimal Portfolio of Divisions

As we have just seen, high-systematic-risk divisions produce sustained divisional growth and adaptation and thus increase divisional profitability over the long term. Therefore, corporate management would do well to have as many of these divisions as possible. The optimal long-term corporate performance results from having all divisions have as high systematic risk as possible.

In specifying the optimal corporation, consideration also has to be given to the correlations among performances of the divisions. The optimal corporate performance would seem to result from having divisions that all have high systematic risk and whose performances are highly, positively correlated with each other. The high systematic divisional risk produces high divisional performance (as seen above). Having divisional performances positively correlated means that the substantial fluctuation of performances of the divisions synchronize to produce substantial fluctuations of corporate performance. Large fluctuations in corporate performance cause it to periodically swing down below the satisficing level so that needed corporate-level adaptations occur, thus leading to further increments of corporate growth. Corporate performance swings over time from high to low and back again, producing recurrent corporate-level adaptations and consequent growth spurts. These incremental corporate changes lead to long-run adaptation and growth for the corporation so that its long-run performance is high. The higher the positive correlation among the performances of the divisions, the more corporate profit mirrors fully the fluctuations in divisional profits, so that corporate incremental growth and adaptation is rapid, producing maximum long-run corporate performance.

A constraint, however, is that if divisional performances are perfectly, positively correlated with each other, the fluctuation in performance of each division corresponds to that of every other division and hence with corporate performance. Thus the divisional beta of all the divisions is 1, that is, medium and not high. Hence there is a limit to how high the divisional beta can be while divisional performances are also highly positively correlated.

For corporate performance to fluctuate maximally, the divisional performances should be perfectly, positively correlated and the divisional betas as high as possible (i.e., divisional beta of 1). Thus optimal corporate adaptation is attained by having a set of perfectly, positively correlated divisions of medium systematic risk. Yet, as seen above, with medium-risk divisions, corporate-level maladaptation is liable to be misattributed to the divisions, thereby avoiding needed corporate-level adaptations. This works to reduce the effectiveness of the portfolio in inducing corporate adaptation. Moreover, with merely medium risk, some of the divisions will remain maladapted (as seen above), and so divisional performance will be less than the maximum. Hence the portfolio of perfectly correlated, medium-risk divisions will not produce the maximum corporate or divisional adaptation and performance. Nevertheless, such a portfolio provides the highest probabilities of corporate adaptation and so provides the optimal long-term success.

The proposition thus is the following:

9.11   Optimal corporate performance results from medium-systematic-risk divisions whose performances are perfectly positively correlated.

We arrive at a corporation beset by volatility in its performance and that of its divisions. This may be thought to be unrealistic as a design for an organization, in that it strains the problem-solving capacity of the managers, especially at the corporate level. Thus management might consider alternative approaches to the issue of what sort of divisions to put together to make up its corporation. The first alternative approach would be to limit divisional volatility by having some divisions with low risk. The second alternative approach would be to limit corporate volatility through the portfolio effect. Each of these two approaches is discussed in turn.

Corporate management might reduce the volatility of the performances of its divisions by having some more stable divisions. This would provide stability in those parts of the corporation and also some stability in overall corporate profits. This means that corporate management would encourage some of its divisions to have low risk. However, such stable divisions, as has been shown above, tend to become chronically maladapted and mediocre, suboptimal performers. Thus the high, long-range performance of the high-systematic-risk divisions would be dragged down by the long-run mediocre performance of the low-systematic-risk divisions so that overall corporate profit was suboptimal.

Nevertheless, because of the bounded rationality problem, corporate management tends to avoid having all high-systematic-risk divisions. Instead, corporate management would opt to have, or allow to develop, some low-systematic-risk divisions in its corporation to make its own task feasible.

The proposition thus is the following:

> **9.12** Due to bounded rationality, corporate management may encourage some divisions to have low systematic risk, but this makes corporate performance suboptimal.

Alternatively, to keep overall volatility manageable, corporate management might be tempted to use a portfolio approach, which involves all its divisions having betas as high as possible (i.e., of more than 1) and being of roughly similar performances. Thus the divisions are those that yield optimal performance over the long run. However, these divisions would also have performances correlating negatively with each other, thereby offsetting each other. Thus even though each division had a volatile performance, the overall corporate performance would be stable. When the performance of one division was poor, reflecting a need for adaptive change, the performance of other divisions would be medium or high. Therefore, corporate management could attend to each division as its performance became poor, which would make the task of corporate management more feasible. However, the stability of overall corporate performance means that despite the poor performance of a division, corporate performance is not poor, and so there is less pressure on corporate management to change the division, which might then remain maladapted or be less than completely adapted, thus impairing its long-run performance.

Moreover, there is also the problem that stable corporate profit levels eliminate episodes of poor corporate performance that are required to trigger changes in corporate-level structure, which are needed as the corporate level becomes maladapted over time through growth and so forth. Thus a portfolio of negatively correlated, high-systematic-risk divisions produces pathological stability for the corporation. The eventual result is a drift into chronic maladaptation of the corporate level, which then interferes with divisional performance, thus leading corporate performance to become mediocre. Thus a portfolio approach to putting together high-risk divisions does not avoid producing suboptimal corporate performance. We see again that the portfolio of negative correlations between divisions leads to the pathological stability of corporate performance for the diversified, divisionalized corporation. The resultant maladaptation at the corporate level eventually reduces corporate growth. Thus the benefits from growth of divisions are limited by the gradually worsening corporate maladaptation over the long run.

Nevertheless, because of the bounded rationality problem, corporate management tends to avoid having the correlations between the performances of all divisions be positive and high. Instead, it opts to have, or allows to develop, some correlations between divisional performances that are low positive or negative so as to make its own task feasible.

The proposition thus is the following:

9.13 Due to bounded rationality, corporate management may encourage the correlations between the performances of some divisions to be low positive or negative, but this makes corporate performance suboptimal.

We now discuss the significance of unsystematic divisional risk for the optimal corporate portfolio. As seen above, unsystematic divisional risk is divisional profit variation that is uncorrelated with corporate profit. It follows that the divisional profit variation from unsystematic risk is uncorrelated with the profit variation of almost all other divisions in the corporation (otherwise the profit variation of the division would be correlated with the corporate profit and the risk then systematic). Therefore, the profit variation due to its unsystematic risk of one division can be thought of as uncorrelated with the profit variations from their unsystematic risk of the other divisions. Unsystematic risk is idiosyncratic, and so the unsystematic risks of divisions are independent of each other. Hence the combined effects on corporate performance of the unsystematic risks of all its divisions are random. On average, the unsystematic risks of the divisions will cancel each other out, producing nil effect on corporate performance, although by chance they will occasionally come together to produce a high or low corporate performance, but this will be a random and rare event.

As just established, the most typical effect on corporate performance of the unsystematic divisional risks will be near zero. Because the unsystematic risks of divisions tend to cancel each other out, there will usually be no additional fluctuation in corporate performance resulting from the unsystematic risks of divisions to boost corporate adaptation and growth. However, the unsystematic risks of divisions will boost their adaptation and growth, so contributing to corporate growth and success. Thus unsystematic divisional risk contributes to corporate success but mainly only at the divisional level. Nevertheless, because of the divisional-level benefits, corporate management will seek to have divisions with unsystematic risk in its portfolio.

Notwithstanding the benefits of organizational risk for adaptation and growth, high risk increases the chance of bankruptcy for the firm. Large fluctuations in organizational performance may fluctuate down to the catastrophically poor level. The greater the organizational risk, the higher the mean performance that can nevertheless experience bankruptcy on the downside fluctuation. Clearly, a corporation bankrupted by its high risk will not survive long enough to reap the long-term growth and success discussed above. Therefore, to increase the probability of survival, a prudent corporate management will reduce the risk of the corporation. This entails reducing the degree of positive correlations among divisional performances and the average divisional risk.

The propositions thus are the following:

9.14   Corporate management will trade off the benefits of greater corporate risk for an increased probability of corporate survival.

9.15   To increase probability of corporate survival, corporate management will settle for less positive correlations among divisional performances and lower divisional risk than is optimal for the adaptation, growth, and performance of the corporation.

The risk reduction resulting from bounded rationality, as discussed earlier, has benefits in terms of corporate survival, so both reasons incline corporate management toward some risk reduction.

Divisions in the Strategic Planning Matrix

In the previous section, we analyzed the effect of divisional risk on divisional and corporate change and sought to specify the optimal corporate portfolio in terms of the risks of divisions and their mutual correlations to produce sustained adaptation and growth at both divisional and corporate levels. However, the corporate portfolio can also be considered in terms of the optimal mix of divisions, given that corporate growth requires capital to be allocated between divisions. This sense of the corporate portfolio is now discussed, bringing out the role of systematic divisional risk in the divisional and corporate adaptations needed to produce corporate growth. As part of the analysis, an underlying cause of divisional risk is identified.

In the diversified, divisionalized corporation, each division can be analyzed as a discrete business in its own industry, subject to the life cycle of the industry.

Divisions in Their Industrial Life Cycle

In the divisional structure, corporate-level management allocates capital between the divisions. Some of this new capital is internally generated within the corporation; that is, it comes from the profits of the corporation itself. These corporate profits are, of course, created by the divisions. Thus the corporate-level management is transferring profit from one division to another; that is, it is making an interdivisional investment decision. One framework that can be used to analyze decisions is the strategic planning matrix associated with the Boston Consulting Group (also sometimes known as the portfolio planning approach or the growth share matrix; Davis and Devinney 1997). This focuses attention on the need for the optimal long-term corporate portfolio to contain divisions that are cash generators and divisions that are cash users.

As is well known, the strategic planning matrix distinguishes two dimensions: market share and industry growth rate (see Figure 9.2). Each division (or business unit) in the corporation is placed in one of the four quadrants defined by cross-classification on the two dimensions. The underlying theory is a model of the industrial life cycle. When the industry is young, its growth rate is high. Many small firms compete, each having small market share, keeping prices and thus profits low. When the industry matures, its growth rate is low. Larger firms enjoy superior scale economies enabling them to lower prices so that smaller firms can no longer compete, leaving the large firms each having high market share. At maturity, there are a few large, major firms setting oligopolistic prices that combine with their low costs to generate high profits. These firms also enjoy barriers to entry, so preserving their high market shares and oligopoly.

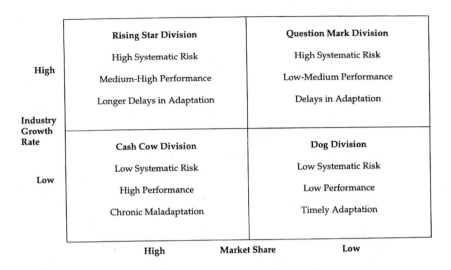

	Rising Star Division	**Question Mark Division**
High	High Systematic Risk	High Systematic Risk
	Medium-High Performance	Low-Medium Performance
	Longer Delays in Adaptation	Delays in Adaptation
	Cash Cow Division	**Dog Division**
Low	Low Systematic Risk	Low Systematic Risk
	High Performance	Low Performance
	Chronic Maladaptation	Timely Adaptation

Industry Growth Rate (vertical axis)

High — Market Share — Low (horizontal axis)

Figure 9.2 Strategic Planning Matrix Showing Systematic Risk, Performance, and Adaptation of Divisions

Thus within an industry there are considerable first-mover advantages to capturing market share, attaining scale economies, and, as a result, becoming one of the few firms to emerge as a major at maturity. At maturity, this business needs little of its cash for reinvestment in itself and so can be "milked," thus being a "cash cow" division. Therefore, the optimal corporate strategy is to invest heavily in a promising division that is in a rapidly growing industry—in other words, a "rising star." The latter can use cash to advantage to build market share and become a major in its industry. Thus cash flow is being internally reallocated within the corporation, from slow to rapidly growing industry and from the wealthy, large, mature business units to the cash-hungry, smaller, younger business units. In terms of the four quadrants of the model, this is from the high market share–low industry growth quadrant (i.e., cash cow division) to the high market share–high industry growth quadrant (i.e., rising star division).

Another quadrant is the business that is low market share in a low-growth industry, where gaining market share is costly and unprofitable; it missed its opportunity by being too small when its industry matured. This is the "dog" quadrant and has low profit and is possibly a candidate for divestiture, there being little that can be done to improve its long-term future. The last quadrant is the "question mark," that is, low market share but high industry growth. This business is not presently dominant in its industry, but the industry has not yet matured and so there is still a chance that it could become a major at maturity. However, this is uncertain and hence the title "question mark." Some funds can be moved from mature businesses into the "question mark" division if it seems to have some promise. Thus the corporation is well served by containing both cash-generating and cash-using divisions. The model implies that the corporation has sufficient diversification that it has both types of divisions.

The whole model is cyclical, in that in time the cash cow may die away as its industry turns from maturity into decline. Similarly, the rising star will become a highly profitable major in its industry, and, as that industry matures, the major throws off surplus cash and becomes a cash cow. In this way, the framework accommodates the cycle of industrial growth and maturity, constantly renewing the set of businesses within the corporation. The strategic planning matrix model is familiar to many scholars; the point here is to tie this to our present theory by analyzing the risk of each of the four types of division and its significance for adaptation and growth.

How would we characterize each of the four quadrants in terms of organizational portfolio theory?

Industrial Life Cycle and Systematic Divisional Risk

The divisions in each of the four quadrants of the strategic planning matrix will, as a result of their industry positions, each tend to have a certain degree of systematic risk. The higher its industry growth rate, the higher the division's systematic risk (see Figure 9.2).

The *dog division* has low systematic risk. It has a low mean and stable profit level. If its mean were higher than low or if its profit fluctuated up into the high or even medium levels, it would not be a dog. On the downside, its profit cannot fluctuate too low or it might be disposed of or disbanded by the corporation. Thus the profits of the dog tend to fluctuate only in a limited range around low to below zero. Therefore, its profitability fluctuates less than the corporation as a whole, and so its systematic divisional risk is low (i.e., divisional beta is less than 1).

The *cash cow division* also has low systematic risk. It has high and fairly stable profits; therefore, its profit fluctuations are limited. Its mean profit level has to be high to have cash surpluses, and if its profit were variable, it could not reliably feed cash to other divisions, so it would not be a cash cow. Moreover, its profits make up the bulk of corporate profits. The other divisions taken together have less effect on corporate profit; otherwise, their propensity to incur low profits or losses would bankrupt the corporation. Thus for ongoing, multidivisional corporations, the cash cow must dominate and be the main determinant of corporate profitability. So too, the fluctuations in the profit of the cash cow are similar to in pattern but less than the fluctuations in overall corporate profit. Fluctuations in corporate profits tend to come from the other divisions that are more unstable, but their smaller magnitude (relative to the cash cow) tends to attenuate their impact on corporate profitability. Therefore, the profit variance of the cash cow is less than that of the corporation as a whole, and so its systematic divisional risk is also low (i.e., divisional beta is less than 1).

The *rising star division* has high systematic risk. It tends to have medium profits because investments are beginning to pay off as its industry grows rapidly. But there are variations in its profit, as investments take time to generate profits. Moreover, there are fluctuations in its profit due to periods in misfit caused by its rapid growth. Therefore, the profitability of the rising star fluctuates more than the cash cow, and so its systematic divisional risk is high (i.e., divisional beta is more than 1).

The *question mark division* also has high systematic risk. It has rapid fluctuations in profit as it moves, more quickly than the rising star, through misfit and fit due to its mediocre average profitability. Hence the question mark moves rapidly through increments of growth, and so its size and profitability change quite rapidly over time. Thus its systematic divisional risk is also high (i.e., divisional beta is more than 1).

To summarize, the cash cow and dog divisions have low systematic risk, whereas the rising star and question mark divisions have high systematic risk. This emphasizes the greater volatility of the rising star and question mark divisions relative to the cash cow and dog divisions.

Systematic Risk and Adaptation of Each Division

Here we explain how the level of systematic risk of each division affects its adaptation and feeds back to affect its longer-run performance (see Figure 9.2). The higher the risk of the division, the more probable that it will make needed adaptive changes.

Adaptation by a division is affected by both the level and risk, that is, volatility, of its performance. A low-level divisional performance triggers adaptive change in the division. Therefore, adaptive change is more probable in divisions that have, over time, low average levels of performance: the dog and question mark divisions. However, the volatility of divisional performance also affects adaptation, so that, despite average divisional performance being satisfactory, large fluctuations can cause it to drop below the satisficing level, triggering adaptive divisional change. Adaptive change is more probable in divisions that are volatile, that is, with high systematic divisional risk: the question mark and rising star divisions. The cross-classification of average level and risk volatility of divisions determines their probability of adaptation. In descending order, from high to low, the probability of divisional adaptation is the dog, question mark, rising star, and cash cow, respectively.

The dog division tends to make timely adaptations. It has poor profit performance. Its low growth means that it only relatively slowly grows from fit into misfit. However, when it does enter misfit, its poor performance is likely to trigger adaptation relatively quickly. Thus the dog division is, on average, in relatively good fit. The reasons for its chronically poor performance lie not in maladaptation but in its low market share and other strategic factors. Structural misfit cannot be an enduring source of low performance because low performance triggers adaptation. In the dog division, changes in contingencies, such as size, are infrequent, but when they occur, they quickly produce adaptations in structure or other aspects, such as human resources or information technology.

The question mark division makes adaptations only after some delays. It is in a fast-growing industry, and as long as its own growth is at least equal to the industry, it will experience fast growth that propels it into misfit. It has, on average, mediocre performance; therefore, when it enters misfit, its performance is liable to decline to low profit fairly quickly and so trigger adaptation. However, because the mean performance level of the question mark division is not as low as the dog division, it will take longer for its performance to sink low enough to trigger a needed adaptation. This divisional adaptation and new fit will contribute to raising its performance. Thus the question mark displays both growth spurts and structural increases alternately, so that it increases substantially both in size and structure cumulatively. The question mark division adapts, though with more time lag than the dog division.

The rising star division makes adaptations, but the delays are expected to be longer. It is rapidly growing, and so this will keep propelling it into misfit. Its profits will not be as high as the cash cow, for the rising star is smaller and faces more price competition in its industry. Relative to the dog and question mark divisions, however, the profit of the rising star tends to be higher, and this tends to delay the onset of adaptation during misfit. Its profits tend to be moderate, and only when they drop to poor performance is adaptation triggered. Thus there will be some delays in making needed adaptations. However, this new fit state is again temporary, as the high industry-growth rate allows the business to grow rapidly and so will cause misfit as the adaptations lag behind the increase in size and so forth. Thus the rising star will cycle recurrently through states of fit and misfit, growing in size and increasing its structure. The recurrent periods of fit will contribute to its performance and its growth. The rapid occurrence of spurts of growth and structural change will mean that the division makes alternating increments in size and structure, cumulating in substantial increases in size and structure. However, there will be substantial time lags before each adaptive structural change and other changes. These lags will be longer than those of the question mark division because of the higher average profits of the rising star division.

The cash cow division, in contrast, tends to fail to make needed adaptations. It is a large oligopolist that is enjoying year after year of high profits. There may be some fluctuation in profit level, reflecting business cycles and so forth, but being a dominant, low-cost producer in an oligopoly tends to mostly make for profitable operations. Moreover, oligopoly tends to stabilize prices so helping to stabilize profits for the oligopolist. The cash cow is more profitable than the other divisions in the corporation and will tend to remain above the average profitability of these other divisions; thus its performance is liable to be seen as acceptable at the least (i.e., above the satisficing level). Therefore, although its growth rate is modest, the successive years of growth mean that the cash cow may drift out of fit because there may be no period of low performance to trigger adaptive change in structure and so forth. Thus the cash cow division has the lowest probability of making needed adaptations of any of the four divisions. Therefore, the cash cow division reflects that combination of low risk and lack of adaptation that leads to pathological stability. Hence the cash cow division will become suboptimal in its performance, despite being initially high relative to some of the other business units. Thus the performance of the corporation will drift down over time as the maladaptation of the cash cow division worsens.

In summary, divisions with higher risk are more likely to make needed adaptive changes that feed back to make their long-term performance more optimal (see Figure 9.2).

The cash cow is the linchpin of the corporate strategy, for this provides the funds for the investment in the other divisions. The paradox is that its success may mean that it performs less optimally than it could because it becomes maladapted. Thus the tendency toward mediocre performance of the cash cow depresses corporate performance.

The negative effect of the mediocre performance of the cash cow division on corporate profitability is amplified by the fact that the profit of the cash cow may be much greater than that of the other divisions. The cash cow division is large and an oligopoly, whereas the other divisions are small and facing more competitive markets (these being tenets of the strategic planning matrix theory). The cash cow division supplies much of corporate profit. Thus changes in the profitability of the cash cow strongly affect corporate profitability. Therefore, the profitability decline of the cash cow will strongly influence the corporate profitability to decline. Further, this may also cause the satisficing level to decline because corporate managers may implicitly come to hold a somewhat depressed view of the possibilities of their industry. This would lead to greater tolerance and so reduce the incidence of adaptations at both divisional and corporate levels, leading to greater performance losses.

On average, over the years the level of organizational adaptation will be greatest in the dog division, followed by the question mark division, then the rising star division, and finally the cash cow division. This reflects the way that divisional performance feeds back to trigger the organizational adaptation of the division.

The propositions thus are the following:

9.16 The probability of making needed divisional adaptations is greater, respectively, in the cash cow, rising star, question mark, and dog division.

9.17 The probability of suboptimal divisional performance is greater, respectively, in the dog, question mark, rising star, and cash cow division.

Thus, whereas the industry position gives each division an underlying performance level, the feedback effects of performance on adaptation work to counter the underlying performance. Hence divisions having high underlying performance suffer maladaptation that works to reduce their performance, whereas divisions having low underlying performance maintain their adaptation that works to raise their performance. These feedback effects are weaker than the underlying industry effects, however, so the feedback effects merely reduce the differences between divisions from that which the underlying industry effects create. Therefore, for example, the cash cow division remains a superior performer to the dog division.

As seen above, high levels of divisional performance when combined with stability in divisional performance, that is, low risk, induce chronic misfit and suboptimal performance of the division. For this reason, the high-performance, stable, low-systematic-risk division, the cash cow, eventually becomes a suboptimal performer. Given the size of the cash cow division within the corporate portfolio, this means that most of the corporate assets are performing suboptimally. However, as noted earlier, the stability from this low-systematic-risk division is liable to be welcomed by corporate management already occupied attempting to manage the more volatile high-systematic-risk divisions, the rising star and question mark, plus the more stable but low-performing dog division. The burden on corporate management is intensified by the attention it must give to transferring resources from the cash cow to the rising star and possibly also to the question mark under the strategic planning matrix concept. The burden of corporate management is further increased in that there may be more than one of each of the four types of divisions, thus straining the critical, managerial resources of attention and problem-solving capacity. Therefore, corporate management is less likely to intervene in the cash cow division, which will remain internally chronically maladapted and suboptimal. Performance lost at the divisional level contributes to suboptimal performance at the corporate level.

Moreover, there is a second source of performance loss for the corporation: Low divisional risk reduces corporate risk. The stability in corporate performance caused by the cash cow and dog divisions tends to cause corporate management not to make needed adaptations at the corporate level because their stability reduces fluctuations of corporate performance down to low levels. (The low level of performance of the dog division depresses corporate performance, but this is more than offset by the high performance of the cash cow division, and so corporate performance is kept above the satisficing level.) Thus the stability of the two low-systematic-risk divisions leads to pathological stability at the corporate level that eventually degrades corporate performance.

In summary, low divisional risk reduces divisional performance, and low divisional risk reduces corporate risk, both of which reduce corporate performance (see Figure 9.3). Thus low divisional risk reduces corporate perfor-

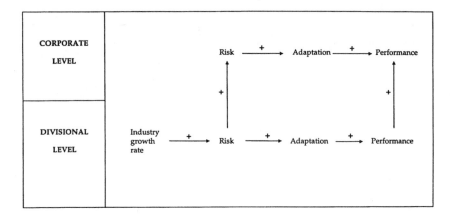

Figure 9.3 Effects of Divisional Risk on Corporate Performance

mance both through lowering divisional performance and through lowering corporate risk.

The discussion of systematic risk and position of the division in its industry brings out the way in which pathological stability can occur for divisions. This drags down the performance of the diversified, divisionalized firm, the main form of large corporation in our society. The effect of these chronically misfitted and underperforming divisions on the corporation is added to the underperformance of the corporation that stems from its own misfitted structure at the corporate level.

The Optimal Corporate Portfolio and the Strategic Planning Matrix

The strategic planning matrix holds that the corporation will maximize its growth and profitability long term if it contains both a cash cow division and a rising star division so that mature profits can be invested in a good future prospect. Therefore, the corporation contains both a low- and a high-systematic-risk division, respectively. The low risk of the cash cow division leads to it becoming maladapted and mediocre while also leading to maladaptation and mediocrity at the corporate level. This illustrates the point made earlier: From a risk perspective, the optimal corporate portfolio contains divisions all of which have medium systematic risk so as to maximize adaptation and long-term growth at both divisional and corporate levels. Thus it is advantageous to replace the low-risk cash cow division with a medium-risk division. The problem is that such a medium-systematic-risk division is unlikely to be a cash cow because it is not able to consistently generate surplus funds. A portfolio of rising stars is attractive in that all of them have medium systematic risk but are cash users, not cash generators, thus leaving the corporation with a deficit to fund.

One solution is to relax the assumption of the strategic planning matrix: that the corporation funds itself and that capital for cash-hungry divisions must come from other divisions. The corporation could raise funds from outside, through equity or debt (i.e., selling shares or borrowing), and in that way fund its divisions, all of which could be cash-using rising stars. We have argued that the optimal corporate portfolio consists of divisions all medium on systematic risk and positively correlated with each other (to foster corporate-level adaptation). This leads to high corporate risk, and so external suppliers of capital to the corporation would charge a premium. However, the superior growth and profitability over the long term that flow from high corporate risk would reduce the cost of equity funds. Thus an optimal corporate portfolio of all medium-systematic-risk divisions could be financed in this way. There would be no cash cow division, the external capital market having replaced it. Therefore, the strategic planning matrix concept of the corporation containing a cash-generating division to fund the cash-using division would be abandoned.

However, we earlier noted that it was unlikely that a corporation would have all medium-systematic-risk divisions, in practice, because of the constraints of managerial bounded rationality and fear of bankruptcy. To keep the task feasible, corporate managers would include some low-systematic-risk divisions in the corporation. These could include cash cow divisions, so that some of the cash needs of the low-systematic-risk rising star divisions would be from capital allocation between divisions (i.e., within the corporation rather than externally). Thus the corporation would be well served to contain mainly medium-systematic-risk divisions but with some low-systematic-risk cash cow divisions, yielding a portfolio that is suboptimal but the best possible under bounded rationality. In this way, some but probably not all of the cash needs of the rising star divisions are met by transfers of capital between divisions. The remaining funds would be raised externally.

Conclusions

The analysis of divisions was taken further in this chapter to increase our understanding of how divisional performance, risk, misfit, and adaptive change interact to affect each other. The concept of systematic divisional risk (i.e., divisional beta) illuminates the relationship between the performance variance of the division and that of its corporation. The systematic divisional risk captures the volatility of divisional profit relative to corporate profit.

A division of low systematic risk tends over time to increase in maladaptation, and so its performance becomes suboptimal. A division of medium systematic risk tends to persist in maladaptation and to lead the corporate center to fail to perceive when it is maladapted. Only a division of high systematic risk tends over time to reliably make recurrent adaptation and, in consequence, to grow, and so its performance is closer to optimal.

The optimal portfolio is a corporation consisting of medium-systematic-risk divisions that are highly, positively correlated. However, the constraints of bounded rationality and survival render this infeasible, so management will encourage some divisions to have low systematic risks and some divisions to have low positive or even negative correlations with the other divisions.

The systematic divisional risk is, in turn, affected by the position of the division in its industrial life cycle as captured by the strategic planning matrix variables of market share and growth rate. These yield the familiar four quadrants of the dog, rising star, question mark, and cash cow divisions. The dog division has low performance and a low systematic divisional risk and so tends to make needed adaptations in a timely manner. Rising star and question mark divisions tend to have high systematic divisional risk and therefore make needed adaptations, thereby restoring their performance. However, because the question mark division tends to have higher performance than the dog division, it tends to make its adaptation after some delay. Similarly, because the rising star division tends to have higher performance than the question mark division, it tends to make its adaptation after a greater delay. In contrast, the cash cow division has high performance and a low systematic risk and so tends to becomes chronically maladapted and suboptimal in performance. This directly reduces corporate performance and is material in that the cash cow division is large relative to the other three types of divisions. Therefore, the way divisional risk affects divisional adaptation reduces the performance superiority of the divisions in the more advantageous industry positions. In this way, divisional risk affects corporate performance through its effect on divisional performance.

Moreover, the financial stability of the cash cow and dog divisions, that is, their low risk, may be welcomed by corporate management but contributes to the pathological stability of the diversified, divisionalized corporation, leading to chronic maladaptation at the corporate level and suboptimality. In this way, divisional risk affects corporate risk. Thus there is an indirect reduction of corporate profit from the low-systematic-risk divisions (the cash cow and dog) through their inhibiting effect on corporate-level adaptation.

Hence low-risk divisions reduce corporate performance both through reducing divisional performance and through reducing corporate risk.

In Chapter 6 we saw that the low risk of the diversified, divisionalized corporation tends to lead to pathological stability and suboptimal performance. In this chapter, we saw that the low risk of certain divisions within such corporations also leads to pathological stability and suboptimal performance of the corporation. This alerts us to further possible disadvantages of the diversified, divisionalized corporation.

10

Conclusions

In this book, we have advanced the model of the organization as a portfolio of variables that interact with each other to affect the performance of the organization. The portfolio characteristics affect organizational performance and risk. These feed back to determine the occurrence and timing of organizational change. This model generates a set of new theoretical propositions that may be used to guide future research efforts. This chapter first summarizes the arguments of the previous chapters, considers interactions, draws together implications of the theory for the divisionalized corporation, and then presents an agenda for future research using the new theory.

Summary of Organizational Portfolio Theory

The structural adaptation to regain fit theory treats organizational performance as the crucial intermediary variable between misfit and organizational change. This leads to a consideration of the organization as a financial portfolio, which results in overall organizational performance. The environmental effects on the organization are conceptualized in terms of the business cycle and competition. In this way, the model is made more dynamic. Moreover, by bringing into organizational theory discourse concepts such as the portfolio and business cycles, concepts usually absent from organizational theory, an integrative link is made with the disciplines of finance and economics. Thus the overall import of the organizational portfolio theory advanced here is to make organizational theory both more dynamic and less insular in a disciplinary sense.

Organizational theory holds that an organization in misfit adopts a new structure or other needed adaptation and moves into fit only after performance declines sufficiently that it drops below the satisficing level (Chandler 1962; Williamson 1964; Child 1972). Poor performance is thus the immediate cause of organizational adaptation. For adaptive organizational change to occur, therefore, performance must fluctuate over time and periodically drop to a low level. Similarly, high performance fosters organizational growth so that performance fluctuating to a high level enhances growth, again revealing the importance of performance fluctuations.

The overall performance of an organization results from causes both internal to the organization, including organizational maladaptation, and external to the organization. These internal and external causes of organizational performance constitute the organizational portfolio. Use is made of portfolio theory from finance to analyze the risk from each cause and their mutual correlation. These interact to cause the level of organizational performance and its fluctuations over time, which, in turn, drive organizational adaptive change and growth. The greater the risk, that is, the performance fluctuation, caused by each factor in the organizational portfolio, the more probable is organizational adaptation and growth. Similarly, the more positive the correlations among the factors, the greater the organizational risk and so the more probable is organizational adaptation and growth. Conversely, the more negative or low positive correlations there are among the factors of the organizational portfolio, the more the factors neutralize each other, so preventing organizational adaptation and growth.

Apart from organizational maladaptation, organizational portfolio theory has identified the following eight factors as key causal components of the organizational portfolio:

◆ Business cycle
◆ Competition
◆ Debt
◆ Divisional risk

- ◆ Diversification
- ◆ Divisionalization
- ◆ Divestment
- ◆ Directors

There are four factors that increase the risk of a firm and thereby increase its likelihood of making needed adaptations and of growing so that the firm may become complex, large, and successful over the long term. These are the business cycle, competition, debt, and divisional risk. Conversely, there are four factors that decrease the risk of a firm and thereby may prevent adaptive change and inhibit growth, leading to stagnation and mediocrity long term. These are diversification, divisionalization, divestment, and directors. The role of each of these eight factors is briefly summarized in turn.

Business Cycle

A major cause of organizational performance for a firm is the business cycle. The constituent fluctuations in economic activity are massive and considerably affect the performance of firms. The business cycle thereby is a high-risk factor in the organizational portfolio. It is therefore highly consequential for whether an organization in misfit adapts or not and for the growth of an organization in fit. The correlation between organizational misfit and the business cycle varies over the cycle. The correlation between organizational misfit and the business cycle goes from negative to positive as the cycle moves from rising to falling. Therefore, the business cycle goes from offsetting the effect of misfit on performance to reinforcing it so that adaptation is prevented during the upswing and triggered during the downswing. Conversely for organizational growth, when the organization is in fit, growth is frustrated by the downswing but facilitated by the upswing. Thus the business cycle fosters adaptation and growth.

The business cycle fluctuates recurrently, causing repeated increments of organizational adaptation and growth. This generates a large, successful organization with an elaborate internal structure and systems. Furthermore, the amplitude of the business cycle varies from industry to industry, so the effects of the business cycle are greater on organizations in industries of larger cycle.

Competition

Competition has strong effects on organizational performance and therefore constitutes an important element of the organizational portfolio—that is, it causes considerable risk. The number of competitors raises competition, especially if they are effective by being themselves in fit. When competitors are in fit, their depressive effect on the performance of the firm is positively correlated with the depressive effect of the misfit of the firm so that its performance becomes low and it would probably adapt. However, when competitors are in misfit, their effect on performance of the firm is negatively correlated with the depressive effect of the misfit of that firm so that its performance is more likely to remain satisfactory and it will thus probably fail to adapt. When competitors are in misfit, a firm that is in fit will find it easier to grow. Thus competition affects organizational adaptation and growth. Although competition may change over time, it does not fluctuate in a recurrent pattern like the business cycle. Thus competition will usually not produce the recurrent increments of adaptation and growth that lead to a large, successful, elaborate organization, so its effect on these outcomes is more moderate than the business cycle.

Debt

Debt increases the level of operating profit that is regarded as satisfactory and reduces the final profit figure of the corporation, thereby increasing the likelihood of adaptation for an organization in misfit. For an organization in fit, debt is a major source of financial resources, so it tends to increase organizational growth. Thus debt increases the probability of organizational adaptation and the rate of organizational growth.

Divisional Risk

A division with high risk has large fluctuations in its performance over time. These contribute to fluctuations in the performance of the overall organization—in particular, that systematic divisional risk (i.e., a higher divisional beta coefficient) increases corporate risk. Thus a corporation that has more, higher-risk divisions has greater corporate risk, and so the chance of corporate adaptation, growth, and long-term success is increased.

Hence the business cycle, competition, debt, and divisional risk are important factors in the organizational portfolio that positively affect organizational adaptation and growth.

When, however, an organization adapts, it may not always display an increase in performance, and the portfolio perspective explains why. An adaptive change occurs because of a temporary positive correlation between organizational misfit and the other causes of performance, resulting in it dropping below the satisficing level. However, after the adaptive change, this correlation often begins to break down and may become negative so that performance declines. This gives a false impression that the change was not adaptive when actually it was. Thus some organizational adaptations may be erroneously perceived as changes that produce no benefits or are counterproductive because of the way the other causes of organizational performance interact with the adaptations to obscure their benefits.

As seen, organizational portfolio theory holds that organizational change is induced by the business cycle, competition, debt, and divisional risk. However, other forces work to prevent organizational change. Often, they work by creating an organizational portfolio whose elements are less positively or even are negatively correlated with each other. The four factors inhibiting organizational adaptive change are diversification, divisionalization, divestment, and directors.

Diversification

Diversification achieves lower positive or negative correlations within the organizational portfolio by adding to it businesses from disparate product markets whose business cycles and fortunes may fluctuate independently of, or counter to, each other.

Divisionalization

Divisionalization is a typical organizational structural response to diversification, and it also reduces corporate risk. Divisionalization reduces the fluctuations in corporate profit relative to functional structure because the divisions tend to smooth their reported profits and also to make their decisions independent of the other divisions. The creation of autonomous divisions further loosens the positive correlations between businesses that diversification causes so that the correlations are more likely to become negative after divisionalization. Thus diversification and divisionalization interact to reduce corporate risk. This risk reduction tends to prevent needed corporate adaptations, leading to mediocre performance in the longer term.

Divestment

Divestment is a possible response to low corporate performance and is particularly feasible in a diversified, divisionalized corporation, which can readily sell some divisions. In this way, divestment can restore performance without the corporation making needed adaptive changes. Thus adaptation of the large corporation tends to be retarded by its diversification, divisionalization, and divestments.

Directors

Non-executive directors and their chairperson reduce managerial discretion, and this leads to less fluctuation in corporate performance over time—that is, directors lower corporate risk. Conversely, executive directors and their chairperson give management freer rein, and this leads to more fluctuation in performance over time (i.e., higher risk). This greater risk leads to episodes of low performance, which triggers organizational adaptation, and also of high performance, which fosters growth. Corporate governance reflects this effect of directors on corporate risk together with other portfolio factors.

Corporate risk causes fluctuations in the level of corporate performance, which, in turn, affects corporate governance. Low organizational performance leads to distrust of the management by shareholders, leading to replacement of executive by non-executive directors on company boards. Conversely, high organizational performance leads to trust of the management by shareholders, leading to replacement of non-executive by executive directors on company boards. Diversification and divisionalization reduce risk and so make episodes of low performance less probable, leading to a higher proportion of executives on the board and to an executive chairperson. However, a preponderance of executive directors on the board subsequently leads to higher corporate risk, which tends eventually to lead to an episode of poor performance that causes some of the executive directors to be replaced by non-executives and possibly also to a non-executive chairperson. Moreover, increased competition, debt, and downturns in the business cycle also contribute toward episodes of unsatisfactory performance, leading also to a higher proportion of non-executives on the board and to the increased probability of a non-executive chairperson. However, subsequent business cycle upturns or divestments lead to a restoration of corporate performance and so of executives on the board. Thus corporate governance is affected by the interaction between the factors that form the organizational portfolio.

In sum, corporate adaptation, growth, and long-term success are increased by the organization being in an industry of larger business cycles and greater competition, with the organization having more debt and more higher-risk divisions. Conversely, corporate adaptation, growth, and long-term success are decreased by the organization being diversified and divisionalized with more non-executive directors and divesting more divisions. Whether the organization adapts, grows, and is successful long term or not is dependent on the strength of the first set of organizational portfolio factors relative to the second.

We can conceive of a continuum of adaptive organizational change varying from low to high (see Figure 10.1). The place that an organization occupies on the adaptive organizational change continuum is affected by how high the organization rates on each of the eight organizational portfolio factors.

As stated in Chapter 9, high-risk divisions tend to occur in high-growth-rate industries, so an organization is more likely to have them if it is in a high-growth-rate industry. (If the organization is an undiversified, functionally structured, single business in a high-growth-rate industry, it will nevertheless experience greater fluctuations, that is, higher risk, on the logic of Chapter 9.) When the organization is in a very cyclical, competitive, high-growth-rate industry and the organization is undiversified, functionally structured, with high debt, with a board dominated by executives, and has made no divestments, it is more likely to make maximal adaptive organizational changes, producing maximal growth and long-term success. Conversely, when the organization is in a stable, noncompetitive, low-growth-rate industry and the organization is diversified, divisionally structured, with low debt, with a board dominated by non-executives, and periodically divests a division, it will make minimal adaptive organizational changes, producing little growth and little long-term success. Most organizations will be at neither extreme but, rather, at some intermediary point on the continuum of adaptive organizational change. This is because their level on the eight organizational portfolio factors will not be all at the extremes; that is, they may rate high on some portfolio factors but low on others (see Figure 10.1).

VALUES INHIBITING ORGANIZATIONAL CHANGE	ORGANIZATIONAL PORTFOLIO FACTORS	VALUES PROMOTING ORGANIZATIONAL CHANGE
	Industry Level	
Small	Business Cycle	Large
Low	Competition	High
	Organizational Level	
Diversified	Strategy	Undiversified
Divisional	Structure	Functional
Non-executives	Directors	Executives
Low	Debt	High
High	Divestment	Low
Low	Divisional Risk	High
Low	**Adaptive Organizational Change**	**High**

Figure 10.1 The Continuum of Adaptive Organizational Change

As an organization matures, its industry growth rate slows, thus inducing less change in the organization. Also, larger-size organizations tend to be more diversified, and this also inclines them toward divisionalization, divestment, and probably debt, so large corporations are somewhat more likely to be toward the low change end of the continuum. However, over time the average level of competition is probably increasing for organizations, so this tends toward increasing organizational change. Thus maturity, growth in size, and changes in competition as well as changes in the other portfolio factors can all lead the organization to shift its position over time on the continuum of organizational change.

At the divisional level, processes occur that mirror and intensify those at the corporate level. The divisions are each elements in the organizational portfolio, so their performances may be only weakly positively or negatively correlated. When some divisions have medium or high performance and other divisions have low performance, corporate performance can still be satisfactory, reducing the impetus for corporate intervention into those low-performing divisions. Again we see a portfolio effect. Adaptive change in a division is more likely when not only it but other divisions are performing poorly. Thus change in divisions is liable to occur only periodically but to be dramatic and protracted when it does occur. Moreover, focus on divisions may preclude needed corporate-level adaptations.

The concept of risk can be applied to the divisions individually. Divisions in misfit of their internal characteristics to their situation tend to adapt when their performance is low and to not adapt when it is medium to high. Divisions in fit are more likely to grow when their performance is medium to high. Hence divisions with high risk are more exposed to large fluctuations in their performance that leads them to repeatedly adapt and grow. In contrast, divisions of low risk are more likely to not adapt and to stagnate. The cash cow type of division has low risk and high performance and so is likely to stagnate, depressing corporate performance. In such ways, a consideration of divisional risk reveals further ways in which divisionalized corporations will tend to become only modest performers over time, due to less than complete adaptation at corporate and divisional levels.

The optimal corporate portfolio would consist of divisions that were all positively correlated with each other and of medium risk. However, this is infeasible given the bounded rationality of corporate management. Moreover, high corporate risk also incurs higher risk of bankruptcy. Therefore, corporations are likely to include some lower-risk divisions in order to lower corporate risk, despite this tending to produce suboptimal performance.

Table 10.1 provides a summary of the main points of this book.

Portfolio Effects Among the Organizational Portfolio Factors

The eight organizational portfolio factors interact additively to determine the position of an organization on the continuum of adaptive organizational change. An organization that has a value of an organizational portfolio factor that lies to the right in Figure 10.1 has a higher probability of making an adaptive organizational change. The organizational portfolio factors add in that the more factors on which the organization lies on the right in Figure 10.1, the higher the probability that the organization will make an adaptive organizational change. Conversely, the more organizational portfolio factors on which the organization lies on the left in Figure 10.1, the lower the probability that the organization will make an adaptive organizational change. If an organization has a value on one organizational portfolio factor that is at the

TABLE 10.1 Summary of Organizational Portfolio Theory

Concept	Theoretical Propositions
Overarching Concepts	
Risk and organizational change	Risk causes organizational change.
	Low performance causes organizational adaptation.
	High performance fosters growth.
	Risk is necessary for adaptation and growth.
Organizational portfolio	The portfolio properties of the organization determine its performance fluctuation (i.e., risk).
	Risk is increased by portfolio elements with larger performance fluctuation.
	Risk is reduced by negative correlations between portfolio elements.
Organizational Portfolio Factors	
1. Business cycles	Business cycles are a major external source of fluctuation in organizational performance.
	Downswings foster adaptation and fit.
	Upswings foster maladaptation and misfit.
	Organizational adaptation cycles in time with the business cycle.
	Industry structure is affected by business cycles.
	Business cycles are in part caused by the cyclical nature of organizational adaptation.
2. Competition	An external cause of organizational performance is competitive pressure.
	It varies according to the extent of fit among the competitor organizations.
3. Debt	Debt raises the satisficing level.
	It increases organizational adaptation and growth.
4. Divisional risk	High-risk divisions increase corporate risk.
5. Diversification	Diversification reduces risk.
6. Divisionalization	Divisionalization reduces risk.
	Diversification and divisionalization interact to reduce risk.
	This leads to failure to adapt and mediocre performance over the long term.
7. Divestment	Divestment creates organizational slack that forestalls adaptation.
8. Directors	Non-executive directors reduce risk.

extreme right in Figure 10.1 and a value on another organizational portfolio factor that is at the extreme left, their combined effect is to place the organiza-

TABLE 10.1 Continued

Concept	Theoretical Propositions
Other Concepts	
Adaptation	Organizational adaptation is triggered by low organizational performance caused jointly by misfit and other causes of performance.
	After adaptation, the correlation between fit and these other causes breaks down, confounding the results.
	Performance variation between organizations is higher after than before adaptation.
Corporate governance	The risk reduction from diversification and divisionalization fosters executive directors.
	Debt and economic downturns foster non-executive directors.
	Divestment fosters executive directors.
Divisions	Divisions have additive effects on organizational performance.
	Poor divisional performance can be compensated for by other divisions.
	When divisional change occurs, several divisions may be performing poorly simultaneously.
	A division may remain performing poorly.
	Poor corporate management may be misattributed to divisions.
Divisional risk	High divisional risk leads to divisional adaptation and growth.
	Dog, question mark, rising star, and cash cow divisions, respectively, are less likely to adapt.
	Cash cow divisions become mediocre performers.
	Optimal corporate portfolio is medium-risk divisions positively correlated.

tion in the middle of the continuum of adaptive organizational change. Thus the position on the adaptive organizational change continuum is the mean of the positions on the eight organizational portfolio factors. (If an organizational portfolio factor affects adaptive organizational change more than other factors, its effect should be weighted accordingly to yield a weighted mean.)

Because the effects of the organizational portfolio factors are additive, portfolio effects are possible from their interactions. If the organization changes its value on the organizational portfolio factors so that they all move in the same direction, then the organization moves in that direction on the continuum of adaptive organizational change. However, if the organization changes its value on the organizational portfolio factors so that half move in one direction but the other half move in the opposite direction, then the effects of the movements of the portfolio factors counter each other so that the organization may move only little on the adaptive organizational change continuum. If the changes in the second direction are equal to the changes in the first, then the organization would remain stationary in its existing position on the continuum of adaptive organizational change. Thus portfolio effects of one factor counteracting or even nullifying another are possible. This is to say that the set of eight organizational portfolio factors themselves form a portfolio. When portfolio effects are dominant, there will be little movement over time by the organization on the adaptive organizational change continuum. The organization could still be changing—that is, it could be in the middle of the continuum—but it would not shift its position because any organizational portfolio factor that moved toward the right would be countered by another factor moving to the left.

Such a portfolio effect among the organizational portfolio factors is a higher-order type of portfolio effect than the type discussed in most of this book. To distinguish this second-order portfolio effect from the first-order portfolio effect, we refer to the second-order portfolio effect as a *meta-portfolio effect*. So far in this book, each organizational portfolio factor interacts with organizational maladaptation to nullify its depressing effect on organizational performance. In contrast, the meta-portfolio effect is among the organizational portfolio factors themselves. Similarly, there is a difference in what is affected. A single organizational portfolio factor affects *the position* on the continuum of adaptive organizational change. In contrast, the portfolio effect among the organizational portfolio factors affects *movement along* the continuum of adaptive organizational change (i.e., shifts in position). Thus the meta-portfolio effect of the organizational portfolio factors is a second-order effect that nullifies second-order change.

As just seen, for meta-portfolio effects to occur, an increase in one organizational portfolio factor needs to be compensated by a decrease in another factor. Such a compensatory effect requires a low positive to negative correlation between the two organizational portfolio factors. Which organizational factors are correlated in this way, and to what degree, is a question best left to empirical research, but some exploratory comments may be offered. For example, diversification is probably negatively correlated with non-executive directors, in that as large corporations have diversified they seem increasingly to have adopted the executive chair and to have appointed executive directors. Therefore, the organizational portfolio factors of diversification and directors seem to move in opposite directions. In Figure 10.1, as a corporation moves to the left on diversification, it moves to the right on directors so that the lowering of adaptive organizational change caused by the increase in diversification is offset to some degree by the heightening of adaptive organizational change caused by the decrease in non-executive directors. Such an interaction between diversification and directors would be a meta-portfolio effect.

Similarly, divisionalization has increased among large corporations apparently concomitantly with their possible decrease in non-executive directors, that is, apparently a negative correlation. Thus the interaction between divisionalization and directors may also be a meta-portfolio effect. In contrast, diversification and divisionalization are quite highly positively correlated according to research, in that firms that diversify subsequently divisionalize (e.g., Rumelt 1974). Therefore, these two organizational portfolio factors illustrate reinforcement rather than compensation, so their interaction is *not* a meta-portfolio effect.

As noted earlier, competition is widely conceived to be increasing over time, thus increasing adaptive organizational change. The effects of this increase in competition are offset, however, by any shifts to the left among the organizational portfolio factors occurring at the same time. Thus, for example, increase in competition on large corporations between 1980 and 1995 is probably countered to some degree by increasing divestment by those same corporations during that period. Hence competition and divestment may be negatively correlated so that their interaction would be a meta-portfolio effect that inhibits organizations from moving along the continuum of adaptive organizational change.

The business cycle is an organizational portfolio factor that has an effect on organizational performance and thereby on adaptive organizational change that may be greater than that of some of the other factors, at least in the short term. However, being a cycle it raises and then lowers and then raises again organizational performance. Thus its effect on the level of organizational performance is not constant. Thus it is difficult to say that the business cycle correlates positively or negatively with any other organizational portfolio factor because it is liable to correlate positively for a few years and then negatively for the next few years so that the correlation over time likely may be nil or low. Therefore, the business cycle, while prominent in this book, may not play a strong role in the portfolio of organizational portfolio factors.

This discussion is purely illustrative. The actual movements by organizations along each of the organizational portfolio factors are empirical questions, as are the correlations between the organizational portfolio factors. The sign (i.e., positive or negative) of each correlation and its magnitude need to be ascertained from research. The discussion brings out that the correlations need to be established separately for each time period—and probably for each group of organizations as well. How far the correlations generalize across different groups of organizations and time periods requires careful empirical examination and should not be presumed.

The correlations between each pair of organizational portfolio factors constitute a semi-matrix. When each correlation in the semi-matrix is known, the overall mean correlation can be calculated. If this is high and positive, then changes in the values of the organizational portfolio factors are likely to produce movement along the continuum of adaptive organizational change.

Many writers hold that the level of adaptive organizational change is increasing (though see Eccles and Nohria 1992). In terms of the present analysis, this presumes that the organizational factors are moving overall to the right in Figure 10.1. (We are here assuming that the eight factors have equal effects; if not, then their scores should be weighted by their effects on adaptive organizational change.) However, if, for the typical organization, its average value on the organizational portfolio factors is moving to the left in Figure 10.1, then its adaptive organizational change is decreasing. Also, if the average correlations among all the organizational portfolio factors are low positive or negative, then their movements offset each other so that, even if the typical organization is experiencing change on its organizational portfolio factors, its level of adaptive organizational change will tend toward being constant. Thus either an average leftward shift on the values of, or an average low positive or negative correlation between, the organizational portfolio factors leads to the level of adaptive organizational change *not* increasing.

Also, when each correlation in the semi-matrix is known, it is possible to establish clusters. When certain organizational portfolio factors cluster together, it will be possible to term each of them as organizational portfolio *factorials* (as distinct from the organizational portfolio *factors* that cluster into the factorials). Again, purely as an illustration, the quite high positive correlation between diversification and divisionalization means that they would quite likely form an organizational portfolio factorial, such as heterogeneity (of strategy and structure). Negatively correlating organizational portfolio factors would also fall into the portfolio factorials, with a negative loading on the factorial. Thus the organizational portfolio factorials would distill the effect of all their factors on the probability of adaptive organizational change. Organizational portfolio factors that loaded positively on a factorial contribute positively to the probability of movement on the continuum of adaptive organizational change. In contrast, organizational portfolio factors that loaded negatively on a factorial reduce the probability of movement on the continuum of adaptive organizational change.

Once organizational portfolio factorials are established in this way, it reduces the complexity of the analysis of the overall effects of organizational portfolio factors on the movement along the adaptive organizational change continuum. Instead of considering the effects of all 28 pairs of correlations among the eight organizational portfolio factors, only the effects of the factorials need to be considered. (Of course, any such use of factorials depends on the results of the factorial analysis producing a limited number of factorials that account for a large proportion of the total variance in the adaptive organizational change continuum.)

Revisions to the Theory of the Divisionalized Corporation

An implication of several of the theoretical ideas advanced in separate chapters is their view of the large, divisionalized corporation. These points are now drawn together.

Prevailing discussions of the large, divisionalized corporation in organizational theory tend to follow the theory of Williamson (1970, 1985): that the divisionalized (i.e., M-form) corporation has distinct advantages over the formerly dominant functionally structured (i.e., U-form) corporation. The divisionalized corporation is held to provide for the effective management of assets and ensure their high-performance use. This occurs both within the divisionalized corporation, by monitoring of the divisional profit centers by the corporate center, and outside the corporation, by pressure on other firms through threat of their being taken over by the divisionalized corporation. Thus the corporate center of the divisionalized corporation effectively polices the businesses in the economy. The main limitation noted in contemporary discussions of the divisionalized corporation is that diversification may be counterproductive (e.g., Rumelt 1982). Although the strategy of diversification is widely called into question, the divisionalized organizational structure has generally been lauded (though see Hill 1985a).

In contrast, the organizational portfolio theory advanced herein takes a different view of the large corporation by revealing negative, long-term effects. Most large corporations are diversified to some degree, but diversification across industries with different business cycles tends to nullify the positive aspects of the business cycle on organizational adaptation and growth. The diversification and consequent divisionalization of the large corporation produce stable overall performance, that is, low risk. The lack of episodes of the organizational performance dropping below the satisficing level means that the organization persists in misfit and fails to make adaptations in structure and other aspects. Thus the large corporation fails to adopt the next set of structural and other innovations that it needs and so its performance is less than optimal and tends to drift downward toward mediocrity. In contrast, increasing competition, such as through new, international competitors or existing competitors becoming better organized, increases pressure on the corporation to adapt. The actual degree of adaptation of the large corporation is thus the net effect of these forces pushing for or against its adaptation. While forces from outside the corporation, such as competition, are pushing it to adapt, there are substantial forces inside the corporation pushing it to not adapt, such as its diversification and divisionalization.

The tendency toward pathological stability of the divisionalized corporation is reinforced by processes at the divisional level. These divisional processes conspire against intervention by the corporate center to raise all poorly performing divisions to their optimal. The center will tend to intervene in divisions particularly when not only the division but also the corporation as a whole is performing below the satisficing level. This means that when the corporation intervenes, several divisions may be performing poorly simultaneously. In such a situation, limits on the information-processing capacity of the corporate center will tend to force it to attend to fixing the problem divisions one after the other. Moreover, this process is liable to be curtailed when sufficient divisions have been fixed to raise corporate performance above its satisficing level. Thus some divisions may endure with low performance for considerable periods of time. Furthermore, problems at the corporate center may be mistakenly attributed by corporate managers to divisions and so delay their rectification. In this way, divisions can also form part of the pathological stability and suboptimal performance of the corporation. Again, divisions with stable performance are liable to drift into maladaptation and suboptimal performance, mirroring the fate of the pathologically stable corporation. Such pathologically stable divisions will tend to include the cash cow divisions, which strongly influence corporate profits, and so substantially depress the performance of the corporation.

When the corporation takes on debt, this works to increase the likelihood of adaptive organizational change. However, the tendency for corporations to not make needed adaptive changes is reinforced further by divestment. When a corporation divests, such as selling non-core businesses, this provides new slack resources that keep its performance satisfactory and so forestall adaptive change. A large diversified corporation that sequentially divested itself of businesses one by one over many years could in this way forestall a performance crisis and adaptive change a long time. Divestment of non-core businesses by large, diversified corporations, that is, downscoping, was a trend among some corporations in the 1980s (Hoskisson and Hitt 1994; Davis, Diekmann, and Tinsley 1994), which then tended to add to their pathological stability.

Thus the various mechanisms in organizational portfolio theory combine to make the overall performance of the large corporation stable at a medium level so that needed structural adaptations are avoided, preventing the emergence of new, better-fitting structures and higher performance. Hence a national economy dominated by large diversified, divisionalized corporations would become quite mediocre and be outperformed by other national economies in which diversified, divisionalized corporations are less dominant or more recent.

The pathological stability of the diversified, divisionalized corporation gives late capitalism a particular hue. Theorists of the political left, in the tradition of Marx, prophesied economic decline ending in collapse of capitalism and replacement by socialism. This has not happened in the advanced capitalist economies. Conversely, the socialist economies have collapsed. Theorists of the political right, in the tradition of Adam Smith, have forecast the triumph of capitalism as the economic system that produces superior performance. Thus, relative to both the left and right of political-economy theory, the suggestion of organizational portfolio theory is neither catastrophic decline nor triumph but, rather, a long, slow decline toward mediocrity for capitalist economies under the influence of their large diversified, divisionalized corporations.

Research Agenda

The main objective of this book has been to present a new theory of organizational change, the organizational portfolio theory. This takes the form of a number of conjectures (Popper 1963) that constitute a set of novel propositions about the interacting causes of organizational performance and the effects of organizational performance on organizational change. It is intended to provide a framework to guide future research by posing interesting questions that have not been asked previously. To aid this process, the major components of the theory have been presented as propositions in each chapter. It is intended that these propositions can be readily turned into research hypotheses. Thus stating the theory as a series of propositions should help make it empirically testable by scholars. Research can then be conducted using this framework to test the empirical validity of the theory and refine it over time. The result should be a more coherent and valid understanding of organizational adaptation and consequent success as driven by organizational performance.

At the heart of organizational portfolio theory is the organization itself reconceptualized as a portfolio, that is, as a number of causes of organizational performance, each of whose performances vary over time and covary with one another to produce fluctuations in overall organizational performance. Empirical research needs to measure the fluctuation in overall organizational performance and in this way to measure organizational risk and then to use it as an independent and dependent variable.

The fluctuation in organizational performance is affected by factors external to the organization. These include the business cycle. A testable hypothesis is that when an organization is in misfit of its structure to its contingencies, it is more likely to adapt a better-fitting structure when the business cycle has turned downward for some time. The explanatory hypothesis is that this occurs because the business cycle helps depress organizational performance below the satisficing level. Similarly, the related testable hypothesis is that when an organization is in fit of its structure to its contingencies, it is more likely to move into misfit when the business cycle has been rising for some time. This occurs because the business cycle helps raise organizational performance, and this leads to organizational growth and other developments that increase the contingencies to the point where the existing structure becomes a misfit. Exactly at what point in the business cycle the changes occur is best left to empirical research to establish.

More generally, all the propositions about organizational performance causing organizational change are, in turn, the results of all the factors that affect organizational performance, including the business cycle.

The second major external economic factor is competition. A testable hypothesis is that an organization in misfit is more likely to move into fit if its competitors are in fit.

Turning inside the organization, a testable hypothesis is that organizational risk is lower in diversified, divisionalized corporations than in undiversified, functionally structured corporations. A second hypothesis is that the lower organizational risk of diversified, divisionalized corporations is caused by the lesser fluctuation of the performance of their divisions and the less positive, or more negative, correlation among divisional performances (relative to the performances of functional departments in the undiversified, functional corporations). The performance variables of interest are profit measures for the corporation and its divisions (and for functionally structured corporations the sales and costs of its functional departments that produce corporate profitability).

Another key idea of organizational portfolio theory is that risk (i.e., fluctuation) is required to trigger adaptive change, so some minimum risk is needed for a healthy firm. Thus a third hypothesis is that the risk of firms that are adapting and growing is considerably greater than firms that are not adapting and growing. The logic is that organizational performance needs to drop below the satisficing level for adaptation to occur.

This implies that the satisficing level, that is, the level of organizational performance that is satisfactory and allows the status quo to be maintained, is substantially below the optimal possible performance of the organization. If this condition is not met, the theory of performance-driven organizational adaptation presented here experiences difficulties. If satisficing is close to and just below the optimal organizational performance, a small drop below the optimal level triggers adaptive organizational change. Thus any internal misfit of the organization to its contingencies would lead quickly to organizational adaptation and restitution of optimal performance. Thus there would be no long periods in misfit, no lags in adaptation, no pathological stability, and no waiting for other factors (e.g., the business cycle) to turn downward before adaptation occurred. Thus the set of propositions outlined in our theory would largely be inapplicable. The theory is more informative to the extent that the satisficing level of organizational performance is significantly below the optimal level. Thus empirical research is required to ascertain the satisficing level and to see how far it is below the optimal.

This in turn raises a set of issues about the measurement of the organizational performance variable. In outlining the theory, the tendency has been to equate organizational performance with organizational profitability. This is likely to be so for most practical purposes in studying most business firms. However, organizational performance is an objective established for the firm by its dominant coalition (i.e., the set of most powerful people, typically managers, owners, and so on). In some firms, these people may have preferences other than profit (e.g., maximum sales growth). For example, senior managers may be concerned about maintaining cash flow, so a drop in cash flow below a certain level may be subsatisficing to them, causing them to initiate action.

Timing is also an issue here in that for some corporations profit may be calculated quarterly, whereas for some firms, profit is calculated only annually for the reported accounts. Thus an awareness among managers that their organization has dropped below the satisficing level may occur only at certain points in the annual accounting cycle. Only then will adaptive change be triggered. Thus an empirical assessment of whether the firm is satisficing or not involves ascertaining the measures used by the dominant coalition, which may be other than profit, and the time period used by the organization to compute such measures and to report them to management. For instance, managers of a large corporation may be galvanized into taking adaptive action by the monthly cashflow turning poor rather than waiting to see the quarterly profit figure. Thus there is a task for empirical research to establish the variables, levels, and time frames that constitute satisficing for an organization.

Moreover, the satisficing level may vary by industry. Social comparison will be made between firms, especially between those perceived as similar (e.g., in the same industry). The growth of information comparing company performances (e.g., investor league tables) enters here as a factor. It may also vary by organizational size, with expectations being higher for large corporations than for smaller firms. It may also vary by country—for example, the satisficing level in the United States may be different from that in Japan. Furthermore, the satisficing level may change over time. Indeed, the present satisficing level is affected by the level of organizational performance that was actually attained in prior periods (Cyert and March 1963). Institutional effects play a role, in that banks and lenders signal their expectations of performance to the focal organization that seeks to meet them (DiMaggio and Powell 1983). The investor activism movement has focused attention on the returns to investors generated by firms and has criticized the performance of some organizations as unsatisfactory (Davis and Thompson 1994), thereby pressuring their managers to revise upward the level of performance that they take as satisficing. Thus satisficing levels will vary by organization and also over time. They need to be studied empirically. As the discussion indicates, satisficing levels are causally determined, and so establishing these causal regularities is itself a substantive topic of research and a part of the whole research agenda.

A similar set of hypotheses applies at the divisional level. Theoretically, higher-risk divisions have a higher probability of adapting and growing over time. This is because their performance drops below their satisficing level recurrently, so triggering the episodes of change. The satisficing level, the performance measures, and their time frame (e.g., annual, quarterly, or monthly) need to be established empirically for the divisions and may vary across divisions and across corporations. Thus there is scope for empirical study of these phenomena at the divisional level as there is for the corporate level.

For both corporate and divisional levels, even if the underlying mechanisms about satisficing and so forth cannot be immediately studied empirically, the hypotheses about adaptive change being driven by low performance and by risk can be studied empirically, at both the corporate and the divisional levels. Thus the relationships between the objective variables readily lend themselves to study even if the intervening psychological variables are less easily accessed.

Turning to corporate governance, two of the empirical research hypotheses are as follows. High organizational performance leads the corporation to adopt boards of directors in which executives play a larger role; that is, a higher proportion of directors are executives, and the chair is also an executive. Conversely, low organizational performance leads the corporation to adopt boards of directors in which executives play a smaller role; that is, a higher proportion of directors are non-executives, and the chair is also a non-executive. Thus poor performance drives toward a board more independent of management that is intended to provide a control on management.

There are many other testable hypotheses that derive from organizational portfolio theory. Each of the theoretical propositions stated in the chapters can be turned into a hypothesis by stating the variables in the proposition in terms of operational measures. The discussion here serves only to suggest some part of this process in order to encourage future researchers.

References

Abrahamson, Eric. 1997. "The Emergence and Prevalence of Employee Management Rhetorics: The Effects of Long Waves, Labor Unions, and Turnover, 1875 to 1992." *Academy of Management Journal* 40:491-533.

Aldrich, Howard E. 1979. *Organizations and Environments*. Englewood Cliffs, NJ: Prentice Hall.

Allen, Stephen A. 1978. "Organizational Choices and General Management Influence Networks in Divisionalized Companies." *Academy of Management Journal* 21:341-365.

Amburgey, Terry L. and Tina Dacin. 1994. "As the Left Foot Follows the Right? The Dynamics of Strategic and Structural Change." *Academy of Management Journal* 37:1427-1452.

Amihud, Y. and B. Lev. 1981. "Risk Reduction as a Managerial Motive for Conglomerate Mergers." *Bell Journal of Economics* 12:605-617.

Amit, R. and J. Livnat. 1989. "Efficient Corporate Diversification: Methods and Implications." *Management Science* 35:879-897.

Argyris, Chris. 1964. *Integrating the Individual and the Organization*. New York: John Wiley.

———. 1970. *Intervention Theory and Method: A Behavioral Science View*. Reading, MA: Addison-Wesley.

Armour, Henry O. and David J. Teece. 1978. "Organizational Structure and Economic Performance: A Test of the Multidivisional Hypothesis." *Bell Journal of Economics* 9:106-122.

Ball, Ray and Philip Brown. 1980. "Risk and Return From Equity Investments in the Australian Mining Industry: January 1958-February 1979." *Australian Journal of Management* 5:45-66.

Barnett, W. P. 1990. "The Organizational Ecology of a Technological System." *Administrative Science Quarterly* 35:31-60.

Barnett, W. P. and T. L. Amburgey. 1990. "Do Larger Organizations Generate Stronger Competition?" Pp. 78-102 in *Organizational Evolution: New Directions*, edited by Jitendra V. Singh. Newbury Park, CA: Sage.

Barnett, W. P. and G. R. Carroll. 1987. "Competition and Mutualism Among Early Telephone Companies." *Administrative Science Quarterly* 32:400-421.

Barney, Jay B. 1990. "The Debate Between Traditional Management Theory and Organizational Economics: Substantive Differences or Intergroup Conflict?" *Academy of Management Review* 15:382-393.

215

Baumol, William J., J. C. Panzar, and R. D. Willig. 1982. *Contestable Markets and the Theory of Industry Structure.* New York: Harcourt Brace Jovanovich.

Baysinger, B. D., R. T. Kosnik, and T. A. Turk. 1991. "Effects of Board and Ownership Structure on Corporate R&D Strategy." *Academy of Management Journal* 34:205-214.

Baysinger, Barry D. and Henry N. Butler. 1985. "Corporate Governance and the Board of Directors: Performance Effects of Changes in Board Composition." *Journal of Law, Economics and Organization* 1:101-124.

Bennis, W. G. 1971. "Theory and Method in Applying Behavioral Science to Planned Organizational Change." Pp. 358-376 in *Personnel Management and Organizational Development: Fields in Transition,* edited by Wendell L. French and Don Hellriegel. Boston: Houghton Mifflin.

Berle, Adolf and Gardiner Means. 1932. *The Modern Corporation and Private Property.* New York: Macmillan.

Bettenhausen, Kenneth L. 1995. "Group Dynamics." Pp. 203-204 in the *Blackwell Encyclopedic Dictionary of Organizational Behavior,* edited by Nigel Nicholson. Cambridge, MA: Blackwell.

Bishop, Matthew and John Kay. 1988. *Does Privatization Work? Lessons From the UK.* London: Centre for Business Strategy, London Business School.

Blau, Peter M. 1970. "A Formal Theory of Differentiation in Organizations." *American Sociological Review* 35:201-218.

———. 1972. "Interdependence and Hierarchy in Organizations." *Social Science Research* 1:1-24.

Blau, Peter M. and P. A. Schoenherr. 1971. *The Structure of Organizations.* New York: Basic Books.

Bowman, E. H. 1980. "A Risk/Return Paradox for Strategic Management." *Sloan Management Review* 21:17-31.

Boyd, B. 1995. "CEO Duality and Firm Performance: A Contingency Model." *Strategic Management Journal* 16:301-312.

Brealey, Richard A. and Stewart C. Myers. 1996. *Principles of Corporate Finance.* 5th ed. New York: McGraw-Hill.

Bromiley, Philip. 1991a. "Testing a Causal Model of Corporate Risk Taking and Performance." *Academy of Management Journal* 34:37-59.

———. 1991b. "Paradox or at Least Variance Found: A Comment on 'Mean-Variance Approaches to Risk-Return Relationships in Strategy: Paradox Lost.' " *Management Science* 37:1206-1210.

Brown, J. A. C. 1954. *The Social Psychology of Industry: Human Relations in the Factory.* London: Penguin Books.

Buhner, R. and P. Möller. 1985. "The Information Context of Corporate Disclosures of Divisionalization Decisions." *Journal of Management Studies* 22:309-326.

Burns, Tom and G. M. Stalker. 1961. *The Management of Innovation.* London: Tavistock.

"That's Chairman Golub to You." 1993. *Business Week,* July 12, p. 35.

Cadbury, Adrian. 1992. *Report of the Committee on the Financial Aspects of Corporate Governance.* London: The Committee and Gee.

Cameron, Kim S., M. U. Kim, and David A. Whetten. 1987. "Organizational Effects of Decline and Turbulence." *Administrative Science Quarterly* 32:222-240.

Cameron, Kim S., Robert I. Sutton, and David A. Whetten, eds. 1988. *Readings in Organizational Decline: Frameworks, Research, and Prescriptions.* Cambridge, MA: Ballinger.

Capon, Noel, Chris Christodolou, John U. Farley, and James M. Hulbert. 1987. "A Comparative Analysis of the Strategy and Structure of United States and Australian Corporations." *Journal of International Business Studies* 18:51-74.

Carew, Edna. 1997. *Westpac: The Bank That Broke the Bank.* Sydney, Australia: Doubleday.

Cascio, Wayne F. 1993. "Downsizing: What Do We Know? What Have We Learned?" *Academy of Management Executive* 7:95-104.

Chaganti, R. S., V. Mahajan, and S. Sharma. 1985. "Corporate Board Size, Composition and Corporate Failures in Retailing Industry." *Journal of Management Studies* 2:400-416.

Chandler, Alfred D., Jr. 1962. *Strategy and Structure: Chapters in the History of the Industrial Enterprise.* Cambridge: MIT Press.

———. 1977. *The Visible Hand: The Managerial Revolution in American Business.* Cambridge, MA: Belknap Press.

———. 1994. "The Functions of the HQ Unit in the Multibusiness Firm." Pp. 323-360 in *Fundamental Issues in Strategy: A Research Agenda,* edited by Richard P. Rumelt, Dan E. Schendel, and David J. Teece. Boston: Harvard Business School Press.

Channon, Derek F. 1973. *The Strategy and Structure of British Enterprise.* London: Macmillan.

———. 1978. *The Service Industries: Strategy, Structure and Financial Performance.* London: Macmillan.

Chenhall, Robert H. 1979. "Some Elements of Organizational Control in Australian Divisionalized Firms." *Australian Journal of Management,* suppl. to 4, 1:1-36.

Child, John. 1972. "Organizational Structure, Environment and Performance: The Role of Strategic Choice." *Sociology* 6:1-22.

———. 1973. "Predicting and Understanding Organization Structure." *Administrative Science Quarterly* 18:168-185.

———. 1975. "Managerial and Organizational Factors Associated With Company Performance. Part 2: A Contingency Analysis." *Journal of Management Studies* 12:12-27.

———. 1997. "From the Aston Programme to Strategic Choice: A Journey From Concepts to Theory." Pp. 45-72 in *Advancement in Organizational Behaviour: Essays in Honour of Derek S. Pugh,* edited by Timothy Clark. Aldershot, Hants, England: Ashgate.

Cibin, R. and R. M. Grant. 1996. "Restructuring Among the World's Leading Oil Companies, 1980-92." *British Journal of Management* 7:283-307.

Clegg, Stewart and David Dunkerley. 1980. *Organization, Class and Control.* London: Routledge & Kegan Paul.

Clifford, Peter W. and Robert T. Evans. 1996. "The State of Corporate Governance Practices in Australia." *Corporate Governance: An International Review* 4:60-70.

Cohen, Allan R., Stephen L. Fink, Herman Gadon, and Robin D. Willits. 1976. *Effective Behavior in Organizations: Learning From the Interplay of Cases, Concepts, and Student Experiences.* Homewood, IL: Richard D. Irwin.

Cummings, Thomas G. and Edgar F. Huse. 1989. *Organization Development and Change.* 4th ed. St. Paul, MN: West.

Cyert, Richard M. and James G. March. 1963. *A Behavioral Theory of the Firm.* Englewood Cliffs, NJ: Prentice Hall.

Cyert, Richard M., Herbert A. Simon, and Donald B. Trow. 1956. "Observations of a Business Decision." *Journal of Business* 29:237-248.

Daily, Catherine M. and Dan R. Dalton. 1994a. "Corporate Governance and the Bankrupt Firm: The Impact of Board Composition and Structure." *Academy of Management Journal* 37:1603-1617.

———. 1994b. "Bankruptcy and Corporate Governance: An Empirical Assessment." *Strategic Management Journal* 15:643-654.

———. 1997. "CEO and Board Chair Roles Held Jointly or Separately: Much Ado About Nothing?" *Academy of Management Executive* 11:11-20.

D'Aveni, Richard A. 1994. *Hypercompetition: Managing the Dynamics of Strategic Maneuvering.* New York: Free Press.

Davis, Gerald F. 1991. "Agents Without Principals? The Spread of the Poison Pill Through the Intercorporate Network." *Administrative Science Quarterly* 36:583-613.

Davis, Gerald F., Kristina A. Diekmann, and Catherine H. Tinsley. 1994. "The Decline and Fall of the Conglomerate Firm in the 1980s: The Deinstitutionalization of an Organizational Form." *American Sociological Review* 59:547-570.

Davis, Gerald F. and Walter W. Powell. 1992. "Organization-Environment Relations." Pp. 315-375 in *Handbook of Industrial and Organizational Psychology,* 2d ed, Vol. 3, edited by Marvin Dunnette and Laetta M. Hough. Palo Alto, CA: Consulting Psychologists Press.

Davis, Gerald F. and Tracy A. Thompson. 1994. "A Social Movement Perspective on Corporate Control." *Administrative Science Quarterly* 39:141-173.

Davis, Jeremy G. and Timothy M. Devinney. 1997. *The Essence of Corporate Strategy: Theory for Modern Decision Making.* St. Leonards, NSW, Australia: Allen & Unwin.

Davis, Stanley M. 1972. "Trends in the Organization of Multinational Corporations." Pp. 231-248 in *Managing and Organizing Multinational Corporations,* edited by Stanley M. Davis. New York: Pergamon.

DiMaggio, Paul J. and Walter W. Powell. 1983. "The Iron Cage Revisited: Institutional Isomorphism and Collective Rationality in Organization Fields." *American Sociological Review* 48:147-160.

Donaldson, Gordon. 1994. *Corporate Restructuring: Managing the Change Process From Within.* Boston: Harvard Business School Press.

Donaldson, Lex. 1979. "Regaining Control at Nipont." *Journal of General Management* 4:14-30.

———. 1982. "Divisionalization and Diversification: A Longitudinal Study." *Academy of Management Journal* 25:909-914.

———. 1985a. *In Defence of Organization Theory: A Reply to the Critics.* Cambridge, England: Cambridge University Press.

———. 1985b. "Organization Design and the Life-Cycles of Products." *Journal of Management Studies* 22:25-37.

———. 1987. "Strategy and Structural Adjustment to Regain Fit and Performance: In Defence of Contingency Theory." *Journal of Management Studies* 24:1-24.

———. 1990a. "The Ethereal Hand: Organizational Economics and Management Theory." *Academy of Management Review* 15:369-381.

———. 1990b. "A Rational Basis for Criticisms of Organizational Economics: A Reply to Barney." *Academy of Management Review* 15:394-401.

———. 1994. "The Liberal Revolution and Organization Theory." Pp. 190-208 in *Towards a New Theory of Organizations,* edited by J. Hassard and M. Parker. London: Routledge.

———. 1995. *American Anti-Management Theories of Organization: A Critique of Paradigm Proliferation.* Cambridge, England: Cambridge University Press.

———. 1996a. *For Positivist Organization Theory: Proving the Hard Core.* London: Sage.

———. 1996b. "The Normal Science of Structural Contingency Theory." Pp. 57-76 in *The Handbook of Organization Studies,* edited by Stewart R. Clegg, Cynthia Hardy, and Walter R. Nord. London: Sage.

Donaldson, Lex and James H. Davis. 1991. "Stewardship Theory or Agency Theory: CEO Governance and Shareholder Returns." *Australian Journal of Management* 16:49-64.

———. 1994. "Boards and Company Performance: Research Challenges the Conventional Wisdom." *Corporate Governance: An International Review* 2:151-160.

Dotsey, Michael and Robert G. King. 1987. "Business Cycles." Pp. 302-310 in *The New Palgrave: A Dictionary of Economics,* edited by John Eatwell, Murray Milgate, and Peter Newman. London: Macmillan.

Dougherty, Deborah and Cynthia Hardy. 1996. "Sustained Product Innovation in Large, Mature Organizations: Overcoming Innovation-to-Organization Problems." *Academy of Management Journal* 39:1120-1153.

Drazin, Robert and Andrew H. Van de Ven. 1985. "Alternative Forms of Fit in Contingency Theory." *Administrative Science Quarterly* 30:514-539.

Dunning, John H., Bruce Kogut, and Magnus Blomström. 1990. *Globalization of Firms and the Competitiveness of Nations.* Lund, Sweden: Institute of Economic Research, Lund University.

Dunphy, Dexter. 1981. *Organizational Change by Choice.* Sydney, Australia: McGraw-Hill.

Dunphy, Dexter and Doug Stace. 1990. *Under New Management: Australian Organizations in Transition.* Sydney, Australia: McGraw-Hill.

Dyas, Gareth P. and Heinz T. Thanheiser. 1976. *The Emerging European Enterprise: Strategy and Structure in French and German Industry.* London: Macmillan.

Eccles, Robert G. and Dwight B. Crane. 1988. *Doing Deals: Investment Banks at Work.* Boston: Harvard Business School Press.

Eccles, Robert G. and Nitin Nohria. 1992. *Beyond the Hype: Rediscovering the Essence of Management.* Boston: Harvard Business School Press.

Egelhoff, William G. 1988. *Organizing the Multinational Enterprise: An Information Processing Perspective.* Cambridge, MA: Ballinger.

Eisenberg, Melvin A., Stanley A. Kaplan, Harvey J. Goldschmid, Marshall L. Small, Ronald J. Gilson, and John C. Coffee, Jr. 1994. *Principles of Corporate Governance: Analysis and Recommendations.* St. Paul, MN: American Law Institute.

Emery, Fred E. and E. L. Trist. 1965. "The Causal Texture of Organisational Environments." *Human Relations* 18:21-32.

Etzioni, Amitai. 1975. *A Comparative Analysis of Complex Organizations: On Power, Involvement and Their Correlates.* Revised and enlarged ed. New York: Free Press.

Ezzamel, M. A. and R. Watson. 1993. "Organizational Form, Ownership Structure and Corporate Performance: A Contextual Empirical Analysis of UK Companies." *British Journal of Management* 4:161-176.

Figenbaum, Avi and Howard Thomas. 1986. "Dynamic and Risk Measurement Perspectives on Bowman's Risk-Return Paradox for Strategic Management: An Empirical Study." *Strategic Management Journal* 7:395-407.

Finkelstein, Sydney and Donald C. Hambrick. 1996. *Strategic Leadership: Top Executives and Their Effects on Organizations.* Minneapolis/St. Paul: West.

Fligstein, Neil. 1985. "The Spread of the Multidivisional Form Among Large Firms, 1919-1979." *American Sociological Review* 50:377-391.

———. 1990a. *The Transformation of Corporate Control.* Cambridge, MA: Harvard University Press.

———. 1990b. "Organizational, Demographic and Economic Determinants of the Growth Patterns of Large Firms, 1919-1979." Pp. 45-76 in *Business Institutions,* Vol. 12, *Comparative Social Research,* edited by Craig Calhoun. Greenwich, CT: JAI.

———. 1991. "The Structural Transformation of American Industry: An Institutional Account of the Causes of Diversification in the Largest Firms, 1919-1979." Pp. 311-336 in *The New Institutionalism in Organizational Analysis,* edited by Walter W. Powell and Paul J. DiMaggio. Chicago: University of Chicago Press.

Fligstein, Neil and Peter Brantley. 1992. "Bank Control, Owner Control, or Organizational Dynamics: Who Controls the Large Modern Corporation?" *American Journal of Sociology* 98:280-307.

Freeman, J. and M. T. Hannan. 1975. "Growth and Decline Processes in Organizations." *American Sociological Review* 40:215-228.

Galbraith, Jay R. 1973. *Designing Complex Organizations.* Reading, MA: Addison-Wesley.

Galbraith, Jay R. and Robert K. Kazanjian. 1988. "Strategy, Technology and Emerging Organizational Forms." Pp. 29-41 in *Futures of Organizations: Innovating to Adapt Strategy and Human Resources to Rapid Technological Change,* edited by Jerald Hage. Lexington, MA: Lexington Books.

Graen, George and William Schiemann. 1978. "Leadership-Member Agreement: A Vertical Dyad Linkage Approach." *Journal of Applied Psychology* 63:206-212.

Grant, Robert M. 1993. *Restructuring and Strategic Change in the Oil Industry.* Milano, Italy: Franco Agneli.

Greiner, Larry E. 1972. "Evolution and Revolution as Organizations Grow." *Harvard Business Review* 4:37-46.

Grinyer, Peter H. and Masoud Yasai-Ardekani. 1981. "Strategy, Structure, Size and Bureaucracy." *Academy of Management Journal* 24:471-486.

Hage, Jerald. 1974. *Communications and Organizational Control: Cybernetics in Health and Welfare Settings.* New York: Wiley Interscience.

———. 1980. *Theories of Organization: Form, Process and Transformation.* New York: John Wiley.

———. 1988. *Futures of Organizations: Innovating to Adopt Strategy and Human Resources to Rapid Technological Change.* Lexington, MA: Lexington Books.

Halberstam, David. 1987. *The Reckoning.* New York: William Morrow.

Hamilton, R. T. and G. S. Shergill. 1992. "The Relationship Between Strategy-Structure Fit and Financial Performance in New Zealand: Evidence of Generality and Validity With Enhanced Controls." *Journal of Management Studies* 29:95-113.

———. 1993. *The Logic of New Zealand Business: Strategy, Structure, and Performance.* Auckland, New Zealand: Oxford University Press.

Hannan, Michael T. and John Freeman. 1984. "Structural Inertia and Organizational Change." *American Sociological Review* 49:149-164.

———. 1989. *Organizational Ecology.* Cambridge, MA: Harvard University Press.

Hannan, Michael T., J. Ranger-Moore, and J. Banaszak-Holl. 1990. "Competition and the Evolution of Organizational Size Distributions." Pp. 246-268 in *Organizational Evolution: New Directions,* edited by Jitendra V. Singh. Newbury Park, CA: Sage.

Harris, Barry C. 1983. *Organization: The Effect on Large Corporations.* Ann Arbor: UMI Research Press.

Helfat, Constance E. and David J. Teece. 1987. "Vertical Integration and Risk Reduction." *Journal of Law, Economics, and Organization* 3:47-67.

Hill, Charles W. L. 1985a. "Oliver Williamson and the M-Form Firm: A Critical Review." *Journal of Economic Issues* 19:731-751.

———. 1985b. "Internal Organization and Enterprise Performance: Some UK Evidence." *Managerial and Decision Economics* 6:210-216.

———. 1988. "Corporate Control Type, Strategy, Size and Financial Performance." *Journal of Management Studies* 25:403-417.

Hill, Charles W. L., Michael A. Hitt, and Robert E. Hoskisson. 1992. "Cooperative Versus Competitive Structures in Related and Unrelated Diversified Firms." *Organization Science* 3:501-521.

Hill, Charles W. L. and S. A. Snell. 1988. "External Control, Corporate Strategy, and Firm Performance in Research-Intensive Industries." *Strategic Management Journal* 9:577-590.

Hofer, Charles W. 1975. "Toward a Contingency Theory of Business Strategy." *Academy of Management Journal* 18:784-810.

Hopkins, H. Donald. 1988. "Firm Size: The Interchangeability of Measures." *Human Relations* 41:91-102.

Hoskisson, R. E., Charles W. L. Hill, and Hicheon Kim. 1993. "The Multidivisional Structure: Organizational Fossil or Source of Value?" *Journal of Management* 19:269-298.

Hoskisson, Robert E. 1987. "Multidivisional Structure and Performance: The Contingency of Diversification Strategy." *Academy of Management Journal* 30:625-644.

Hoskisson, Robert E. and Craig S. Galbraith. 1985. "The Effect of Quantum Versus Incremental M-Form Reorganization on Performance: A Time-Series Exploration of Intervention Dynamics." *Journal of Management* 11:55-70.

Hoskisson, Robert E. and Michael A. Hitt. 1994. *Downscoping: How to Tame the Diversified Firm.* New York: Oxford University Press.

Jaques, Elliott. 1951. *The Changing Culture of a Factory.* London: Routledge & Kegan Paul.

Jegers, Marc. 1991. "Prospect Theory and the Risk-Return Relationship: Some Belgian Evidence." *Academy of Management Journal* 34:215-225.

Jennings, Daniel F. and Samuel L. Seaman. 1994. "High and Low Levels of Organizational Adaptation: An Empirical Analysis of Strategy, Structure and Performance." *Strategic Management Journal* 15:459-475.

Jensen, Michael C. 1986. "Agency Costs of Free Cash Flow, Corporate Finance, and Takeovers." *American Economic Review* 76:323-329.

Jensen, Michael C. and William H. Meckling. 1976. "Theory of the Firm: Managerial Behavior, Agency Costs and Ownership Structure." *Journal of Financial Economics* 3:305-360.

Johnson, G. 1987. *Strategic Change and the Management Process.* Oxford, England: Basil Blackwell.

Kesner, Idalene F. 1987. "Directors, Stock Ownership and Organizational Performance: An Investigation of Fortune 500 Companies." *Journal of Management* 13:499-508.

Kesner, Idalene F. and Dan R. Dalton. 1986. "Boards of Directors and the Checks and (Im)Balances of Corporate Governance." *Business Horizons,* September-October, pp. 17-23.

Khandwalla, Pradip N. 1973. "Viable and Effective Organizational Designs of Firms." *Academy of Management Journal* 16:481-495.

———. 1974. "Mass Output Orientation of Operations Technology and Organizational Structure." *Administrative Science Quarterly* 19:74-97.

———. 1977. *The Design of Organizations.* New York: Harcourt Brace Jovanovich.

Kraatz, Matthew S. and Edward J. Zajac. 1996. "Exploring the Limits of the New Institutionalism: The Causes and Consequences of Illegitimate Organizational Change." *American Sociological Review* 61:812-836.

Kuczynski, M. G. 1986. "Recent Developments in Business Cycle Theory." *Journal of Economic Dynamics and Control* 10:255-260.

Lant, Theresa K. and David B. Montgomery. 1987. "Learning From Strategic Success and Failure." *Journal of Business Research* 15:503-517.

Lawrence, Paul R. 1993. "The Contingency Approach to Organizational Design." Pp. 9-18 in *Handbook of Organizational Behavior,* edited by Robert T. Golembiewski. New York: Marcel Dekker.

Lawrence, Paul R. and Jay W. Lorsch. 1967. *Organization and Environment: Managing Differentiation and Integration.* Boston: Division of Research, Graduate School of Business Administration, Harvard University.

Likert, Rensis. 1961. *New Patterns of Management.* New York: McGraw-Hill.

Lorsch, Jay W. and Stephen A. Allen. 1973. *Managing Diversity and Interdependence: An Organizational Study of Multidivisional Firms.* Boston: Division of Research, Graduate School of Business Administration, Harvard University.

Mahoney, Joseph T. 1992. "The Adoption of the Multidivisional Form of Organization: A Contingency Model." *Journal of Management Studies* 29:49-72.

March, J. G. and H. A. Simon. 1958. *Organizations.* New York: John Wiley.

March, James G. 1988. "Variable Risk Preferences and Adaptive Aspirations." *Journal of Economic Behavior and Organization* 9:5-24.

March, James G. and Zur Shapira. 1987. "Managerial Perspectives on Risk and Risk Taking." *Management Science* 33:1404-1418.

Mayer, Roger C., James H. Davis, and F. David Schoorman. 1995. "An Integrative Model of Organizational Trust." *Academy of Management Journal* 20:709-734.

McLennan, Roy. 1989. *Managing Organizational Change.* London: Prentice Hall International.

McNamara, Gerry and Philip Bromiley. 1997. "Decision Making in an Organizational Setting: Cognitive and Organizational Influences on Risk Assessment in Commercial Lending." *Academy of Management Journal* 40:1063-1088.

Merton, R. K. 1949. *Social Theory and Social Structure.* Chicago: Free Press.

Miller, Kent D. and Philip Bromiley. 1990. "Strategic Risk and Corporate Performance: An Analysis of Alternative Risk Measures." *Academy of Management Journal* 33:756-779.

Miller, Kent D. and Michael J. Leiblein. 1996. "Corporate Risk-Return Relations: Returns Variability Versus Downside Risk." *Academy of Management Journal* 39:91-122.

Miner, J. B. 1982. *Theories of Organizational Structure and Process.* Chicago: Dryden.

Mintzberg, H. and James A. Waters. 1982. "Tracking Strategy in an Entrepreneurial Firm." *Academy of Management Journal* 25:465-499.

Mintzberg, Henry. 1979. *The Structuring of Organizations: A Synthesis of the Research.* Englewood Cliffs, NJ: Prentice Hall.

Murphy, Kevin J. and Jay Dial. 1994. "General Dynamics: Compensation and Strategy (A) and (B)." Harvard Business School case.

Ocasio, William. 1995. "The Enactment of Economic Adversity: A Reconceptualization of Theories of Failure-Induced Change and Threat-Rigidity." *Research in Organizational Behavior* 17:287-331.

Orton, J. Douglas and Karl E. Weick. 1990. "Loosely Coupled Systems: A Reconceptualization." *Academy of Management Review* 15:203-223.

Palmer, D., R. Friedland, P. D. Jennings, and M. E. Powers. 1987. "The Economics and Politics of Structure: The Multidivisional Form and Large U.S. Corporation." *Administrative Science Quarterly* 32:25-48.

Palmer, D., P. D. Jennings, and Xuegang Zhou. 1993. "Late Adoption of the Multidivisional Form by Large U.S. Corporations: Institutional, Political, and Economic Accounts." *Administrative Science Quarterly* 38:100-131.

Parsons, Talcott. 1961. "Suggestions for a Sociological Approach to the Theory of Organizations." Pp. 32-47 in *Complex Organizations: A Sociological Reader,* edited by Amitai Etzioni. New York: Holt, Rinehart & Winston.

———. 1963. "On the Concept of Political Power." *Proceedings of the American Philosophical Society* 107:232-262.

Pavan, Robert J. 1976. "Strategy and Structure: The Italian Experience." *Journal of Economics and Business* 28:254-260.

Perrow, Charles. 1986. *Complex Organizations: A Critical Essay.* 3d ed. New York: Random House.

Pettigrew, Andrew M. 1973. *The Politics of Organizational Decision-Making.* London: Tavistock.

———. 1985. *The Awakening Giant.* Oxford, England: Basil Blackwell.

Pfeffer, Jeffrey. 1982. *Organizations and Organization Theory.* Boston: Pitman.

Pfeffer, Jeffrey and Gerald R. Salancik. 1978. *The External Control of Organizations: A Resource Dependence Perspective.* New York: Harper & Row.

Pitts, Robert A. 1974. "Incentive Compensation and Organization Design." *Personnel Journal* 53:338-344.

———. 1976. "Diversification Strategies and Organizational Policies of Large Diversified Firms." *Journal of Economics and Business* 28:181-188.

———. 1977. "Strategies and Structures for Diversification." *Academy of Management Journal* 20:197-208.

Popper, Karl. 1963. *Conjectures and Refutations: The Growth of Scientific Knowledge.* London: Routledge & Kegan Paul.

Porter, M. E. 1985. *Competitive Advantage.* New York: Free Press.

———. 1990. *The Competitive Advantage of Nations.* New York: Free Press.

Powell, Thomas C. 1992. "Organizational Alignment as Competitive Advantage." *Strategic Management Journal* 13:119-134.

Powell, Walter W. and Paul J. DiMaggio, eds. 1991. *The New Institutionalism in Organizational Analysis.* Chicago: University of Chicago Press.

Pugh, D. S., D. J. Hickson, C. R. Hinings, and C. Turner. 1968. "Dimensions of Organization Structure." *Administrative Science Quarterly* 13:65-105.

———. 1969. "The Context of Organization Structures." *Administrative Science Quarterly* 14:91-114.

Rumelt, Richard P. 1974. *Strategy, Structure and Economic Performance.* Boston: Division of Research, Graduate School of Business Administration, Harvard University.

———. 1982. "Diversification Strategy and Profitability." *Strategic Management Journal* 3:359-369.

Saloner, Garth. 1994. "Game Theory and Strategic Management: Contributions, Application and Limitations." Pp. 155-194 in *Fundamental Issues in Strategy: A Research Agenda,* edited by Richard P. Rumelt, Dan E. Schendel, and David J. Teece. Boston: Harvard Business School Press.

Salter, Malcolm S. and Wolf A. Weinhold. 1979. *Diversification Through Acquisition: Strategies for Creating Economic Value.* New York: Free Press.

Samuelson, Paul A. 1980. *Economics.* 11th ed. New York: McGraw-Hill.

Scott, Bruce R. 1971. *Stages of Corporate Development.* Boston: Harvard Business School Press.

Scott, W. Richard. 1987. "The Adolescence of Institutional Theory." *Administrative Science Quarterly* 32:493-511.

———. 1992. *Organizations: Rational, Natural and Open Systems.* 3d ed. Englewood Cliffs, NJ: Prentice Hall.

Sharpe, William F. 1970. *Portfolio Theory and Capital Markets.* New York: McGraw-Hill.

Simon, Herbert A. 1976. *Administrative Behaviour: A Study of Decision-Making Processes in Administrative Organization.* 3d ed. New York: Free Press.

———. 1979. "Rational Decision Making in Business Organizations." *American Economic Review* 69:493-513.

———. 1983. *Reason in Human Affairs.* Stanford, CA: Stanford University Press.

Singh, Jitendra V. 1986. "Performance, Slack, and Risk Taking in Organizational Decision Making." *Academy of Management Journal* 29:562-585.

Smith, Chris, John Child, and Michael Rowlinson. 1990. *Reshaping Work: The Cadbury Experience.* Cambridge, England: Cambridge University Press.

Stace, Doug and Dexter Dunphy. 1994. *Beyond the Boundaries: Leading and Recreating the Successful Enterprise.* Sydney, Australia: McGraw-Hill.

Staw, Barry M., Lance E. Sandelands, and Jane E. Dutton. 1981. "Threat-Rigidity Effects in Organizational Behavior: A Multilevel Analysis." *Administrative Science Quarterly* 26:501-524.

Stopford, J. M. and L. T. Wells, Jr. 1972. *Managing the Multinational Enterprise.* New York: Basic Books.

Suzuki, Y. 1980. "The Strategy and Structure of Top 100 Japanese Industrial Enterprises, 1950-1970." *Strategic Management Journal* 1:265-291.

Thompson, James D. 1967. *Organizations in Action.* New York: McGraw-Hill.

Tricker, R. I. 1984. *Corporate Governance: Practices, Procedures and Powers in British Companies and Their Boards of Directors.* Aldershot, Hants, England: Gower.

Usher, John M. and Martin G. Evans. 1996. "Life and Death Along Gasoline Alley: Darwinian and Lamarkian Processes in a Differentiating Population." *Academy of Management Journal* 39:1428-1466.

Utterback, J. M. and W. J. Abernathy. 1975. "A Dynamic Model of Process and Product Innovation." *Omega* 6:639-656.

Van de Ven, Andrew H. and Robert Drazin. 1985. "The Concept of Fit in Contingency Theory." Pp. 333-365 in *Research in Organizational Behaviour, Vol. 7,* edited by B. M. Staw and L. L. Cummings. Greenwich, CT: JAI.

Van Duijn, J. J. 1983. *The Long Wave in Economic Life.* London: Allen & Unwin.

Vroom, Victor H. and Philip W. Yetton. 1973. *Leadership and Decision-Making.* Pittsburgh, PA: University of Pittsburgh Press.

Weber, Max. 1968. *Economy and Society: An Outline of Interpretive Sociology,* 3 vols., edited by Guenther Roth and Claus Wittich. New York: Bedminster.

Weick, Karl E. 1976. "Educational Organizations as Loosely Coupled Systems." *Administrative Science Quarterly* 21:1-19.

Whetten, David A. 1980. "Sources, Responses, and Effects of Organizational Decline." Pp. 342-374 in *The Organizational Life Cycle: Issues in the Creation, Transformation and Decline of Organizations,* edited by John R. Kimberly and Robert H. Miles. San Francisco: Jossey-Bass.

Williamson, Oliver E. 1964. *The Economics of Discretionary Behavior: Managerial Objectives in a Theory of the Firm.* Englewood Cliffs, NJ: Prentice Hall.

———. 1970. *Corporate Control and Business Behavior: An Inquiry Into the Effects of Organization Form on Enterprise Behavior.* Englewood Cliffs, NJ: Prentice Hall.

———. 1985. *The Economic Institutions of Capitalism: Firms, Markets, Relational Contracting.* New York: Free Press.

Williamson, Oliver E. and Narottam Bhargava. 1972. "Assessing and Classifying the Internal Structure and Control Apparatus of the Modern Corporation." Pp. 125-148 in *Market Structure and Corporate Behaviour: Theory and Empirical Analysis of the Firm,* edited by Keith Cowling. London: Gray-Mills.

Wiseman, Robert M. and Philip Bromiley. 1991. "Risk-Return Associations: Paradox or Artifact? An Empirically Tested Explanation." *Strategic Management Journal* 12:231-241.

———. 1996. "Toward a Model of Risk in Declining Organizations: An Empirical Examination of Risk, Performance and Decline." *Organization Science* 7:524-543.

Wiseman, Robert M. and Anthony H. Catanach, Jr. 1997. "A Longitudinal Disaggregation of Operational Risk Under Changing Regulations: Evidence From the Savings and Loan Industry." *Academy of Management Journal* 40:799-830.

Woodward, Joan. 1965. *Industrial Organization: Theory and Practice.* London: Oxford University Press.

Yukl, Gary. 1994. *Leadership in Organizations.* 3d ed. Englewood Cliffs, NJ: Prentice Hall.

Index

About the Author

Lex Donaldson is Professor of Organization Design at the Australian Graduate School of Management. He holds a B.Sc. in behavioral sciences from the University of Aston and a Ph.D. from the University of London. His research interests are organization theory, organizational structure, and corporate governance. He has authored six books, including *For Positivist Organization Theory: Proving the Hard Core* (Sage, 1996) and *American Anti-Management Theories of Organization: A Critique of Paradigm Proliferation* (Cambridge University Press, 1995). His professional activities include being on the editorial boards of *Corporate Governance, Organization Studies,* and the *Strategic Management Journal.* He has held visiting appointments at the universities of Aston, Iowa, Maryland, Northwestern, and Stanford. Address: Australian Graduate School of Management, University of New South Wales, Sydney, NSW 2052, Australia. [E-mail: lexd@agsm.unsw.edu.au]